The Transformation of Capitalist Society

The Transformation of Capitalist Society

ZELLIG S. HARRIS

ROWMAN & LITTLEFIELD PUBLISHERS, INC.
Lanham • New York • Boulder • Oxford

ROWMAN & LITTLEFIELD PUBLISHERS, INC.

Published in the United States of America
by Rowman & Littlefield Publishers, Inc.
4720 Boston Way, Lanham, Maryland 20706

12 Hid's Copse Road
Cummor Hill, Oxford OX2 9JJ, England

British Library Cataloguing in Publication Information Available

Library of Congress Cataloging-in-Publication Data

Harris, Zellig S. (Zellig Sabbettai), 1909–1992
    The transformation of capitalist society / Zellig S. Harris.
        p.   cm.
    Includes bibliographical references and index.
    ISBN 0–8476–8411–3 (cloth : alk. paper). — ISBN 0–8476–8412–1
(paper : alk. paper)
        1. Decision-making. 2. Capitalism. 3. Economic policy.
    4. Management—Employee participation.   I. Title.
    HD30.23.H372   1997
    330.12'2—dc20   96-44876
                                                                       CIP

ISBN 0–8476–8411–3 (cloth : alk. paper)
ISBN 0–8476–8412–1 (pbk. : alk. paper)

Printed in the United States of America

⊖™ The paper used in this publication meets the minimum requirements of American
National Standard for Information Sciences—Permanence of Paper for Printed Library
Materials, ANSI Z39.48–1984.

Contents

ON BEHALF OF THE AUTHOR   IX

FOREWORD   XI
WOLF V. HEYDEBRAND

PREFACE   XV

1. OVERVIEW: THE POSSIBILITIES OF CHANGE   I
    APPENDIX: CRITICIZING CAPITALIST SOCIETY   9

2. BASIC TERMS IN DESCRIBING SOCIETY   11
    2.1 THE RELEVANCE OF STRUCTURE   11
    2.2 OCCUPATIONS   11
    2.3 POWER   13
    2.4 DECISION-MAKING ON PRODUCTION AND CONSUMPTION   16
    2.5 ECONOMIC EFFECT ON SOCIAL FORMS   17
    2.6 THE ECONOMY AS SOCIETY AND SYSTEM   19
    APPENDIX: METHODOLOGICAL CONSIDERATIONS   21

3. CAPITALIST DECISIONS ON PRODUCTION   23
    3.1 THE CONDITIONS OF DECISION-MAKING   23
    3.2 DYNAMICS OF THE SYSTEM   28
    3.3 STRENGTHS AND FLEXIBILITIES   32
    3.4 INSTABILITIES   33
    3.5 BYPASS VIA GOVERNMENT   36

4. CONSIDERATIONS IN ANALYZING SOCIAL CHANGE   43
    4.1 CONTINUITY   43
    4.2 INTERNAL CHANGE   43
    4.3 SOCIAL FORCES   44
    4.4 ACTIONS   47
    4.5 INDIVIDUALS   48
    4.6 WHAT INDUCES ACTION?   49
    4.7 THE COURSE OF CHANGE   52
    4.8 THE DIRECTION OF CHANGE   53
    4.9 CONCLUSION   54

5. POTENTIALLY POST-CAPITALIST DEVELOPMENTS   57
    5.1 ONGOING CHANGES   57
      5.1.1 INTERNAL TO THE DECISION SYSTEM: PROFIT   57
      5.1.2 INTERNAL FACTORS: DISTANCE FROM PRODUCTION   59
      5.1.3 UNIVERSALIZATION   63

5.1.4 THE PHYSICAL ENVIRONMENT   69
5.1.5 DECLINE IN PRODUCTIONAL KNOWLEDGE   70
5.1.6 OPPOSITION FROM BELOW   72
5.1.7 LIMITS TO CAPITALISM   74

5.2 RELINQUISHING OF DECISION-MAKING   76
5.2.1 TO "BEHIND" THE CAPITALIST ADVANCE   77
5.2.2 TO BELOW CAPITALISM   82

5.3 THE SUCCESSOR TO CAPITALISM   84

6. HOW CAPITALISM BEGAN   **87**

6.1 LEARNING FROM THE PAST   87
6.2 DEVELOPMENTS THAT CONSTITUTED FIRST STEPS TOWARD
     CAPITALIST DECISION-MAKING   88
6.3 THE DEVELOPMENT OF BUSINESS INTO AN ECONOMIC SYSTEM   94
6.4 THE DEVELOPMENT OF A CAPITALIST SOCIETY   97
6.5 THE ENVIRONMENT THAT CAPITALISM PRESENTS TO
     POST-CAPITALIST DECISION-MAKING   99
6.6 POSSIBLE FIRST STEPS TOWARD COOPERATIVE
     DECISION-MAKING   104

     (1) STEPS TOWARD WORKERS' VOICE IN DECISIONS   104
     (2) STEPS TOWARD A NEW SOCIETY   107
     (3) PROSPECTS   110

7. SELF-GOVERNED PRODUCTION   **113**

7.1 DEMOCRACY IN PRODUCTION   113
7.2 IDEOLOGICALLY DRIVEN INNOVATIONS IN
     PRODUCTION RELATIONS   114

     7.2.1 COLLECTIVES   114
     7.2.2 COOPERATIVES   118
     7.2.3 WORKERS' COUNCILS   124

7.3 ECONOMIC PROCESSES TOWARD EMPLOYEE SELF-
     GOVERNING IN PRODUCTION   126

     7.3.1 WORKERS' PRESSURE FOR ECONOMIC AND
            WORKPLACE CONCESSIONS FROM THE BOSS   126
     7.3.2 WORKERS' PRESSURE FOR DECISION POWER   128
     7.3.3 BUSINESS PRESSURE FOR EMPLOYEE OWNERSHIP   131
            (1) EXTENT   131
            (2) ADVANTAGES FOR THE EMPLOYER   133
            (3) OTHER REASONS FOR ESTABLISHING AN ESOP   134
            (4) ADVANTAGES AND DISADVANTAGES TO
                 THE EMPLOYEES   135
            (5) BUYOUTS   136

(6) NEW COOPERATIVE ENTERPRISES 137
(7) PENSION FUNDS 139
(8) THE IMPLICATIONS OF OWNERSHIP 140
7.3.4 BUSINESS MOVES TOWARD ACCEPTING WORKER DECISION-MAKING 141
7.4 SUPPORT WITHIN CAPITALISM FOR STARTING SELF-GOVERNED PRODUCTION 145
7.4.1 DUE TO THE OPEN-ENTRY STRUCTURE OF CAPITALISM 145
7.4.2 AREAS OF LESSER PROFITABILITY 146
7.4.3 SITUATIONS SUPPORTING SELF-GOVERNED PRODUCTION 148
(1) JOB PROBLEMS 148
(2) COMMUNITY NEEDS 148
(3) PRODUCTS 149
(4) ECOLOGICAL CONCERNS 150
(5) SIZE 150
(6) BUSINESS INTERESTS 151
(7) GOVERNMENTAL CONSIDERATIONS 152
7.5 VIABILITY 152
7.5.1 DUE TO THE INTERNAL STRUCTURE 152
7.5.2 TECHNOLOGICAL NICHE 154
7.5.3 REDUCED DISTANCE BETWEEN DECISION AND PRODUCTION 156
7.5.4 FREEDOM FROM PROFIT MAXIMIZATION 157
7.5.5 DIFFICULTIES 159
7.6 GROWTH 161
7.7 PRESERVING THE PARTICIPANT CHARACTER 165
(1) MANAGEMENT 166
(2) HIRING NON-MEMBERS 167
(3) BUREAUCRACY 169
7.8 RELEVANCE TO SOCIAL CHANGE 171
APPENDIX: ON EMPLOYEE OWNERSHIP 177

8. IN THE AFTERMATH OF SOVIET COMMUNISM 183
8.1 POLITICAL STRUCTURE 183
8.2 ECONOMIC POLICIES 185
8.3 SOCIAL POLICIES 187
8.4 THE GLOBAL VIEW ON THE COMMUNIST REGIMES 191
8.5 THE ROAD FROM COMMUNIST REGIMES 196
(1) THE GOVERNMENTS 196
(2) THE MIDDLE-CLASS ELEMENTS 200
(3) THE WORKING CLASS 203
(4) THE "MASSES" 204

8.6 ASSESSMENTS IN RESPECT TO SOCIAL CHANGE   204
   (1) ON THE DECISION SYSTEM OF COMMUNIST REGIMES   205
   (2) ON THE FAILURE OF COMMUNIST REGIMES   206
   (3) ON THE COLLAPSE   206

9. INTERVENING IN THE HISTORICAL PROCESS   209

9.1 AWARENESS AND INTERVENTION   209
9.2 AGAINST WHAT?   210
9.3 FOR WHAT?   220
9.4 STRATEGIES AND ISSUES   225
9.5 TACTICS AND TOOLS   229

INDEX   235

ABOUT THE AUTHOR   245

On Behalf of the Author

The author of this work was a world-renowned linguist. A complete bibliography of his published writings appears in *Historiographia Linguistica*, xx: 2/3, 509-522 (1993).

Professor Harris was also a polymath with a profound knowledge of history, economics, sociology and anthropology. This accounts for his interest, toward the end of his life, in writing a book on ongoing changes in capitalism. Upon his death in 1992, he left a manuscript entitled *The Transformation of Capitalist Society*. Several of his old friends collaborated in preparing the manuscript for publication.

MURRAY EDEN
WILLIAM M. EVAN
SEYMOUR MELMAN

FOREWORD

This book deals with the possibilities of economic democracy and employee ownership and control as viable, socio-economic strategies of transformation of capitalist societies. It sees this transformation as a non-political, non-violent potential growing out of existing and possibly increasing tendencies within contemporary capitalism itself.

Harris presents a compelling interpretation of the self-transformative capacities of capitalism from a left-libertarian perspective. He is critical of both managerial capitalism and the politically instituted or state-oriented alternatives to historical capitalism, notably Stalinist state socialism and national socialism. But he recognizes certain positive and constructive elements in liberal capitalism, such as individualism and the flexibility, fluidity, and openness of social patterns that grow out of it, as well as the dynamic growth of technology that permits rising productivity, higher levels of living, and certain improvements in the quality of life. The non-centralized and self-regulating properties of liberal capitalism permit the mechanisms of decision-making as well as actual decisions to be either delegated to democratic government or to be relinquished to employees. This is not seen as an unconditional or automatic mechanism, but as a potential that arises both from internal weaknesses and contradictions of capitalism and from legal and constitutional rights already achieved, such as political and social rights as well as employee share ownership plans (ESOP) and, generally, gradual growth of employee ownership and control.

This book radiates a cautious optimism, although Harris does not shrink from highly critical discussions of corporate and governmental rule or extant theories of political revolution. The book opens with a general, fairly non-technical and quite accessible discussion of the possibilities of social change. Chapter 2 lays out the conceptual framework in terms of which social structures can be described most profitably, for example, the importance of occupation is emphasized over that of social class as a basic building block of society and as a way of describing power and decision-making. Chapter 3 focuses on the structure and process of economic and managerial decision-making as the key variable in understanding and explaining the functioning of a capitalist society and its transformation. Chapter 4 is a general discussion of social change that emphasizes gradual structural and economic change over rapid political and revolutionary transformation. These ideas are then applied to the specific possibilities of transformation in capitalist production systems.

The key argument is that capitalist decision-making power can be, and is frequently, relinquished to two non-capitalist levels of decision-making: (1) governmental regulation of the economy, mainly in the form of neo-Keynesian and post-Keynesian strategies of intervention in the affairs of private economy; and (2) the delegation of certain technical and managerial types of decision-making to the level of employees and workers in order to elicit their cooperation and participation in an increasingly complex and technically vulnerable production process. The development of computer-integrated design and production as well as new forms of work organization such as project teams, task forces, flexible specialization, and matrix organization are cited as examples. The consequences of these structural possibilities and tendencies are spelled out in Chapter 6 where the development of cooperative and group-based decision-making as strategies of systematic transformation is discussed at length.

Chapter 7 presents the empirical centerpiece of the argument that self-governed production is possible and feasible. Harris discusses the historical role and possibilities of collectives, producer and consumer cooperatives, and workers' councils, the latter being the main (and largely unsuccessful or ineffective) form of worker self-management in state socialist societies. He then turns to Employee Share Ownership Plans and, generally, the idea of employee ownership as the key tendency that promises to combine worker ownership and management within a capitalist economic context, albeit initially in labor-intensive, low profit/low competition areas and industries. There is nothing unrealistic about the argument here, but it leaves open the crucial question whether employee control on behalf of "employee interests" would transcend narrow issues of profit and income and would advance to broader issues of organizational and social policy. Harris is conscientiously concerned to discuss the difficulties associated with such a program of transformation and considers the need (and the problems) of preserving the participant character of self-governed production, e.g., insider vs. outsider (shareholder) management control, hiring non-members, and corruption due to bureaucratic tendencies.

In Chapter 8, Harris deals with the current social and economic transformation of Eastern European reform societies. This is an excellent, magisterial, and politically sensitive discussion of a complex topic that helps to illuminate the overall theme of this book. Harris clearly demonstrates the shortcomings of pre-1989 state socialist economic reform policies as well as post-1989 obstacles to effective privatization and economic development.

Chapter 9 concludes the argument with an injunction against political and revolutionary strategies of social change and a frankly normative appeal for the desirability of economic democracy to be realized within a democratic constitutional framework.

Harris draws on a broad range of historical, social, political, and economic data and materials to support his thesis. While the book is not devoid of a normative component (e.g., the prefigurative idea that democratic goals must be pursued democratically, or that reformist change is imperative, given persistent problems of the existing system), it argues for limited change on the basis of concrete, existing premises. Given the globalizing tendencies of contemporary capitalism, it seems especially important to consider the remaining options of internal self-transformation under democratic auspices. This book will empower readers to do so in a particularly appealing and compelling way.

WOLF V. HEYDEBRAND

Professor of Sociology
New York University

PREFACE

This book has a two-fold purpose. First, to bring together an orderly set of evidentially-supported generalizations (Chapters 2,4) on the basis of which one can usefully analyze the socio-economic changes in our world and the possibilities of a future more humane society (Chapters 3,5). Second, to present a conclusion: that a step, perhaps a necessary one, toward such a possibility is the development of viable cooperative and employee-owned enterprises, non-employing and not based on profit maximization, within capitalist society (Chapter 7).

The two purposes are interrelated. For this conclusion to seem anything but arbitrary and unrealistic, it is necessary to show (Chapter 5) that while capitalism was expanding it was also relinquishing various parts of its profit-based decision-making on various aspects of economic life, bypassing the methods of business via the differently made decisions of government and public bodies. To understand ongoing developments in this way, it is necessary to describe capitalism (Chapter 3) not monolithically but as a bundle of interrelated social and economic properties, in which the basic criterion is profit making, which leads necessarily to profit maximization. To arrive at such a description of capitalism and of its course of change, it is useful to present (Chapters 2,4) certain methodological generalizations about how to describe societies and their change.

The argument in this book involves issues that had been widely discussed for centuries. The relevant data fill countless books and also the pages of daily newspapers. Only the briefest reference has been possible here to the major discussions of these issues or to the more telling data. In the face of all this extant material, the reason for this book is primarily to relate the conclusions to the picture of capitalist development today, so that they are seen not as a forlorn hope but as a possible outcome, growing out of the particular extant conditions.

This book deals with the development specifically of the old capitalisms, primarily of Western Europe and North America, because the issues elsewhere differ in important respects from those in the old capitalist lands. The data noted here are limited largely to the United States; the dynamics of relinquishing decision-making (as also the struggles against such relinquishing) is clearer there.

ZELLIG S. HARRIS

CHAPTER I

Overview:
The Possibilities of Change

The failures of the Communist (more correctly Bolshevik or Leninist) regimes raise the question of whether fundamental long-range economic and social changes — in any case, changes toward a democratic economy — can be achieved by fiat or by purely political means. Of course, one could say that the major communist revolutions were steps of national industrialization rather than direct moves toward egalitarianism and freedom. Certainly, the declared goal of an equitable society, with the producers freed from exploitation by others, was not achieved. Whatever the particular historical circumstances in each of these countries, one can hardly avoid the question of whether the social and economic goals which were understood to motivate these revolutions were at all achievable by a political victory, in the absence of prior economic developments toward these goals.

If now we turn to the capitalist countries we meet again the problem of how social and economic improvement may be expected. Despite the success of capitalism in production, and its attendant acceptance through much of the world, essential problems are looming. Perhaps the chief of these is one that was hardly thought of fifty years ago: the destruction of the earth's resources and environment. Capitalism cannot avoid a conflict of values because any proposed activity in this respect is likely to be at a cost of reduced short-term profit. This can conflict with the maximization of profit, which is in essence the criterion by which economic decisions are made in capitalism. Another central problem is the large unemployed and impoverished segment of the population excluded from the benefits of capitalist production and society. A third is the essential need in profit-making, and especially in profit maximizing, for an ever expanding domain of operation — an expansion which cannot be maintained forever.

This book looks ahead to a time when the decline of capitalist production in various countries, economic sectors, and companies, leaves workers without job prospects and sectors of production inadequately covered for the needs of the population. The book examines the possibility that under these conditions worker-controlled enterprises, where employees are included in sharing control, may be able to arise and to fill an economic niche, and thus to survive within a capitalist environment. The book suggests that if, and as, such enterprises become a significant part of a country's economy, they will give rise to new social economic understandings and different political attitudes. They may pave the way for a more humane and equitable society. Indeed, politically-centered changes toward such a society may well fail — even if only after decades — unless such enterprises have become part of the economy by the time the political changes are made.

The issue raised here does not put political attitudes or activities into question: these have to be decided on their own merits in each historical situation. Rather, it will be argued here that local economic developments toward worker-controlled production are a necessary, though not sufficient, condition for the establishment of a more equitable social order. The changes in attitudes, institutions, and political structure will be unstable unless they are related to ongoing developments in the social arrangements of production in appreciable sectors of the economy.

In view of this, we ask whether, in spite of its success, the capitalist system will end or change substantially in the foreseeable future. If so, what are the possibilities that the change will foster more equitable socio-economic conditions?

First, we ask what processes, if any, lead out of the existing shape of capitalism into a different character of society. Capitalism characteristically proceeds by means of an unorganized multiplicity of self-initiating enterprises, each making decisions which ultimately determine aggregate production and consumption based on an expectation of profit, and leading to a concentration of accumulated capital at the disposal of capitalist decision-makers. Capitalism has evolved through many changes over the last several centuries. While some parts of this development were a result of internal dynamics, other parts came in response to broad problems in profit-making (obtaining resources, inducing employees to work for sufficiently low wages), and to the inadequacy of the chaotic multiplicity of enterprises as a framework for essential common action; e.g., for creating a national economic infrastructure such as roads, and, more recently, for basic research in science.

Some of the successful responses to these problems were reached not by business decisions, but by businessmen leaving these problems to government (and to a lesser extent to public bodies such as universities, churches, scientists' associations), which resolved them by applying other than profit criteria. As responsibility is shifted, parts of the domain of the profit criterion are relinquished to government. This domain is thus decreased "behind" capitalism even as that domain increases by capitalism's forward expansion, both geographically and into more aspects of life.

Once this process is exhibited, one can see that there are possibilities of a second, different, way of relinquishing bits of profit-guided decision-making, replacing them from "below" by production decisions not based on profit maximization. Such possibilities arise from certain characteristics of the business process: ongoing changes in relative profitability, or in convenience for the capitalist mode of decision-making, among the various sectors of production (manufacture, commerce, finance) and among the various individual enterprises (companies). Some areas become less profitable or less attractive, and are abandoned by the aggressive business players. Among companies, there are bankruptcies, inadequate profitability, closing and sales for one reason or another, and various opportunities for new starts (new enterprises). Such events may be expected to occur more frequently, as the problems of late capitalism increase (e.g., the possible rising costs of depleted energy, raw materials, pollution reduction, and the greater profitability of producing in third world plants).

In many such cases, employee purchase of the plants or companies could be a viable alternative. Employee ownership, even with hired professional business and marketing management, may be viable in industries and companies that had become unattractive to capital. In today's strong capitalism, the record of employee-owned enterprises has been mixed. However, future difficulties and possible decline in profitability in various sectors of business production may change the climate for employee-owned enterprises. Creditors may favor purchase by employees over bankruptcy; some (smaller) banks may consider loans to employee purchasers more secure than to corporate raiders floating junk bonds. Employee owners can better weather depressions and downturns because they can accept whatever livelihood they can get at such times, whereas capitalist owners would have to close or simply lose money. Employee owners may have greater incentive to keep plants up-to-date and to innovate, because their fate is tied uniquely to the products and customers of their company, whereas capital can be shifted to other enterprises or to financial investments. In time, employee owners may learn how to oversee their management more adequately than is done by the directors of stock-owned companies, where the interests of the company and of its management do not always coincide.

We note that the market does not require that the internal structure of an enterprise be employment as against shared ownership, only that the input (materials, equipment) and the output (sales) go through the market. It is profit maximization that in effect requires businessmen to employ workers who do not share fully in the profits. It is employment rather than the market mechanism that creates the concentration of decision power and wealth, the political status of big business, and many of the social ills that result therefrom.

There is an apparent problem. If there is any trend toward employee ownership it is more likely to develop in the less profitable industries and companies. However, this does not mean that such ownership is relegated to unimportant corners of production for, if anything it is more likely that the humdrum essentials of life are what will become the less profitable.

Thus we arrive at a possible basis for non-capitalist production growing inside capitalist society, the more easily because (at least in its early stages) it is not in confrontation with the pure capitalist production, but rather a special-case complement to it. Although employee-owned companies fit into the capitalist economy in that they buy and sell in the market, and have to make a profit, they may not share the capitalist fate in several respects:

they do not have to maximize profit; they do not have to accumulate wealth beyond the needs of reinvestment; they have no necessary conflict of interest between owners and workers (so long as they do not employ non-owning workers); their business decisions remain close to their production decisions; and they may be less susceptible to the vagaries of the stock market, depressions, and other features of capitalist conditions.[1]

It appears, then, that as capitalism develops, and as it leaves a greater number of decisions in the hands of government, it may also come to leave various segments of production decisions in the hands of employee owners and cooperatives. If capitalism comes to a time when its need to expand is no longer satisfiable, in part because of the finiteness of the earth, these two together or separately may have advanced sufficiently to occupy the decision-making position in various sectors of production, with some sectors perhaps remaining as business.

What is important is that these two are very different from each other in social-political character. If the successor to capitalism is governmental control of the economy, it may well be oligarchic and dictatorial with frozen social strata (with the remaining capitalists possibly merging into the governmental stratum), though conceivably it might be superficially democratic in some respects. In contrast, the employee-owned and cooperative production arrangements would presumably yield a democratic social and political system controlled from below.

The growth of employee ownership within capitalism is certainly not in itself enough to create a democratic successor or even a democratic partner in a mixed economy with capitalism. But, though it is not sufficient, it is necessary. For one can hardly imagine a democratic successor to capitalism unless a recognizable portion of social production has moved into employee-owning and cooperative forms before any large post-capitalist political changes are reached. The failure of East European communists today to move toward any more egalitarian economy than a typical (not even Swedish type) capitalist one, and the repeated failure of past peasant revolts to produce any important changes in their

---

1. Officers of trade union locals that have bought major ownerships shares in steel industry firms have observed a change in orientation and behavior of managers. Formerly, managers of all grades followed top management orientation and focussed on measures to produce maximum profits toward the familiar quarterly report. After the union buyout managers began to reorient themselves toward measures directed toward stabilizing worker employment.

contemporary economic and political systems, are examples of how hard or indeed impossible it is for social upheavals to establish economic systems other than such as are already available in some degree to the population at the time.

In the past, such political-economic shifts have always amounted to transferring power to a new elite, conductors of new, and in some respects, more productive economic (and attendant social) arrangements, whose ideas helped predispose the political actors (whose own motives are in the first place geared to their immediate interests) toward historically important action. However, it is the concept and availability of such new arrangements, rather than the status of a new elite, that is the essential contribution. If the available more advantageous productional alternative does not involve a new elite, we may expect that the change will be to a more egalitarian system.

We can hope, then, that a cooperative successor to capitalism is not likely to be established simply in the wake of political upheavals, whether a massive revolution or a sequence of partial political changes. Rather, a system of cooperative production controlled from below may be expected only if arrangements of this type are available in sufficient measure within the capitalist society of the time to make them extendable to the point of becoming the main form of decision-making on production.

There remains the question of whether capitalist society will ever reach the point of major political changes, at which the availability of alternative decision-making forms would become relevant. Such a situation is bound to be reached, though not necessarily at a single moment of crisis or upheaval: because capitalist decision-making will continue to undergo changes and to be increasingly removed from production; because the expansion needs of capitalism ultimately conflict with the limits of the earth and with its growing population; because the wastefulness of capitalist technology, notably in military form, which cannot be circumvented in a system of profit maximization (5.1.4), pollutes man's environment and dislocates his ecology; and because capitalism's diminution in the role of making decisions on production will reduce both its available wealth and its influence in society.

The unexpected collapse of Communist regimes shows how suddenly political power can decline when the minimally acceptable level of consumption by the population is no longer being maintained. And despite the current economic and political success of capitalism, there is some reason to think that massive difficulties — in internal relations, in ecological limits, and in social decline and upheaval — are still to come.

Our knowledge of social forces and of the sweep of history has deflected our attention from the detailed conditions and motivations of the component groups that act — intervene — in social change. This the more so that in many cases these actors fail to achieve an acceptable measure of what they are acting for. What succeeded and what failed both in the initiating of the East European uprisings of 1989 and in their outcomes is a good example. A more detailed analysis of the interplay between history and the specific actors in it suggests why the actors in social history failed to get what they intended, and in what circumstances they might be expected to come closer to satisfaction.

Criticizing Capitalist Society

A note about what is implied in criticizing capitalist society: Given what we now understand (let alone what may come to be understood by future generations), it is clear that man has moved historically (with many setbacks) to better material conditions and higher cultural levels. What constitutes better material conditions is hard to formulate because some of them come with deterioration in the "quality of life." What constitutes higher cultural levels is also hard to formulate, because there are no clear or agreed upon scales of emotion and art, or thought and science, and there is no imaginable level to which man is ultimately approaching, and no infinite future for man. Nevertheless, both the material conditions of life, and the richness of art and science and understanding, are greater today than a few thousand years ago or a few hundred years ago. The human life span has been extended markedly, as have advances in medicine and public health.

Many people today decry the notion of progress, because it is promoted as tantamount to the development and product proliferation of capitalism. But whatever progress may mean, there has been not only a slow progression but also some kind of progress in the long history of man, at least as judged by many people alive today. And it is also undeniable that there has been particularly great progress in art and science and thought (including thought about a better society) during the last few centuries in Europe and its cultural extensions. It is also true that the social conditions which grew with industrial capitalism were a causative factor in this. This is not a matter of a self-congratulatory "white man's burden," but it does reflect on the value of the productional activism and social individualism that came with capitalism (together with all its ills). Of course, the ills of capitalism do not imply that different social systems do not have similar or other ills: we cannot find a haven in admiration of other societies and cultures, or in uncritical social relativism.

For these reasons, discussing the possibilities of moving from the social conditions of capitalism to more humane ones does not devalue all that capitalism has brought to the life and culture of man. Any social system that may be expected to be more humane than capitalism, on the grounds of being based on more egalitarian control, would not wish to forego the preceding cultural progress that capitalism has brought.

CHAPTER 2

Basic Terms in Describing Society[1]

2.1 THE RELEVANCE OF STRUCTURE

In the present discussion, social relations and actions will be considered primarily in respect to social groupings, whether fixed or fluid, rather than in respect to individuals. Beyond this, as the purpose of this book is to consider the possible direction of change in the society of today, we have to deal with the specific situations and actions constituting both the stability of society and its change; in other words, with the micro-sociology of politics. Accordingly, the discussion here will avoid purely abstract or hypothetical concepts, in favor of specifiable types or aggregates of specifiable institutions, groups, and actions.

Two major sets of social relations are considered below. One is the division of labor (occupations), with its attendant difference in consumption levels, social power, and conflicting interests. The other is the economic political "system" that interconnects economic arrangements, political power, social institutions, and cultural ways and attitudes.

2.2 OCCUPATIONS

The interdependences within large populations in respect to production, consumption and social life have led to specific divi-

---

1. For methodological considerations see Appendix to this chapter.

sions of labor with their attendant technology, communication, communal knowledge, and science, as well as to more or less fixed social relations which are in many cases, as notoriously in the Hindu castes, related to the occupations.[2] In these perceptions and activities, the participation of the individual is not arbitrary or entirely free, but is with or like others in those subsets of the population to which he "belongs" (for as long as he belongs).

There is in most societies and times a rough correlation between status in respect to production and status in respect to consumption. But in many societies birth into ethnic or religious sectors also determines social status and even consumption level. In many societies, the individual's membership in occupations or social classes is determined by birth or habitation; but this restriction is looser in capitalism. Successive periods of capitalism have also brought forth various changes in the types and statuses of occupations, such as the development of commercial and later professional middle classes.

Important conditions and aspects of life are similar within (and correlate with) particular occupational groupings: income (consumption) levels; "perks"; social status and power; life-conditions which place a person in a particular occupational grouping; freedom of choice; opportunity for an individual to rise within the occupation (e.g., within medicine or acting, in contrast to within truck-driving); education; many social attitudes; fate under major economic-social crises and catastrophes (e.g., even, as suggested by Sen,[3] famine). Many individuals take on the special interests and perceptions of their specific occupation. It is not surprising that the answer to "What is he?" is generally the person's occupation ("He's a carpenter," "He's a dog-breeder").

---

2. In each society, the availability of the physical essentials of life depends on the division of labor and the technology, on the utilization of natural resources (with provision for generational continuity), and on the differential allocation of consumption among social groups.

In the large and productively complex societies (not considering, for example, those societies in which extended families and moieties, or religious communities, constitute crucial social entities), many of the relevant groupings have been largely occupational in a broad sense, i.e., by type of work in respect to production and to decision-making on production and consumption.

In sum, people's position in production and in respect to economic decision-making will be seen to constitute, by and large, a major factor in their social and political character.

3. A. K. Sen and A. Sen, *Cultural Deprivation and Mental Retardation* (New Delhi: Northern Book Centre, 1984).

In respect to many of these properties, there is in many societies a rough grouping of these occupations into a few socio-economic levels or "classes" traditionally so-called, largely by status in respect to decisions over large productional activities and the production tasks.

There are certain advantages to analyzing in terms of occupation rather than in the more general terms of class. A consideration against "class" is that it combines production status, income, and social power into a single characteristic. Indeed these are correlated but not in all cases, and their changes are partly independent of each other. For example, a ruling class may maintain traditional power while losing much of its decision role in production; and a government may have total political power but be unable to change the relations of production; for example, which sectors decide the productional activities of others, or to prevent them from changing.

Also, asking about a person's actual occupational activity, especially in relation to decision-making, enables us to distinguish leadership as constituting a kind of occupation. It has been observed that many individuals change their views and social character after changing their economic relation to production and its decision-making, even without entering an occupation recognized as new. A worker who has become a top union official (or even perhaps a "professional revolutionary") becomes occupationally a manager rather than a worker. It may be politically confusing to consider leadership as a status within each occupation; rather, in some respects it is itself an occupation. However, the correlation mentioned above, and the utility of the concept of occupational groups, is not compromised by unclear borderline cases.

2.3 POWER

All large societies have had power structures, whereby particular groups could control various aspects of the people's lives, with the power-wielders generally living better than the rest of the population. In many Third World societies today the military is the overt power, though it operates with the support of the large landowners and (usually) the major businessmen. In some, the military is the arm of an occupying country. In the main capitalist countries and in some economic structures derived from them, e.g., Japan, the overt power is in elected governments, in which the overriding influence is commonly "Big Business."

Aside from direct force, the power of government and social institutions such as religion rests on having the organization of basic social needs routed through them. Similarly, the power of the owners and top managers of business and land rests on the organization of production and consumption being routed through their decisions. This routing may be maintained by being the one arrangement into which people grow and which they usually take for granted. In large societies such taking for granted militates against change because too few people are likely to see beyond it to make a change possible. With the increased variegation of religions in the large modern societies, the power of each religion and of religions in general is reduced, and power then rests increasingly in the inability of people to obtain a livelihood except by taking employment from those who in one way or another are accepted as controlling the means of production.

In general, the power is used to maintain itself. In many cases, it is also used for enrichment, both before capitalism and within capitalism. This includes the economic use of people as in the enslavement of the Caribbean Indians by Columbus and his followers, the slave system of the southern United States before the Civil War, the overworking of employees (in mines, in agricultural labor, etc.) whether in colonial areas or at home. Related to this was the depopulation of territory by invaders, as in the killing off of the Tasmanians, the massed displacements and killings of the Native Americans in the United States and of the Aborigines in Australia.[4]

In addition to these crucial sources of social power, there are secondary but important loci of power in society. One is the accumulation of large wealth or prestige, for these enable individuals to advance their self-interest through the institutions and people they support or direct, and through popular deference. Newspapers are sensitive to the political and economic attitudes of their large advertisers, but also of business in general. Many churches support the world-view that accepts ownership of the means of production, profit-making, and the world-view of the main pres-

---

4. In any case, power is not unique or monolithic: there are grades of power, different and even competing power bases, and changes in the character or strength of power. Even if somewhere the power has started in the hands of a single person or small group, the people through whom it is then mediated become secondary wielders of power in their own interest. In this power-spread actions in self-interest that are not officially or commonly accepted as being the normal costs of power are often considered to be "corruption"; but these are all of them parts of the costs of power.

tige groups of the present economy. American universities fill their governing boards with rich businessmen and donors who then control policy, even though the tax-deductible contributions of these donors are supposed to be made only for philanthropic reasons, or at most for the honor they receive.

But the social power of wealth and prestige is mainly reserved for the controllers of the economy — of production and distribution. Wealth and prestige not related to this productional status have far less importance and influence in society. People such as successful artists, writers, and lottery winners (or even widows of industrialists), whose wealth is not directly related to their wielding economic control, have a much greater scatter of social attitudes than do the top industrialists and businessmen; in general they neither seek to nor can they exert their influence as strongly or in as uniform a direction.

Another secondary but important locus of power is the reigning culture of the society. The large established religions, the attitudes and actions and kinds of people that are accepted and respected and admired, the world-views and the perceptions of what is taken to be natural in individuals and social relations — all these usually fit well with the interests of the established wielders of economic and governmental power and often specifically support them. This might seem to be just a natural response of the people to their social environment. But in very many cases there is a constant expenditure of energy to reinforce these social values and cultural attitudes: e.g., in the institutions of religion and education, in the press, in patriotic celebrations, in the mainstream entertainment, in pressures (persuasion and threats) for socialization and conformity.[5]

The social costs of power are of two kinds: the restriction of social interactions to those that fit the power interests or, in any case, do not conflict with them (granted that any standardized social arrangements involve restrictions); and the specific prevention of dissidence. Elites maintaining their power in the face of possible dissidence have illustrated perhaps the most obvious evils in social history: the many ways of indoctrinating the population or particular sections thereof to the point of trying to "domesticate" them, the controls on culture and information, and

---

5. One might wonder how the cultural features supporting the status quo would fare without such constant fostering. But that question is of little practical moment, for the economic and governmental powers will in any case actively promote their self-interest.

the many ways of controlling and destroying opponents as in the tortures perpetrated by the authorities in old China and Japan, feudal Europe, the church hierarchies of Medieval Europe, the Stalinist and Nazi repressions, and untold others.

2.4 DECISION-MAKING ON PRODUCTION AND CONSUMPTION

Even among societies in which the basis of power has been military or religious, there have been many in which particular individuals or groups had economic power, either through accumulated wealth or through control of something necessary to production. In feudal societies, the local lords, who had the status of rulers in their area, were the owners or controllers of "their" land, water, or other productional necessities on which their subjects worked. In post-feudal societies, people who arrange for the availability of goods by commerce, or arrange for the production of goods (and, later, services) by providing machinery (or arrangements) and employing people to do the work, have become the main wielders of economic power and the main political influence. Their role in production has changed over time, from commercial and productional entrepreneurs to managers, and more recently to financiers who mediate vast business deals.

The common property of all their roles — roughly, what is called business — is that they make decisions which directly or ultimately determine productional work performed by others, with resulting availability of goods and services. It is not just making decisions about money and its transfer from one to another; for example, individual wealth such as that of entertainment stars and purely money activities such as gambling do not have this importance in society, even if they make some individuals rich and others poor.

Decision-making on production is an occupation. The economic activity of many people consists solely in making such decisions, without contributing any specific knowledge, skill, or work relating to the physical production or to how it is carried out. Some make decisions about how much of what to produce. Others decide about who shall work — including who shall make the more specific decisions — and at what pay. Still others decide about collecting the capital on the basis of which the preceding kinds of decisions can be made.

For a given form of decision-making to be widespread in a society means that the activities involved in it are standardized into some kind of structure, not merely the whim of one group or another. Such a structure is characterized by certain properties. One is the criteria on which a decision is made; for there must be some basis on which a person can make a productional decision and which other people can accept as an operative decision.

Another structural property is the specification of persons who can make an accepted decision; that is, how a person enters that status, and how he leaves it. In feudal societies, the status was passed from the lord to his heir, much as was the political power of kings (and leaving the status was usually by death); although in both cases the first holder of that status (within a given lineage) had to enter it differently (e.g., by force or by election). In early capitalism, entry was open to almost any person who could find a way (machinery, a bit of capital, etc.) to employ people for production or commerce (or enable others to do so); and exit was simply by failing to be able to do it any longer (by bankruptcy, by lack of opportunity or wherewithal, etc.); but, in effect, only a limited number of people could become successful as employers.

A third property is the interrelation of the decision-making status and activities with the forms of physical power and of status-quo maintenance, such as government and army, social institutions, wealth, and the reigning culture and acceptance (compliance) by the population. This is relevant because decision-making itself is not usually exercised with physical force, so that the support of the physical and life-organizing components of society is important for it.

The centrality of the ultimate decision-making to the economic structure and power will be seen in the particular descriptions of capitalism (Ch. 3) and of its changes (Ch. 5) offered below.

2.5 ECONOMIC EFFECT ON SOCIAL FORMS

The social and political arrangements in a society are in general continuations, possibly modified over time, of the earlier arrangements. However, arrangements for production, and especially the power which inheres in making the ultimate decisions on production, affect the social and cultural and political ways, and alter them deeply. Correlations between productional arrangements and social political forms are visible in any survey of social history and diversity.

To mention a scatter of examples: Societies in which the division of labor is traditionally hereditary maintain decision-relations by the full force of the reigning culture, as can be seen from the traditionalist character of the higher castes' opposition to occupational liberation of the Indian Untouchables. In social environments in which almost everyone decides his own work, such as the American Frontier (up to the later 1800's), there was less of class distinctions or of great differences in wealth. In areas where small family farms contributed a major form of production, a spirit of individual independence or self-directed cooperation was characteristic. In periods of increasing industrial employment and agricultural mechanization there has been increasing pauperization and class conflict, and the accumulation of political power in the hands of the large employers and the wealthy businessmen. And in periods of massive corporations and large complex financial activities, there is massive control of social institutions and manipulation of the market, great accumulation of wealth, and overriding political influence for big business in contrast to small. Such developments are common knowledge, but are mentioned here in order to note the importance of the form of productional decision-making (not just wealth or technology) for the social economic relations in society.

It is not simply that the existing powers control social institutions and cultural life. For it is clear that as new arrangements of production develop within an existing power system, they create new socio-economic relations, new attitudes. and new local power-bases long before they become the dominant economic form for the central political power. This is seen in Europe of the 13th to 19th centuries (Ch. 5), in the development of a growing commercial economy and community, and of profit-making and employment and banking, in the burghers' way of life, in Protestantism, in the decline of the "divine right of kings" and the growth of democracy and attitudes opposed to aristocracy, all well before capitalism reached its majority. These effects of an incoming economic form can be seen even where a total overthrow of the former political structure was never completed, as in England. One can see from the history of late Medieval Europe that the new productional arrangements were developing well before the new social forms and attitudes began to take shape.

In any case, the argument made in the following chapters does not rest upon a general theory of decision power, but upon the effects of productional decision-makers in the capitalist world.

2.6 THE ECONOMY AS SOCIETY AND SYSTEM

Two properties of the economy are seen in the discussion above. One is that an economy or even just an economic sector is a set of social arrangements around production and consumption, and that it builds and maintains around itself a set of social and cultural ways. The other is that various strands can be distinguished in the economy and in the society. These strands are largely interdependent and most often intersupportive, but nevertheless do not constitute a single undifferentiated holistic entity. Rather, the economy and its society are best described as a bundle of properties, of component groups and interactions and ways, which despite their interrelations may have differences of interest and development, may have different sources and directions of change, with some strands even coming into conflict with others. This last can be seen, for example, in the way money activities began as ordinary actions within feudalism but came to fill a niche that enabled them to grow out of feudalism. Even societies and institutions that are formed monolithically, like the communist regimes or the large centralized religions, developed different strands with different potentialities and interests. Aside from this, many societies contain marginal islands of different economic and social characteristics, which may or may not grow to play larger roles in the whole society.

In this sense we may speak of a socio-economic system as an interrelated bundle of economic and social arrangements.

In this spirit, we did not speak directly of class (2.2), but recognized the descriptive importance of occupations with their specific social properties; the conflicts of whole contrasting classes come in part from the similarities, self-interests, and joint actions of groups of occupations. And economies were not assumed to be monolithic entities such as "capitalism" and "communism" (despite the use here of those terms of convenience; and what of European fascism, or Swedish welfare capitalism, or mixed economies, or Third World dictatorships?). Rather, one should consider various component properties or areas present in some or all of these: political power, the military (as an independent factor in some situations), control over production and consumption, social institutions (especially, in various countries, religion), and attitudinal consensus. These components may be tied together by the positive feedback of power (nothing succeeds like success) which gives the leaders in one area a strong status in other areas, and partly by the resulting intersupport of these properties one for the other. Nevertheless, there can be different developments and divergences in different properties which can co-exist in the same institutions and even the same individuals, but can also lead to contradictions and disruptions.

Methodological Considerations

Before trying to analyze social change, we should ask what are the relevant terms for describing society.

In biology, each organism's structure affects the kind of behavior it carries out; for example, whether it walks, flies, swims — well, poorly, or not at all. Similarly, each language has its own structure affecting the kinds of meanings it can carry, and the way the meanings are expressed. In the same way, the major standardized interrelations within a society delineate the social behavior of people in it, and the kind of changes that are possible in it.

The prime determiners of each person's actions may be assumed to be his needs and desires — his self-interest. But since he lives in a society, these desires and actions are informed by his social relations — mediated (which does not necessarily mean obstructed) through the accepted social ways and institutions. His interests are understood and judged by others and by himself, in respect to the accepted social norms. In addition, most people in a society learn to accept and support the world-views and attitudes common in their sector of society, many of which are fostered by the institutions that promote acceptance of the existing power-wielders in the society. To this extent, many people support existing social arrangements even when these are counter to what one would suppose to be their own self-interest. In fact all they are doing is trying to satisfy their needs and interests and inculcations in the means available to them, which are those that have been standardized over many years of social interaction, or that have been established by the current wielders of social power. It is for this reason that the adversarial nature of capitalist actions can remain largely unrecognized. To the extent that this adversarial nature is indirect, a net effect of the interrelation among social interactions rather than an open confrontation, it can remain an unrecognized aspect of standard social behavior.

The most telling social matrix of individual action arises from the ongoing behavior and interests that are common to members of the same social sub-groups. There are many attitudes and actions which are in the self-interest of individuals, yet are similar to those of other individuals who are (since they all fit into the same society) in much the same social situation at the same time. Some of these actions may be taken separately by the individuals, in parallel; others may be carried out by collaborations of these individuals in crowds or in organizations. In either case, what is similar and is reinforced by the acts of others has social weight. In contrast, the social effect of individually different attitudes and actions is washed out. In effect, then, actions common to a group express the self-interest of whole social groupings, though the actors may be individuals rather than groups; in some cases actions that are opposed to the existing authorities may be harmful to the individuals who carry them out as part of the group.

More generally, the physiological and psychological structure of the individual, and his or her individually characteristic personal needs, constitute universes of their own, but are, because of their singularity, not directly relevant to the relations and actions that constitute social behavior and social change. This is the case, though the reigning culture and institutions, whether in capitalism or in the Soviet "insanity" convictions, like to attribute political opposition to personality disorders.

To summarize: the interrelation of those actions that are based on the actors' participation in particular social sub-groups constitutes a more or less stable structure of social relations, which affect or determine much of the participating individuals' behavior.

CHAPTER 3

Capitalist Decisions on Production

This chapter presents a particular way of describing capitalism, one that will be found relevant to the discussion of changes presented in Chapter 5. (Below, the term capitalism will be used not so much for capitalist society as for the characteristic way in which business decisions on production are arrived at.)

3.1 THE CONDITIONS OF DECISION-MAKING

The common property of capitalist activity, from its early development down to today, is that it consists in making decisions involving the availability of goods and services, in a way that leaves the businessman with the expectation of profit, i.e., of receiving more money than he started with. This expectation — sometimes with a risk of failure — is the criterion that has to be satisfied. Without it the decision to go ahead is not made, at least not as a business act. If a businessman consistently fails to operate under this criterion, or consistently fails to achieve the profit, he eventually disappears from the business arena, leaving it populated by the others.

Since the profitability of producing depends on how much is spent on wages and materials and equipment and how much is obtained in prices, businessmen prefer to pay their employees as little as possible and to charge their customers as much as possible, thus tending to lower their consumption (even while increasing the production, as a way of increasing the amount of profit, hence increasing the need to sell).

The profit criterion has a characteristic crucial to its social effect, and to its development through the centuries: it is indirect with respect to production. True, the entrepreneurial actions ("investments") of the early commercial and industrial capitalists were not indirect, having been specifically aimed at certain products and their consumption. But the common property of all investing was not how it dealt with specific products or production, but the requirement that the entrepreneur end up with profit with more money than he started with. Hence the decision-making process is not based on considering the productional possibilities (work-force, resources, and technology) and the consumptional needs for their own sakes (which would entail, for example, also the husbanding of resources, even as early farmers had learned to do), but only on whether the businessman can expect a profit. One result is that business activities are neutral in respect to the production determined by them, and production is neutral and in principle interchangeable in respect to the business actions that initiate it. Profit made in one kind of production is not essentially different from that made in another. Given whatever information and expertise a businessman needs in each case — which can be obtained as part of his investment costs — he and his profits can move from one area and type of production to another. It will be seen below that this indirectness of the profit criterion in respect to production is a factor in important capitalist developments.

A crucial additional characteristic is the fact that the domain of activities which are decided on is not closed, as it is in the limited and allocated control of land (and, in some cases, serfs) in feudalism. If one has the requisite materials or money to make goods available, one can seek further areas of commerce and production from which to make a profit. Thus there are in principle unlimited possibilities for making further profit (reinvestment) out of one's profits.

The accumulation of capital from profit is the feature that enables capitalism to be a dynamical system which has been able to extend over the world. The possibility of reinvestment is one of the properties that distinguish the capitalist process from other ways of obtaining money, such as the earnings of medieval craftsmen. A gambler can plough his earnings back into further gambling, but only until he reaches the bank's limit. And a best-selling writer cannot plough his vast earnings into producing without limit more money-earning books. In contrast, within capitalist activities, profits can be made from the steps of other businessmen's decision-making, as is seen in the modern development of business consultants, accountant services, advertising agencies, corporation lawyers, brokers, and even commercial banks that put together whole business deals and mergers and takeovers. In the latter case, the question of who is the primary businessman and who just provides a step for his money making may become open to question, as in the case of venture capital today and in the case of early capitalist participation in the commercial, industrial, and agricultural activities of specialized occupations.

To the openness of capitalism is related the fact that entry into capitalist decision-making is not a priori restricted to an otherwise determined set of individuals (different from birth restrictions in aristocracy, and the like). Anyone who has the initial capital, or can put together a loan or a profit-promising plan, may be able to make an investment, that is to say a piece of capitalist decision-making. The vaunted individualism of capitalist ideology may arise not so much from the equality of the buyers in the market-place, to which it is often attributed, as from the openness of capitalist decision-making to any person who can supply the initial conditions. Hence competition among would-be decision-makers for the same production-consumption (risk-taking) niche (market-share, and the like) is in principle open. Departure from the activity of capitalist decision-making is also open and depends merely on a person no longer being able or willing to invest or make a profit-promising deal.

All the properties noted above give capitalist decision-making a non-organized and uncentralized character — determinate only in the aggregate, if there — which will be seen to be a strength as well as a weakness of the system. No person or group plans or knows in advance, or can control fully, what capitalist activities will be carried out, or when, or how they will change (except to some extent in government-capitalist joint "industrial policy," as in modern Japan).[1] For such reasons, businessmen cannot in gen-

---

1. Cf. Chalmers A. Johnson, *M I T I and the Japanese Miracle. The Growth of Industrial Policy 1925-1985* (Stanford: Stanford University Press, 1982); Chalmers A. Johnson, ed. *The Industrial Policy Debate San Francisco* (ICF Press, 1984).

eral accept reduced profits of their own volition. Success, and in many cases even survival, depends on pushing all the time to stay competitive, to expand, and to maximize profit.

In earlier periods, certain areas of business such as small shopkeepers and family farms could operate without profit maximization, and indeed with no more profit than to cover their living costs. But this situation pre-existed capitalist production relations, co-existed within capitalism, and did not have the properties of capitalism noted above. By now, most of these earlier activities have been replaced by larger capitalist employee-based enterprises, based on employing labor and on profit maximization.

The making of profit is locally — in each individual instance of decision-making — a zero-sum situation. To the extent that it has near-term winners, it necessarily has losers: the employees (whose wages are a cost against profits), and the customers in the markets (especially given "caveat emptor"); later, in modern corporations, also the small shareholders vis-à-vis the big capitalists and managers of the corporation, and, in a different way, the competitors (especially the smaller ones). In the aggregate, technology and market expansion and the savings due to mass production can nullify the zero-sum effect, yielding gains to all concerned, though often at the cost of undeveloped areas (colonial and Third World). In important periods of capitalism this has indeed taken place.

That the adversarial position against customers is a property of capitalism is seen in the standardized justification "caveat emptor," which was needed not to cover the occasional case of an unsatisfactory purchase (something which could have occurred also in pre-capitalist purchases from a craftsman) but to cover the constant push of the businessman to increase profit by taking every advantage possible, including higher prices or more cheaply made goods. A pressure in the opposite direction is the business advantage of "goodwill," especially relative to competitors, which is based on reputation for reliability, on warranties, and the like. But this has generally been a secondary factor.

The adversarial position with respect to employees is far more central to capitalism and to the injury it causes, because the power of the businessman against his employees (who in many cases cannot wait for better wages to become available, because they cannot eat without working) is far greater than his power against the customers in the market. This power is used to keep wages down, to keep employees obedient, and (in the institutions of inculcation and control) to keep the employees from opposing this power. The central characteristic of capitalism and of the injury (as well as good) it brings about is therefore not the market mechanism but the employment relation, and above all the fact that the vast majority of the population cannot satisfy their needs as consumers without becoming employees.

The ill that is wrought to the losers, and the waste of the earth and the degradation of comity and culture, are not considered here except insofar as they lead to change in capitalism — directly or via the opposition of the losers.

Recognizing the decision-makers and the employees as the two major categories in production does not mean that all occupations can be put into a scale in respect to capitalist status. Some occupations fit into intermediate, more or less necessary, slots: e.g., management, and supporting groups such as lawyers. But other occupations do not fit here naturally: e.g., medicine, entertainment, the personnel of social institutions (education, religion, etc.), and the government bureaucracy. Large and important as these are, they do not seriously affect the developments and problems of capitalist production, or the difference of interest between it and its employees.

The discussion above centered on the motive force in the capitalist system, rather than on the structures through which this motive force operates. In his massive *Civilization and Capitalism* (e.g., in Vol. I, p. 94), Fernand Braudel distinguishes two main forms of economic interaction (aside from barter and the like, "beneath" the market). One is the market as a presumably self-equilibrating method of exchange carried out by certain occupational groups that produce and sell, or else buy and sell. The other is what Braudel calls the "real" capitalism, above the market, which consists in powerful capitalists utilizing market processes to promote their wealth. Braudel considers this to be a manipulation of the market, though he recognizes it as a separate body of activities carried out for the most part by a particular group of people, the large capitalists. From the viewpoint of the market as a system of exchange this is indeed a manipulation. But in terms of the present book, it can be seen as a separate criterion of action, consisting of investing one's money for profit and indeed for maximum profit, which is engaged in not by all participants in the market but only by a particular sector of the population, a particular occupation, for whom indeed the market may be simply an available mechanism.

The market, and the exchange system in general, operates largely in terms of money, though these terms are modified in such activities as barter, exchange plans between countries or companies, and captive markets. In the competitive market of the neo-classical economists' theories, the interests of the participating individuals do not have much effect on the general course of activity, and on its "tendency to equilibrium." In investing for profit, given its positive feedback and its open-endedness, the most successfully active production decision-makers have the incentive and the ability to develop new mechanisms within the system, and new effects arising from the use of the existing mechanisms, thus affecting its modern development and its future history. The new structures of corporations, holding companies, diversification, and raiding create new mechanisms where money is less a medium, and where its strength is replaced in part by the strength of hierarchical and political maneuvering in the boardroom, or the machinations of seizing control.

3.2 DYNAMICS OF THE SYSTEM

As noted above, the profit criterion for capitalist decision-making translates in the aggregate into profit maximization both as a property of the whole capitalist class and as the goal of the individual businessman. Maximization of profit is the more sought for as the investor, in many cases, takes the risk of a negative outcome — no profit, or even loss of his investment. This goal leads to several further goals or common features of capitalist activity. One is to employ labor, for if the businessman sells only what he himself has made or brought, his profits will be quite limited. Another is to regulate wages to his advantage, and also the cost of materials and equipment; but the businessman has less leverage in the latter than in wage levels. Requiring low costs can also favor wasteful technology, since avoidance of wastefulness can be at an immediate cost for the businessman. Yet another goal is to sell at the highest price consonant with keeping the customer ("what the traffic will bear"), and to avoid responsibility thereafter (the old "caveat emptor," and the modern sidestepping of customers' complaints or of damage claims). In the presence of competition, the selling price is in general determined by the market, but business may circumvent this where possible by price-fixing and cartels. (These two goals affect the finances of the workers, suppliers, and customers, so that capitalist decisions on production become also decisions on the consumption levels of the people involved.) A third goal is to raise productivity, that is, to get more product per employee, which spurs technologic development.

The pervasive attempts to produce and sell more, and to find opportunities for investing, create in the aggregate some well-known effects of capitalism: the production of quickly-obsolescent goods (to be replaced by new purchases); the promotion of consumerism, i.e., the desire to obtain goods; the status value of Thorstein Veblen's "conspicuous consumption"; the extension of business into more areas of life in capitalist countries, so that profit can be made out of ever more needs and activities of the population; and the expansion of business into more areas of the world, either by European and American businessmen operating in other countries (for resources and cheap labor), or by new local businessmen arising in countries where capitalism was not previously widespread. As the potential market fills up, companies turn to market research to investigate product preferences and previous purchase-choices (down to privacy threatening pinpointing of potential customers), and concentrate on market manipulation by targeting products at particular purchasing sectors, and above all by massive and highly manipulatory advertising. Finally, the desire to sell more (to increase one's market share) and to have more power in all the respects noted above lead the bigger businessmen to try to eliminate the smaller ones — which leads to mergers, and, in general, to increasing concentration of capital and decision-making in relatively fewer hands.

This set of developments constitutes the dynamics of profit maximization as a direction of change inherent, in the aggregate, in this criterion of business decisions. These developments are assured by the positive feedback in successful profit-making, since every such success puts the capitalist, and capitalism in the aggregate, in a stronger position to succeed in the next attempt. With this goes the positive feedback of wealth and status and of influence in social institutions and in government.

The dynamics of profit-making requires that there be further opportunities for investment, i.e., that the domain for profit not be closed and indeed that it be expandable — a condition that may not be possible without end.

In addition to the well-known dynamics of profit surveyed above, there is another and less frequently discussed dynamical feature, which inheres in the indirect relation of capitalist decision-making to the content of the production decided by it. Since the criterion for a decision is only the (relative) amount of profit that can be expected from it, without any requirement as to the character of the product, or its relation to other production, or its social good, the only relevant question for business decisions is whether people will pay for the product or service, i.e., whether a market can be developed for it. Hence it does not matter for capitalist decision-making whether the product or service involved is of use to people, or only satisfies subjective wants of people which business itself has inculcated (in order to create markets), or meets no need of theirs (e.g., much of weaponry), or simply participates in the steps of the decision-making process itself.

It may be that the less useful products and services are increasingly attractive to business because they are less constrained by the limitations of the real world (e.g., how many physical things can actually be used by the population). Hence the products which are not geared to real use can proliferate more widely than those which are more directly needed. For example, the number of advertisements that business can use is in principle unlimited, especially the intra-business ads designed to give one company a larger market share at the expense of other companies; but the number of apples that a population can consume approaches a finite limit. Hence, expansion of people's wants, and business expansion into more areas of life, and into more geographic areas become more difficult; but the expansion of business into a more complex decision-making process [e.g., by intervening financial steps, or by more advertising] depends only on the fecund imagination of profit-seekers. Finally, the artifact nature of decision-making about decision-making makes this artifact potentially more profitable: it involves fewer struggles with dissatisfied workers, fewer restrictions on the price one can demand (consider, for example, what a bank charges for making a loan or for putting together a deal), and higher ceilings on what the personnel can be paid (consider, for example, the six-figure incomes of junior brokers in the futures market).

For all these reasons, the fact that profit-making does not depend on whether it leads directly or only very indirectly to a product or service, or whether the end result is useful, leaves room for more and more capitalist activity being divorced from any immediate use by consumers. This includes the stock market and corporation structure, where the de facto capitalists are the top management (although the technical owners are the share holders). They are capitalists both in incomes (including perks, etc.) and in decision power, with a frozen bureaucracy in which the criteria for advancement of individuals differs from that which guided entrepreneurs formerly. The distance between decision-making and production is greatly increased, although the bottom line remains as the sole consideration in decisions. (In contrast, family enterprises, whose number and importance in the economy is decreasing, have commitment to product which may limit their bottom line considerations.)

The result of capitalist dynamics and of contemporaneous developments is a considerable change in the process and milieu of capitalist decision-making, a consequence readily recognized if one looks at capitalist history in, say, 50-year intervals. Distinctions have been made between: early capitalism with its expropriation, rapid industrialization, and major pauperization of the population; a middle period with internal and external expansion of production and market, and later with a need for a more orderly and reliable work force, leading to improvement in the workers' consumption level and in their civil rights; and finally a late period with increasing complexity of capitalist activities and increased power of finance capitalism, and with major innovation coming now not so much in technology but in managerial and financial manipulation.

A final note may be added as to the societal character of capitalist decision-making. What gives capitalism a whole socio-economic structure is a set of interrelated properties: the more or less universal acceptance (in capitalist areas) of a single criterion for production decisions. It can cover a whole society (leaving out sectors such as small self-employed, permanent welfare recipients, homeless), and can be established in the whole of a country and in almost any country. The inherent dynamics of this criterion directs its change into more extreme (and purer) forms of the same criterion. The self-strengthening features result from the internal tendency to concentration of capital, from the accumulation of wealth and prestige, and from the resultant activity to influence and control (for capitalist self-interest) the social institutions and government, and to deflect and defeat the opposition of those who lose from the decisions on production and consumption.

3.3 STRENGTHS AND FLEXIBILITIES

For all its ills — large sectors of poverty, injustices, unfair-
nesses and falsities, degraded mass culture, waste of the earth's
resources — capitalism today is at a peak of its popular acceptance
and strength. Interestingly enough, this is not only due to its own
developmental strengths, but also because businessmen and their
governments in the old capitalist lands have by now accommo-
dated to some of the needs or wants of large sectors of their home
populations. Capitalism's own strength comes from various properties: its tremendous advances in technology and quantity of production; its development of a network of middle class occupations
in the population as intermediate buffers between it and the often
oppositional workers (this includes supervisory workers, lower
white collar occupations, various "free professions"), and the separation of powers between itself and the government.

It was the very indirectness (in respect to production) of capitalist decision-making that made possible the pragmatic division
of functions between the ideologically almost identical practitioners of business and government. The separation of powers
between the economic hegemony of capitalists and the political
leadership of government which cooperates with it gives both of
these greater political freedom of action. It also strengthens both
of them against the occasional anger of the victims, which tends
to be aimed at one or the other according to circumstances (leaving the other of the two unscathed or in position to mediate).

But what gives capitalism its overriding current success is the
acceptance of its controls by vast populations in its own countries
in return for services rendered in organizing work and other facets
of life, and in the would-be middle-class elements of communist
lands, as well as in various parts of the Third World populations.
As suggested above, this acceptance, going beyond the attitudes of
populations in previous periods of capitalism, is due to the accommodation capitalism made during the middle of the 20th century
toward the purchasing power of its home workers: raising the
wage-level and improving the work conditions so that the standard of living (though not so much the "quality of life") of most
employed workers and especially of much of the middle class is
well above that of previous and current non-capitalist populations; and admitting civil rights, individual freedoms and opportunity, and democratic political processes to a level well above that

of the rest of the world (for all the controls and manipulations that constrict these gains). Most of these popular gains were reached by sustained struggles on the part of the people most involved. Nevertheless, capitalist economic powers and capitalist governments developed sufficient flexibilities to make such accommodations, and have gained greater acceptance thereby.

The flexibilities of capitalism were not of its original nature. They arose in the course of its growing need for a reliable work force and of struggles by the employees (and in some cases by small businessmen). The flexibilities may have been possible due to the chaotic and partly individualistic structure of capitalism, which permits various capitalist interests to push against each other, thus providing for a range of choice in the actions of different industries and governments.

These accommodations of capitalism to its home workers deflected the economic and political class struggle that had been brewing since the early 1800's and that was erupting in England and in America in the late 1800's and early 1900's. The accommodations created a non-poor, if hardly affluent, working class (in particular sectors) which came to support the existing capitalism and was sufficiently quiescent to enable the business interests (and in some cases the Mafia in America) to gain considerable influence over the governing apparatus of many unions. That big business would not rest with this influence, but seized upon this period of capitalist strength to try to roll back the workers' gains, constituted the motive force of the Reagan-Thatcher period in America and Western Europe.

3.4 INSTABILITIES

In contrast to the strengths and stabilities of capitalism, there are major instabilities which may ultimately pave the way to a different kind of economic political system. Some of these arise from inherent developments which may present no problem now but are bound to cause massive trouble sometime in the future. Chief of these is that the profit criterion for decision-making cannot be satisfied forever.

It is possible to satisfy the requirement for profit, and especially for profit maximization, only so long as the domain of profit-making continues to expand, whether internally over more of people's activities or externally over more populations; but this expansion cannot continue forever. The problem is exacerbated by the tendency in industry and agriculture to increase technology in production: this lowers costs by raising productivity (more production per employee), but leaves a smaller employee base on which to make profit (unless the sales of the enterprise expand, which in the aggregate cannot go on forever). Concentration of capital in fewer enterprises also in general increases the profits of the enterprise, but decreases the room for further concentration.

A related problem is the impossibility of reining in the domain of capitalist decision criteria, even at points where these serve no social purpose for capitalism. For example, the organized accountants in the United States demanded in 1990 that all museums put a dollar value on every item in their holdings, otherwise the accountants said they could not formulate a complete accounting system for the museums; they rejected the museums' argument that it was impossible to put a price on many of these items.

As a result of capitalist decision-making's inability to stop its own activities except for a loss in profitability, its need to expand and to extract ever more profits out of the population may go on beyond what is needed to maintain the capitalists and their associates as rulers and privileged classes over their populations, and to maintain the society in which they can function. That is, the profit-making criterion for deciding on production may some day become a burden on the privileged classes themselves, a politically expensive way of holding on to their privileged position.

Aside from these distant threats to the profit-making criteria, there are many ongoing costs which detract from the status of capitalism as the desirable society which, for example, middle class East Europeans think it to be, and may detract from its success. Some of these are common, in one way or another, to all societies that maintain a privileged class at the expense of the unprivileged. They include unequal consumption, opportunity, and freedom ("poverty amidst plenty," etc.); pervasive unfairness, injustice and political dishonesty (maintaining a privileged class entails that the standard ways of the society include much evil, whether in the official legality or in the unofficial ways called corruption: the evil of what is banal is more relevant than the claimed banality of what is evil); brutality toward opponents and potential opponents (radicals, the poor, minorities, occupied areas such as colonies); conformity and vacuity in public culture not only for the ruled but differently also for the privileged (as in the well-known posturings and mendacity of life in high society and in corporations).

Other social and economic costs are more special to late capitalism: the exceptional waste in production, the destruction of the physical and biological environment, the downgrading of public culture to lower than the lowest common denominator (as in the competition for larger television audiences).

To mitigate some of these costs, when they present problems to capitalism, is difficult within the terms of the profit criterion. The difficulty arises because the profit criterion has no adequate provision for negative feedback. For example, whistle blowers within the system are discouraged and eliminated in capitalist activity, as they are throughout this society (even in the scientific establishment), even though they threaten not the existing system but only its excesses. The victims of the profit criterion, whether employees or customers, have no inherent avenue for affecting the decision-making — witness the economic weakness of the employees vis-à-vis their employer, and the lack of customer recourse embodied in "caveat emptor." Indeed, as noted above, as soon as the American workers and poor won major gains in the first half of the twentieth century (culminating in the welfare state), American business supported a counter-attack to undo the gains by means of resurgent ultra-conservatism. When workers or others injured by business succeed in winning court suits against companies, the companies, after the usual denials of responsibility, find many ways to minimize and delay compensation, going even so far as to enter bankruptcy for this purpose. And when customers succeed in winning suits for damage against a guilty company, the company often gets the judge to seal the court record so that information about the damage is not available to the public.

Mitigating the costs of capitalism is difficult also because of the chaotic structure of capitalist decision-making, which makes it difficult to address or resolve systemic problems. The in-principle free entry and multiplicity of capitalist endeavors give a sporadic character to response in the capitalist system. This on the one hand provides greater adaptability and quickness of response to changing situations. But on the other hand, while capitalism as a whole and its various sectors have characteristic self-interest responses to ongoing or changing conditions, they have no orderly process of coordinating, organizing and timing their reactions to economic problems and to working class opposition, or of adjudicating among different sectors of business. There is no fixed hierarchy or specifically businessmen's parliament, and such industry bodies as exist are mostly specialized to labor, government, and public relations. Capitalism and its business divisions do not even develop directly the accumulation and organization of information that could be useful in considering economy-wide and society-wide arrangements, nor do they have any machinery to make, carry out, or enforce such wide decisions, even if only intracapitalist. Thus, the same chancy structure, which enabled the profit criterion to be established within scattered spots of the feudal economy, stands in the way of its addressing systemic problems.

Also, the same indirectness in respect to production and consumption that characterizes the profit-criterion makes it intractable in respect to some society-wide problems of production and consumption, where the conditions of people and resources have to be taken into consideration.

3.5 BYPASS VIA GOVERNMENT

At various points when faced with difficulties such as have been noted above, the occupational groups with economic decision-making power have ceded decision-making to the government (pure laissez-faire having always been an abstraction) — as when it became necessary to extricate the system from the Great Depression. This is not simply a matter of government and the business community (or Big Capital) being loosely "the same" or "on the same side of the fence." In the early period of capitalism, and later as well, governments often abetted the establishing, operating, and expanding of capitalist decision-making and profits: by expropriation, by pauperization of the worker-pool, by "pacification" of colonies in which companies could operate, by financing or guaranteeing industrial infra-structure (e.g., railroads), by suppression of worker opposition (such as machine-bashing, demonstrations, strikes, forming of unions), by specific laws and regulations protecting and aiding not only profit-taking, but also profit-maximizing, and by a general legal stance in which sacrosanct "property" meant (indistinguishably) ownership of resources and workplaces for employing others no less than ownership of objects for one's own use.

More recently, there are pervasive cases of government protecting the profit-making of individual industries (U.S. right-of-way grants to railroads enabled the railroad owners to become major real estate dealers, who thereupon almost bankrupted their railroads so as to increase their real estate profits); defending industries against their workers or their customers or the public or the environment (for example, governmental denial that a danger from acid rain exists, and the courts' agreements to permit companies to continue with essentially unchanged management or control after the companies have declared bankruptcy in order to escape their contractual obligations); helping companies evade their responsibility for injury to their workers or to the public (for example, court-sealing of injury data, as mentioned above). Administrations in the United States take into serious consideration as a matter of course whether a governmental action will affect adversely the profit interest of one or another sector of big business.

In the early period of capitalism the reasons for government to aid business were varied, having much to do with the immediate financial interests of individual kings and noblemen. There have been rulers favoring one industry or businessman over another, and even (out of various self-interest considerations) favoring small farmers and the working people against the rising capitalists. However, with the great increase in wealth and economic importance of merchants, bankers, and the early industrialists, from the point of view of the political rulers there were an increasing number of cases of business usefulness or similarity of interests. The support of the interests of capitalists became a general property of governments and, more recently, as virtually the central function of government.

In the modern period, business is so pervasive and has such concentration of wealth and power that politicians and social institutions are heavily dependent on big business. In the United States, big business is the source of massive contributions to the ever more costly electoral campaigns, and a source of lucrative jobs when the politicians and military officers retire from government. In social life, major businessmen and major politicians and governmental or institutional personnel all belong to the same social class and often the same clubs. (Even in Communist China, when the post-Mao regime tried to establish capitalist activity, the new capitalists had entree into the restricted clubs of the high government personnel.)

What is important is that, beginning in the late 1800's and much more since the U.S. depression of 1929, the participation of government in production decisions changed. In addition to aiding business in its profit activities, there have been many instances of government carrying out its own decision-making on production and related economic matters, added to or replacing capitalist decision-making, or limiting it.[2] Some of these involve special cases where the multiplicity of enterprises in capitalist societies requires government intervention (for example, the grid-lock of freight trains in the eastern U. S. during World War I which was resolved by the government taking temporary unified control of rail transportation).

More important are large-scale needs of production (above all, the partial cessation of business decisions because of a lack of profitability) or of pressure from human needs or from the workers and poor. Companies concerned cannot meet the pressure either because it would involve profit reduction (e.g., pollution decrease; governmental regulations on various industries; or in the case of a particular industry, rent control) or because it would require economy-wide arrangement (e.g., minimum wage). There are also problems in weighing conflicting interests of various sectors of business: anti-trust laws; laws against price fixing and insider trading; detailed differences in tax policy; such decisions as to permit a company to declare bankruptcy in order to avoid paying medical liabilities, or to prevent companies from dropping their health insurance commitments; "industrial policy" such as that adopted in Japanese government-planning. Furthermore, there are some resources and production decisions so broad that government (or quasi-government) operation is found natural (especially) outside the United States): water, PTT, roads, railroads, airlines, TV, and nationalization of weak but needed industries (such as coal mines). Finally, there are society-wide pressures from the population that only government can meet: universal suffrage, legalization of unions and strikes, progressive taxation, public health services, the welfare state.

In these cases what is important is not that the government intervenes in productional activities, but that it makes the decisions about how those activities are carried out. Some steps by government are only incipiently in this direction, as in establishing government insurance for bank deposits (the FDIC in the United States after the Great Depression's bank crisis). Other steps have greater (though often unused) potential for affecting

2. Cf. Seymour Melman, *Pentagon Capitalism* (New York: McGraw-Hill, 1970).

business decisions: witness the recent massive bailouts of failing businesses — several large banks, the Chrysler automobile corporation, and above all the whole Savings and Loan industry in the United States. Here the government has merely supplied the necessary funds; but in the Chrysler case government people involved in the bailout suggested that the government should put certain conditions on Chrysler's further activities, as business lenders would have done, and as the World Bank does in lending to third world countries.

But in many other cases of the types cited above, government actions in recent decades have affected and regulated, in more intricate detail than previously, the decisions that business could make. This holds particularly in wages and working conditions, in pensions and the safety and health of workers and the public, in sales and export conditions, and in maintaining the environment. Other actions of government during this period constitute direct decisions on production and services and on consumption. This includes the vast bureaucracy of government services and also direct government production. It includes the Keynesian devices by which government tries to rescue capitalism from depression (as in the 1930's, when success in reestablishing profitability came only with the war). And in consumption it includes direct payment to the unemployed and the poor, and in the large governmental share in paying health-care costs, and in some countries the comprehensive welfare state system.

The increased government involvement in business decision-making is not simply an event, perhaps accidental, in history. It is the product of identifiable continuing pressures. Some of these are recurring or continuous conditions that invite governmental action designed to rein in the headlong flow of capitalist activities. Such activities are excesses of competition which can lead to local instabilities, runaway inflation, the cutting edge of modern financial manipulation (so far only barely regulated by government), with corporate raiding, insider trading, unfriendly takeovers, junk bonds, and cycles of taking a company public (offering shares on the market) followed by a leveraged buyout by the management to make it privately held again; and finally the grinding of capitalist decision-making down to a halt as in the depression of the 1930's. Keynes's economic theories served to fit governmental intervention into a theory of capitalism, and they were popular when capitalism had to be saved by a deus ex machina, but later they were unpopular among businessmen and their economists when the resurgent capitalism wanted to free itself of certain governmental reins.[3]

Other pressures coming from the world of business invite other entries of government into decision-making on production and on allocation of consumption. Such are conflicts of interest among sectors of capitalism, which invite governmental adjudication; also desires of the sectors engaging in financial speculation to reduce their risks, as in their acceptance of government insurance for bank deposits. Such also are the intractable problems of wasteful capitalist manufacture as in the pollution, depletion, and destruction of the environment. In these matters business is slowly beginning to accept government regulation — always as little as possible and as late as possible. Finally, there is a problem which by definition lies beyond the scope of business decisions, namely the long-term unemployed and the unemployable. Business may not mind having them around, for their existence helps to keep wages down and presents an ever-ready pool of "replacement" workers ("scabs") for countering the demands or strikes of employed workers. But as the number of unemployed increased, business had to accept the government's creating a minimal (or subminimal) welfare system for them.

The reason government can do such things while business cannot is that while business is bound by its bottom line profit criterion, government is free of that limitation (indeed it cannot use that criterion in any relevant way) and can make its decisions on the basis of the rock-bottom needs of people, and the physical possibilities for meeting them. Thus, government affords a bypass for capitalism, whereby the intractable problems of the profit criterion can be resolved by methods not based on profit calculation; in other matters, capitalism — that is, profitability — can continue on its way. What makes such a bypass available to capitalism is the indirectness of profit calculation in respect to the realities of production and consumption, so that when the method of business is unable to function there is always an alternative method available, namely the direct consideration of needs and possibilities. Indeed, one of the reasons for the 1990 Soviet government's inability to overcome the failure of communism's "command

3. John Maynard Keynes, *General Theory of Employment, Interest and Money* (New York: Harcourt, Brace and Co. 1936); Lawrence R. Klein, *The Kernsign Revolution,* 2nd ed. (New York: Macmillan, 1966).

economy" is that the arsenal of decision methods available to the 1990 government was not essentially different from that used by the command bureaucracy earlier.

The ability of capitalism to avail itself of a governmental bypass is thus a flexibility of capitalism, because capitalist decision-making has no intrinsic built-in stabilizing negative feedback mechanism. Nevertheless it is made possible by an inherent character of capitalism — the indirectness of its decision-making, and to some extent also made possible by the chaotic way in which decision status is exercised.

Two developments are crucial here. First, in addition to making the kind of productional decisions that capitalists would have made if they could, or would have to make if the government did not intervene, the government does make different decisions, on different facets of life and the economy (the right to strike, suffrage, the environment, welfare) going beyond what capitalist decision-making deals with, even in the sphere of production and consumption and social institutions. Second, no matter how pro-capitalist the government may be, and no matter how its choices in resolving problems are intended to aid capitalism or return it to profitability, the decisions which it makes are made on criteria other than profit. Indeed, as noted above, the reason government can make successful decisions (or, in some cases such as the Great Depression, make decisions at all) is that the government is free of the profit criterion and can make its decisions far more freely when necessary on direct (no matter how miserly) consideration of needs and materials and possibilities (as well as considerations of restoring profitability).

If capitalist decisions are in the last analysis based explicitly on profit calculations, then the government's different ways of deciding in various areas of socio-economic life mean that those areas are not, or are no longer, in the direct domain of capitalist profit-based decision-making. Thus, while capitalism is expanding into more aspects of people's lives and into more populations of the world, it is relinquishing decision-making on various areas of production, consumption, and socio-economic life in the capitalist populations. Indeed this happens more often in the democratic welfare states of old capitalism than in the "naked capitalism" of recent expansion. The resulting picture of capitalist activity is therefore less one of a rising tide covering the world than of an advancing wave front which leaves increasing areas of non-capitalist decision-making behind it.

The relinquishing is not a simple matter, as witness the constant struggle of big business against laws that constrain it, or the overflowing hatred of almost the whole American capitalist class against Franklin Roosevelt and his New Deal. Nevertheless, business has found it necessary to accept such tangible evidence of workers' pressure as unions and the right to strike (even if only when business can afford that luxury), and such limitations on excessive profit-makings as anti-trust and anti-price-fixing laws (under populist small-business pressure), and wholesale reining-in and recognition of the population's elementary needs in the New Deal regulatory and welfare measures (under pressure of the Great Depression). Indeed, Keynes's theory of capitalism left intrinsic room for government (and, more fundamentally, generally non-profit) decision-making on the economy to be fitted in under various circumstances (aside from its long-range implications). And, as noted, it is no accident that Keynesianism became the reigning theory of capitalist economy during the mid-century period of difficulties in capitalist decision-making, and that it was shunted aside and derided in the later period of capitalist expansion.

Thus if we do not think in terms of capitalism as a monolithic whole, but only of the profit-based decision system which determines its actions and its course of change, we see that while modern capitalism-supporting governments are not (at present) replacing the power or social system of capitalism, government decision-making is affecting or replacing capitalist decision-making in important areas of the economy and of social life. This relinquishing is, at least at present, visible just in the decision-making but not in the complete picture of socio-economic life, which remains essentially capitalist. This development in decision-making is important because if and when governmental decision-making becomes the major part of economic activity we may reasonably expect that the character of social life will become increasingly governmental — presumably oligarchic — rather than capitalist as we know it now. This future possibility will be discussed at the end of Ch. 5.

CHAPTER 4

Considerations in Analyzing
Social Change

Before asking about the possibilities for social change in the system described above, we note a few methodological conditions.

4.1 CONTINUITY

It is clear, from surveys of many known changes in many societies, that there is considerable continuity in the forms of social life. People in a society grow up into particular ways of providing for their needs and of relating to others; they cannot readily adjust to massive change in these ways, even if it were to be "objectively" in their interest. A simple example is the difficulty in changing common food habits, when it becomes necessary for reasons of public health or of shortages of customary foods. Sharp socio-economic changes, due to sudden physical or political events, usually affect only particular aspects of life; most ways of living change gradually.

4.2 INTERNAL CHANGE

Certain change-potentials ("dynamics") are inherent in certain socio-economic structures: for example, the possibility for moneyed Romans to buy the land of free peasants, thereby creating the rural latifundia on the one hand and the urban proletariat on the other. In the case of capitalism there are massive inherent potentials for change: the profit criterion, which leads to capitalist expansion; the indirectness of profit-calculation in respect to the production thereby decided, which can lead to increased distance between the two, and lead also to the wastefulness and destructiveness of technology; the detriment to employees and customers due to profit-maximization, which can only be compensated for by technologic advance or by extra-capitalist (e.g., governmental) intervention. These potentials contribute to the historical direction of change in the society.

Aside from such specific causes of change and decline, it has been argued by some socio-historical theorists that all social systems age and decline, even if the reasons are unknown. In particular, the question of whether the "autumn" of feudalism was in part independent of the "spring" of capitalism has been debated (cf. Wolff). Interesting as this issue may be, it is not essential to the discussion in the present book, which relates primarily to the actual situation of capitalism and its visible pressures for change.

4.3 Social Forces

One can distinguish in a society what may be called its systemic social forces, which affect its stability and its changeability. The social forces making for stability include in the first place the make-up and structure (including the conditions for entry and exit) of the ruling entity. This entity may be an individual such as a chief or king or dictator; or it may be an institution such as the priesthood or the military, or even a socio-economic group: the large landowners or the landed aristocracy or the business class. The most important property of a ruling entity is the particular basis on which its position and power rest. As noted, this power basis may be military, control of the resources and equipment of production (maintained by physical force or by tradition), exercise of control functions that are vital for production and distribution, or social position in a religion or a tradition which the population accepts.

Stability, or at least resistance to change, comes also from the complex organization of production and consumption, and of the many details of social arrangements embodied in existing social institutions and traditional customs. These generally conform to the existing social powers (irrespective of the extent to which the powers were created by traditions, and to what extent traditions were molded by the powers). The whole existing organization of society makes it hard for people to think otherwise than in terms of the status quo. It is even harder for them to act differently than in those terms.

In addition, in many societies there is explicit acceptance of the current social powers and relations. This is especially so when large sectors of the population are living reasonably well in respect to their material and political expectations, or when the culture (e.g., religion) inculcated into them imbues them with a firm acceptance of the status quo (e.g., Confucian respect for authority, or the Hindu caste system) or of their religious and national ingroup against all others (e.g., Catholicism during much of its history, Islam, Orthodox Judaism, and the many fervent nationalisms and political neighbor-hatreds of modern times).

Even aside from the attitudes inculcated by the institutions of society, the social attitudes of a given people's traditional culture are greater shackles than is generally realized — intellectually, artistically, morally and humanly. Tradition has to be considered a major conservative and divisive constraint, though individuals and even whole subgroups of the population can occasionally outgrow it, especially when other cultures are known to them or when broader life opportunities become available. Even then, people may no longer be able to follow their own traditions without being able to accept or understand or be accepted into other cultures; this situation is well known in immigrant or conquered populations such as the American Indians in the United States today.

Conformity of most people to the existing order, even when they are dissatisfied, should not however be considered "complicity" on their part. It is difficult for most people to depart from existing social arrangements unless alternative arrangements are available to them. Conformity in the absence of choice does not have the implication of complicity. Indeed, nonconformity — opposition to one's social environment and refusal to fit into it — requires particular social conditions and developments, except for occasional cases of one individual or another.

By the same token, ideology in support of the status quo may not be essential for maintaining people's passive fitting in to ongoing social ways. Ordinary conservative governments (say, the last pre-Thatcher Tory regime under Edward Heath, or Republican presidencies before Reagan) do not need to press any explicit ideology (other than the constantly reinforced conformities of the ruling culture), since they coast on the ongoing way of life which constitutes the status quo. It was only Thatcher and Reagan (or for that matter Khomeini in Iran) who had recourse to strong reactionary ideology, in order to buttress their major and quick increases in conferring favor on the power groups in their society. Political attitudes, ongoing or novel, take the explicit character of ideology when they are used in a struggle for change, to the right or to the left. More generally, one can say that all social life is imbued with an implicit ideology, which becomes explicit only in the course of attempted change. Or alternatively (and almost equivalently) that social life in general is a nonideological fitting of individuals into the existing social structures, while awareness of these structures and attitudes toward them (ideology) arise only in the course of attempted change.

In contrast to all this, there are the social forces making for change in the relations among the main socio-economic sectors of a population. Two major types of such forces have appeared in various social situations. One is an alternative "elite," a would-be successor ruling or privileged group, waiting in the wings. For them to become the new rulers usually involves a change in the socio-economic control base. Such were: the growing capitalist class in the late 1700's and early 1800's; the technical, managerial, and politician (people-manipulating) occupations in many countries in the early 1900's (whose members mostly ended up as managers for and within late capitalism); the educated and would-be entrepreneurial elements in Russia and China in the late 1980's. In most cases such elites have too little economic or numerical power to change the control-structure of their society; but with their drive and ideology they can help direct the dissatisfaction and strength of the disadvantaged population to overthrow existing controls, with the elites then becoming the new leaders of the changed society.

The other major social force for change is the disadvantaged sector of the population. Such a sector exists in every society in which there is a heavily privileged sector. The existence of disadvantaged as residue of privileged would be unavoidable in any zero-sum aspects of social life i.e., in any aspects where limits hold because expansion is unavailable. In many societies, this disparity is not a political factor. In societies and periods in which the ruling groups enjoy wide acceptance, upper class privileges can be maintained without precluding various circumscribed freedoms of the population as a whole. In societies in which many of the disadvantaged have a standard of living at least reasonably acceptable to them, the rulers need little force and perhaps not much manipulation to keep the population in place. And in societies and periods when production is expanding, most of the population can attain an acceptable standard of living and range of personal freedoms, even while the privileged groups have far more.

In spite of all the social forces and forms that defang the victims of a regime, the mass of disadvantaged people remains a source of possible change. The intensity and the extent of bitterness of many people against the regime, and their ability to create an upheaval when some occasion offers, is not a thing of the past. It came to the fore in the satellite countries of the Soviet Union in the fall of 1989 once the military umbrella of the Soviet Union was removed by Gorbachev in the summer of 1989. And it appeared in the Soviet Union (no matter how directionlessly) in August of 1991 when the dramatic coup of the KGB gave it its occasion.

In societies in which the victims are strongly opposed to their privileged classes, the people and their interests cannot be permanently defeated. This is so because the power and privileges of the ruling groups are in general based on the differential between them and the bulk of the population either at home or in subject lands. Rulers cannot be rulers without presence of the ruled, and without the ruled being worse off than the rulers. However, the whole society may meet some other catastrophe before this internal conflict is played out.

4.4 ACTIONS

Aside from changes arising out of the decision system itself (4.2), or out of external pressures (military, economic, or of the physical environment), there may be changes arising out of the opposition of the victims of that system. In the latter case, what can be best counted as elementary entities in the course of social change is not the individual opponents as persons, but rather their acts. The individuals may later change, or die, while the effects of their actions may remain. Acts which can contribute to social change are not those of single individuals, no matter how large the act may be for the individual, but actions done at about the same time by many individuals or groups reacting in parallel to a common situation, or acts carried out jointly by groups or crowds (which may be different from what the participating individuals would or could do alone).

Because the actions that count here are those common to a socially relevant group or are reinforced by that group, the types and ranges of ideas and actions taken up in a given social group may be less varied and less complex than the welter of actions by one individual or another. Consistency of individuals in their social actions is generally due to continuity not only in their ethnic and religious groups but also in their occupational position. Often, such group actions are directed toward single issues, or overriding socio-economic difficulties common to many people at the same time. The groups whose actions affect the economic (production-consumption) system and the related political system are the broadly defined occupational groups mentioned in 2.1.

It is clear from all this that what actions are at all possible, and what actions have a chance of being relevant to social change in a particular direction, depend on the directions of change possible in the society at the time and on the social forces involved. An objective description of social potentialities is thus a prerequisite for any consideration of scenarios of change. However, the kinds of action then possible, and the room for intentional intervention in these potential processes, is not automatically determined by the objective social description. The status, effect, and possibilities of intervention have to be investigated as aspects of a separate political problem.

4.5 INDIVIDUALS

Although the reaction to bad conditions, the decision to act, and the carrying out of an action are all done by individuals, the individuals are small as to both size and lifetime in comparison with society and social change. This limits the importance of the individual in respect to actions for change, though not in respect to ideas about social change. Ideas about society and the individual's relation to it generally arise and are kept alive on the basis of people's social experiences and awarenesses. The role of individuals as idea-makers can be considerable, though even here there are limits because the changes of social conditions can limit cultural memory.

This limitation on the importance of individuals applies even to leaders. Idea-makers and leaders are different in their occupations. Commentators and analysts look for large patterns and implications in political action, and often ascribe such broad considerations to the leaders in the society, whereas the leaders in fact are acting either of themselves in their own immediate interests or those of the ruling groups (current or incoming) of their society. The historical importance of their individual actions is less than is commonly claimed. Even in the case of oppositional and revolutionary leaders, whose historical importance can be considerable, there are limits on the long-range effect of their individual actions, as the rollback of the Russian Revolution has underscored.

There is an additional problem with leadership. Given the effects of traditional culture and institutional indoctrination, the disadvantaged have in many situations been confused about their economic self-interest. Their choice of leaders has in many cases been even more confused, as witness the many false prophets that have been followed by radicals, liberals, and labor. One may also consider the attitude of the early 20th century American socialist leader Eugene V. Debs, who said that he would not lead the people to socialism even if he could, because if he could lead them into it someone else could lead them out of it.

More generally, as noted above, there are two considerations that limit the importance of the individual in social change. First, the attitudes and actions which the individual shares with others of his occupation or group are more likely to affect social change than the actions in which the individual is divergent or unique. Second, whatever the individual's intentions, his acts have their own life and effect: the individual may change his intentions but the effects of his actions may continue.

All this suggests that in political change action may be more important than intention or justification. In particular, the end cannot justify the means: A revolutionary leader may have high ideals and may then feel it necessary to create controls to push people toward the desired changes; however, he dies before his ends are achieved, and what remains after him is the apparatus of control he had created. Rather than the Stalinist justification that "there is no white road to socialism," this suggests that there is no black road to socialism.

4.6 What Induces Action?

In considering what leads to action for social change, one cannot assume that there exists, or that we know, a set of "real" interests of the people or specifically of the workers. The "real" as against the learned (conforming) interests are in general not distinguished by people. There are many societies in which religious, nationalist, and traditionalist attitudes and behaviors are fiercely maintained by the bulk of the population, relegating any individuals who doubt these values, or seek forbidden freedoms, to the scorned fringes of this society. Nevertheless, there are certain relevant differences between the "real" and the learned values. By and large, the learned interests are actively promoted (taught) by the social-cultural institutions and the centers of power, and are maintained by a constant input of control and — in the modern world — of money. How they would fare today without this continuing input is perhaps in question. There is historical and sociological evidence that in the course of meeting relevant difficulties or new potentialities, people can go through vague or explicit "consciousness raising" in which they divest themselves of some of these learned attitudes: for example, the growth of anti-royal republican attitudes, the anti-slavery movement, the recent feminist and anti-war movements.

The major social and occupational groupings differ in their readiness to act (2.2). The ruling groups are more or less always on guard to thwart opposition and to protect their interests. This is seen in the self assurance, vigilance, and defensive activities in almost every set of rulers and of super-privileged groups. Even in the early Gorbachev years there were letters in the Soviet press in which the bureaucrats — and their wives — expressed disdain for the masses and self-assurance about their privileges in terms such as are commonly associated by us with Marie Antoinette. There are, however, many cases of ruling groups decaying and losing their readiness to fight back (or their ability to fight back), especially when their economic base and their public acceptance erode to the vanishing point. Consider the late period of Rome, and of European feudalism, and in recent years the Argentine military junta after its defeat in the Falklands, and in some respects the Gorbachev regime.

The new elites are waiting in the wings. They become aggressively active in pushing for social and political power as their importance or their potential usefulness in production begins to outweigh that of the old order. This is seen in the creation and fostering of whole ideologies — even in fundamental opposition to the existing power system — which fit the interests of the given elites; examples are the philosophers and economic theoreticians of early capitalism, or the ideologues of Leninist vanguard communism. It is also seen in the direct activism of demonstrations, attempted uprisings, and socio-economic plans of various educated groups: the fascist-oriented students in Central Europe of the 1930's (Polish Endeks and the Nazis), the Chinese students of Tiananmen Square in June 1989, the intellectuals and the entrepreneurs in the East European satellites in late 1989 and in the Soviet Union in 1990.

In contrast, the oppositional attitudes of the disadvantaged population develop slowly, and do not in most cases reach explicit ideological form on their own. Their adversarial actions consist typically of disorganized or only partially organized sporadic acts such as those of the Luddites and "Captain Swing" in England, and of sudden eruptions of rebellion such as the many peasant revolts of medieval Europe after which the peasants usually simply returned to their homes. Compare also the explosion of Laborite opposition to England's Expeditionary Force sent by Churchill in 1919 to fight the Bolsheviks, which subsided without continuation as soon as the force was withdrawn.

The experience of history is that the "masses" act primarily when special openings arise — specially unbearable situations or special opportunities for action — and that they then act for matters of immediate relevance to them, although their actions can be directed against the whole existing order, and can utilize oppositional ideas learned from rising new elites. (Cf. George Rude, *The Crowd in the French Revolution*, OUP 1959.) As a case of this pattern of action, it is characteristic that in industrial society, where many workers work together or in comparable jobs, the action of the workers in respect to their work and their workplace are much more likely to be organized and focused than the actions of workers, or people in general, in respect to the over-all social and political ills of the existing order.

What is primary, then, is action in response to situation. The understandings and ideas come with such attempts at action or come as their consequence, important as the ideas may be for further development and action. None of this is surprising, if we accept the views about thought and understanding in the writings of pragmatist philosophers, sociological Marxists, critical theorists of the Frankfurt School, or, in developmental psychology, Jean Piaget.

In any case, people's understandings, and existing social ideas and ideals (or new ones growing out of people's experience or out of rising elites), count here primarily as predispositions to action; they seldom are the direct determinants of action. In many situations, immediate issues called forth or triggered by the situation itself or by how it unfolds outweigh all others in determining action. (Cf. the work of Eric Hobsbawm and of George Rude.) For confusions of interest in an uprising, note the relative inaction of East European and Soviet workers in 1989-90, in contrast to the sharp focus and activity of people in middle-class-type occupations — and in contrast to the focused Polish shipyard workers acting in their workplace in the early days of Solidarnosc.

The uprisings in East European countries under Soviet imposed governments show that mass uprisings can still occur, even though they took place in the special conditions of the weakening of the Soviet military control. However, the contrast between their success and the lack of comparable and immediately successful mass uprisings in the Soviet Union proper and in China shows that the East European events are better characterized as uprisings against a foreign occupation more than against a local privileged class (which in any case was hated not only as a repressive regime but also as a Quisling government).

4.7 THE COURSE OF CHANGE

In different situations, change may follow different courses: a revolution (sudden or not), successive piecemeal political or economic upheavals, or long drawn out small though telling changes.

There may be several, partly parallel, courses of change within a single society and period, and different changes may be of different magnitudes. There may even be substantive changes in the economic and political conditions of a country without complete replacement of its ruling groups and individuals (for example, in the change from the landed aristocracy as the fundamental economic elite of England to its present capitalism). Members of the old ruling groups may manage to locate themselves in the developing new system.

It is even possible for major social and economic changes to take place with only partial change in the political structure. This is especially the case when the changes are carried out in a never completed sequence of partial upheavals, as in England from the pre-capitalist Magna Charta and on, or in the German lands in the 19th century. Such a course, especially if it does not crucially involve the intensity and direction supplied by the "masses," carries the price of retaining vestiges of the old political power even though it may have no use in the new economic and cultural system except as a reactionary bulwark for the new privileged classes once they in turn are in power.

4.8 THE DIRECTION OF CHANGE

Several factors make for a more or less consistent direction of change in a society over long periods. One is the potential for change, if any, inherent in the system itself. Another factor is the nature of potentially available, alternative, more desirable socio-economic arrangements (with possibly their own distinct elites) which having been able to grow within the existing system has given them the status of challengers against the existing system. Important social changes have been directed by the opportunities available to new elites, although they were brought about by the activity of the victims of the old society, acting subjectively in their own oppositional direction with at most some additional ideals stemming from the new elites.

In the case of action stemming primarily from the disadvantaged rather than from new challenging elites, one might think that nothing general can be said about the character and direction of social change (especially if intellectuals of the left are not a guiding force), seeing that the workers' actions are geared primarily to the short range and to the situation from which they are coming rather than to the situation toward which they are moving. But in fact there is in each society at each period an approximate delimitation of the further socio-economic possibilities and of the possible directions of development. In the case of capitalism, this comes in part because the workers' rise to action is not arbitrary. They respond in terms of their position in a productional-consumptional and social-cultural system, and in terms of their needs and interests in respect to this system. At any given place and time, with its current productional and social structure and difficulties, there are only a few possible courses toward the future. In particular, only a few types and directions of action can be taken by workers or other groups of the disadvantaged with any possibility of success, and only a few can be taken by them at their workplace.

This is not to denigrate the great importance of political awareness and of radicalism. History includes the effect of individuals in such concerted actions, so long as what they are doing is at least somewhat in keeping with what is possible in the ongoing socio-economic situation, and so long as it can lead to betterment in the consumption level and civil liberties of the population.

But it does not conform to history to believe that change, and more specifically a constant direction of change, must require an awareness of society and history. It is even more clearly not in conformity with history to believe that change cannot take place without a leader or vanguard at the helm. Changes may be made by individuals finding new methods or new niches in the course of seeking their own advantage or the advantage of their populational subgroup. If these methods and niches are useful for others too, a direction of change is born. Changes may also come from barely perceptible differences in equipment and its use or in ways of interacting, made in successive generations in response to some continuing pressure in respect to what leads to a more satisfactory result. Over long periods such cumulative changes constitute a direction or what some may consider a causal chain of one stage leading to another.

4.9 CONCLUSION

The general conclusion from the preceding discussion is that large-scale change is sociological more than political, and productional more than ideological. The sociological and productional developments determine the long range direction and the limits of what is possible. Political and ideological interventions in the process can affect the immediate local conditions. However, these interventions can be rolled back even if they have been instituted. The interventions can be important for hastening, triggering, and focusing change; but they have little chance of a lasting success unless they are supported by ongoing and continuing sociological and productional developments. Indeed, the ability of governments to change the economy and social arrangements is limited, both in a right-wing direction, as is seen in the Thatcher and Reagan endeavors, and in a left-wing direction, as is seen in the social democratic governments, or for that matter in the Communist regimes.

There is also the question of morality as a factor in social change. Without discounting the validity of subjective morality — insofar as such exists — as a value in itself, its status as a social force is most dubious. Whatever morality means, it cannot mean favoring one person or group as such over another. No matter what and how strong a person's (or group's) belief, its only status is that it is his belief. Having the belief does not make it an objective fact outside ones own mind; calling a fertilized human egg a human person, or saying that a braindead hospital patient is still alive no more makes it so than calling a dog's tail a leg makes it so (in the joke about how many legs a dog has if you call its tail a leg — still four). Thus there is no status to one person's or group's belief controlling the belief or action of another person (such as that of the abortion-seeking mother, or the relatives and doctors of the brain-dead patient).

The only politically relevant morality, then, is not a person's beliefs but his participation in the ongoing social choices between what he considers to be better or worse for the population as a whole. People's moralizing and feeling of moral justification can serve to strengthen their disposition to act; but this may simply be a self-justification for controlling others.

CHAPTER 5

Potentially Post-Capitalist Developments

5.1 ONGOING CHANGES

There are various developments within capitalism that may lead to socio-economic conditions which would be at least in part no longer capitalist. Some of these developments were implicit or incipient in earlier periods but have reached a stage in which their post-capitalist potential can be recognized.

5.1.1 Internal to the Decision System: Profit

Some changes are due directly to the exigencies of profit maximization. This criterion requires reducing costs, reducing risk, seeking areas of greater profitability, and maximizing sales by expanding into new areas or into greater market share.[1] Reducing costs involves fighting the workers over wages and conditions (5.1.5) and wasting the environment (5.1.3), as well as seeking cheap resources in the "colonies" and nowadays cheap labor in the third world. Reducing risk has been a factor in many activities such as manipulating the market, forming cartels and mergers, and soliciting government protection, subsidies or guarantees.

During the 20th century the press of profit maximization has led to many situations that differ from those of earlier periods of capi-

---

1. Defense contractors in the U.S. have maximized profit by maximizing both costs and subsidies from the government. This pattern of micro-economy also prevailed in much of the industrial system of the former U.S.S.R.

talism. The search for greater sales has supported a massive advertising occupation, with ever more pervasive and manipulatory
advertisements and commercials, and ubiquitous "hard sell" pressure to buy. The attempt to reduce risk by assuring sales has promoted market research, which first seeks statistical information
about consumer response to products and to advertisements, but
then grows into manipulation such as attempts at subliminal advertisement, or such as identifying likely consumers in order to aim
specific products and advertisements at particular subsets of the
population. With this, business activity has extended into new
areas of business information, including invasion of privacy, as in
selling lists of likely consumers, or in phone companies selling their
information about subscribers to advertisers and sales agencies.

There is of course the expansion of profit-making into countless new products and variations on old products, and into more
areas of consumption (in effect, of living), which has always characterized capitalism. More recently there has also been expansion
of profit-making into new areas of services, entertainment and
information, as in interactive telephone and cable-television services. The expansion of business into more of the social and cultural activities of the population (in effect creating new items of
consumption) not only brings new profits but also puts business
in the position of having the initiative in determining the content
and the political character of popular culture. The influence of
business over public life is increased by the expansion of profit-
making into ever more activities. It has made political campaigns
and such public necessities as the publishing of newspapers cost
so much money that only big business can support them. There
has also been an expansion of business into scientific research,
with not a few scientists becoming entrepreneurs, and many
becoming direct consultants or science-administrators for business (mostly while continuing in their university posts).

Vaster and more dramatic expansions are seen in governments'
privatization of public services: for example, in the United States
the change of the postal service to a privately managed body, and
the growth of profit-making letter and parcel companies; the
growth of profit-making hospital chains, and the plans for profit-
making schools and prisons; the past and recent give-aways of
public lands to industrial corporations, the assigning of public
television channels and airline rights to private companies (as in
England and France); the plans to privatize national railroads; and

in Thatcher's England the plans to privatize water distribution and to make university courses depend on student choices (with government money given not to the schools but to the students, who would pay only for the courses they choose).

In addition, one of the major internal expansions of profit-making has been into the business (profit-making) process; the still rapidly growing maze of financial activities and agencies that make profit by serving or manipulating the steps of business. These include ad-men, market researchers, speculators, brokers, bankers, and the like.

There have also been major expansions of profit-making into new areas of the world. Where the old geographic expansion of business was primarily for resources in conquered "colonies," and also for specialized markets (e.g., in cotton) in particular countries, the new expansion was for international markets (both mergers and investments in foreign capitalist lands, and sales — such as films and cola drinks — in all foreign countries) and for investments and work (e.g., heavy public works) in "developing" countries. For these foreign activities, various large companies in the capitalist countries took on the form of giant multinational corporations. In addition, many manufacturing companies in the old capitalist countries have opened factories in Third World countries, especially in the Pacific Rim and Mexico, because labor there was so much cheaper and more subservient than at home and pollution was disregarded; but much of the market for the products remained in Europe and America.

The search for profit-maximization also fuels a search for immediacy of profits (the issue being maximum profit per unit time). Thus in many cases it discourages long-range planning, or acceptance of lower profits immediately for some long-range reason. Thus, a few quarter-years with low profits makes an American stock-owned company vulnerable to hostile takeover attempts, even if the company could continue to operate profitably in its productional niche.

5.1.2 Internal Factors: Distance from Production

The dynamics of the profit calculation toward bottomline purity, sketched above, fits in with the dynamics of the indirectness of profit as a decision system on production. As has been noted, this indirectness leads to increased distance between decision-making and the production thereby decided. This distance increases because there is nothing that ties the profit decisions to the content of the production. In consequence profit opportunities that are irrelevant to the production in question will sooner or later be seized. The distance increases also because there is nothing to prevent intermediate decisions from intervening between the making of a decision and the production in question; if profits can be made out of intervening steps those steps will sooner or later be taken.

The development of corporate management and corporate life, with its Byzantine structure and attendant culture, fits well into this picture, as does the fact that the evolution of the stock market is culminating in corporate raiding.

The very structure of the stock market indicators, like that of television ratings, focuses on momentary performance and militates against continuity and loyalty and long range considerations. Founders and family owners of a successful company eventually sell out to an industry giant, or take the company public by selling shares.

At an early stage, the shares provided capital for expansion while the owners-managers kept control as "minority stockholder," owning only a few percent of the shares, but which constituted the largest and most focused block. The executives became increasingly an independent self-perpetuating extremely high-paid management. Management had to defend itself at annual stockholders meetings first against scattered discontented shareholders, and later against investors who controlled blocks of shares, and obtained proxies to vote additional shares, seeking to replace the existing management. More recently, the banks' readiness to make high-risk loans or sell junk bonds enabled raiders to buy a majority of the shares (using little or no money of their own) and so remain free to do as they wished with the company, instead of cajoling the shareholders for proxies and thereafter having to justify their managerial actions to the shareholders. Management itself has concerns in addition to high profits in the short term, namely its own survival and income, and the strength of the company and its products in the middle term. The shareholders, however, have in many cases no other interest than immediate profits, and will sell to anyone who offers a high price per share even if this is achieved by junk bonds which may cripple the company thereafter.

The corporate raiders carrying out a takeover have no interest except to capture (or be in position to capture) the company. They can then make their own profits either immediately from greenmail — selling their shares back to the company — or from the operations of the company after they take over, or from selling off large parts of it, or even from bringing it to bankruptcy under certain conditions. The banks and bankers and brokers who give the corporate raiders the loans with which they buy up the shares at inflated prices (or who sell the junk bonds of the raiders) make their vast profits up front, whether the takeover succeeds or not and whether the company under attack survives or not.[2] A typical related development is the purchase of a company whose products or services have achieved a high reputation (of excellence or of prestige), whereafter the new owner cuts costs and cheapens the product until its good name is lost, making his profits in the meantime.

With all these developments, the bottom line becomes not only a necessary consideration for a business decision, as it always has been, but increasingly the only consideration. Investment money moves more and more freely from one company or industry — or country — to another, depending on immediate profitability. The difference between finance capitalism and speculation is decreased.

The growing distance from the eventual production is also seen in the decrease of a company's continuity and loyalty to its products. This is perhaps more pronounced in the diversified conglomerates, in which a company invests its profit not in improving or increasing its production, or in related production that can strengthen its manufacturing process or its profit share, but rather in acquiring completely unrelated companies. There may be a business logic to this, in the face of the vagaries of the market, but there is hardly a productional logic.

As has been seen, the increasing separation of decision-making from the production decided by it has fostered profit-making activities which do not deal with products or services at all but only with the steps of capitalist activity, that is with the process of decision-making itself. In its oldest form this profit made out of profit-making appears as an aid to the ordinary profit-making steps, as when banks give investment loans, in the course of which they check not so much the profitability of the ultimate production as the reliability of the businessman's credit and col-

---

2. John C. Coffee, Jr., Louis Lowenstein and Susan Rose Ackerman, eds., *Knights, Raiders and Targets: The Impact of the Hostile Takeover* (New York: Oxford University Press, 1988); Paul M. Hirsch, *Pack Your Own Parachute: How To Survive Mergers, Takeovers and other Corporate Disasters* (Reading, Mass.: Addison-Wesley, 1987).

lateral. Such banking activity has now advanced to the point where banks and other financial and legal services provide advice on the business steps, on how to move with respect to tax laws and government regulations, and finally on how to put together the loans and deals that make the original decision-making possible. Such intra-capitalist profit-makings constitute the current finance capitalism, which is powerful because its profits are very great (given the vast amounts of money which are involved) and because its activities are essential to many major deals. The removal of financial activities from the ultimate production becomes clearer in the recent growth of financial manipulation such as corporate raiding, leveraged buyouts, junk bonds, kiting of holdings (e.g., by selling oil, land, etc. back and forth between two companies — or two entities under the same holding company — in order to increase its paper valuation), and other "paper entrepreneurialisms," insider trading, and also corruption (even in respect to capitalist laws and customs) such as the massive bankruptcies in the American Savings and Loan industry in the late 1980's.

That all these activities are not aberrations, but natural outgrowths of the nature and demands of capitalist decision-making, is seen in the fact that even the illegal extremes of current financial manipulation are hardly spoken against or acted against by the financial or business establishment. Indeed, corporate raiding and the like, and even junk bonds, have been explicitly defended by representatives of the most august financial houses and even participated in by them.

Some economists have ex post facto written angrily against the frauds perpetrated by the leading Savings and Loan operators in America.[3] However, these operations were only marginally more extreme than the mainstream capitalist activities whether legal or not (including major banks that laundered Mafia and drug millions, and bribes such as those given to officials by Lockheed Corporation, let alone the way John D. Rockefeller first made his fortune, or the way the Robber Barons made their profits in the late 1800's).

In any case, neither capitalist leaders nor the institutions of the business world disavowed the recent questionable ways of making huge profits in banking, brokerage, real estate, and the like. The government's deregulation of the Savings and Loan industry was done in a way that invited the kind of unstable and

---

3. Lawrence J. White, *The S and L Debacle: Public Policy Lessons for Bank and Thrift Regulation* (New York: Oxford University Press, 1991).

manipulated profit-making that indeed took place. Both the big business community and the public accepted the sharp dealings and frauds of the aggressive and large concerns and their innovations in financial manipulation, which constitute the cutting edge of capitalism.

Here one cannot say that the financial activities are merely accessory steps to the productionally relevant decision-making, so that their profits are simply parts of the total profit made in the given decision activities. For these manipulations are largely productionally irrelevant activities, not for example the act of a takeover financier seizing a company and taking for himself the profits from its further activities, but rather the act of a bank making profit on a deal no matter what its outcome may be, or of a corporate raider making his profit by agreeing to stop trying to capture the company (greenmail), or by capturing it and selling off large parts of it, and the like. Such profits are indeed made purely out of the business profit process itself, without regard to any outcome in product or service. For the society as a whole, such activities are possible because of the indirectness of decision-making with respect to production; and they increase this indirectness.

The importance of this increasing indirectness can be seen in various economic and social developments. The greatest profitability and economic power today is in the financial sector. The greatest occupational growth is in finance, management, government, law (largely on economic issues), and advertising and films (where the big money is in commercials). Far more college students go into these fields than into the humanities, let alone science; in applied sciences and engineering third-world and Asian students are the major presence in American universities. The most active innovation in today's society is not in technology or pure science but in advertising, market manipulation, financial operations, and the financing and managing of electoral campaigns.

5.1.3 Universalization

Several expansionist pressures in business make for a universalization of capitalism. One example, which arises from profit calculation to the exclusion of all other considerations, is the insistence (by countries that stand to gain from it) on the free-trade principle. Countries that produce food cheaply oppose agricultural protection (tariff, subsidies, etc.) in other countries, as has happened in the new European Community, and above all with the U.S. pressure in GATT, with no consideration that the other countries might not want to be left without a local agriculture (what would happen if some catastrophe prevents the food transport?), or if they might want to exercise some control over the quality or health-dangers of the foreign food.

With all the pressures for bottom-line considerations enshrined now in the yuppie culture of today and the single-minded businessmen, various corporations are dropping the old continuities and loyalties, to product and to company (top executives of a company sometimes switch to its competitor) and even to country. American executives of multinational companies which originated in America and are still essentially American have now been reported as saying that they have no commitment or responsibility to America (this in superficial contrast to the well-known statement of the head of General Motors in the 1940's that "What is good for General Motors is good for America"). In the words of C. Siewert, chief financial officer of the originally American, now multinational, Colgate-Palmolive Company: "The United States does not have an automatic call on our resources. There is no mindset that puts this country first"; and R. H. Galvin, the chairman of Motorola, Inc., which has a plant in Kuala Lumpur in addition to its American plants, says: "We'd try to make a balanced decision that took everyone into consideration, Malaysians and Americans. We need our Far Eastern customers, and we cannot alienate the Malaysians. We must treat our employees all over the world equally" (The *New York Times* 5/21/89). Despite this stance of internationalist even-handedness, the corporations' turn to third-world plants had been actuated by a search for the cheapest and most pliant labor, for tax savings, and in some cases for easier entry into foreign markets, all without regard to job loss at home or to the needs of the home market and balance of trade. Furthermore, these heady internationalisms of the multinationals disregard the possibility that if these companies ever need their home government to protect them abroad, it may be less easy for the government to justify doing so if the home population no longer looks upon them as part of their country, economically or socially.

With the internal and external expansion of American and West European capitalism, one should consider one additional and more abstract development: the expansion of capitalism — profit-making — as a system, independently of who makes the profits.

The prime case here is Japan. Although Japan had been pushing since before the turn of the century to become an industrial country, it would not necessarily have succeeded on its own in overcoming the status that it had reached before the Second World War, as a producer of cheap low-quality light-industry products. When the Second World War ended, the U.S. government decided to change defeated Japan from the autocratic state that it was to a successful democratic capitalist country, as a way of tying it to the United States and thus creating a bulwark against the Soviet Union (and then against China); this perhaps on the basis of anthropological analyses as to how the Japanese would respond to American authority over them. (In 1946-47 there was a comparable but much weaker attempt by the American government to establish a functioning countrywide capitalism in Chiang Kai-Shek's China, partly in the hope of forestalling a victory by Mao's Communists.)

In the event, Japan went on beyond this to become a major capitalist country, gradually advancing from its previous shoddy and light-industry products to becoming a world leader in consumer electronics, computers, household appliances, automobiles. Like all miracles, the Japanese miracle was no miracle. It was aided actively by continuing economic policies of the United States government, and passively by a failure of American corporations to compete vigorously. Japan started with the advantage of a very low paid and obedient worker population, and with autocratic managers prepared to be energetic entrepreneurs, and autocratic governments willing to serve as partners of the new capitalism in "industrial policy"; that is, in deciding in what productional areas to concentrate the efforts of government and capital. As against these advantages, Japan has virtually no natural resources for industry, lacks the bits of innovative individualistic culture that are left over in the old capitalist countries from the early capitalist period; and it has contributed little fundamental research to its productional activities. When Japan attempts to advance its own research lines, it shows little of the easy success of its more applicational activities in production. Thus, Japan's repeated promise to produce a "fifth generation" of computers able inter alia to "understand language" has not been fulfilled.

Japan's success lies in that its production is carefully geared to the consumers in the old capitalist countries, trying to meet their needs and preferences and to make at low cost products that are satisfactory to them. The success of Japanese production lies also in the lack of enough competitive response from American manufacturers, who (by their own statements) saw Japanese wages as a pressure for lowering American wages, and who failed to encourage and use technologic innovation and to design for the convenience and safety of the users as well as to win more cooperation and interest from the workers (if for no other reason than as counterbalance to the lower wage cost and the more obedient discipline of the Japanese workers). For its part, the United States government has time and again refused to help American industry withstand Japanese competition or to curb Japanese imports; the latter on the plea that only free trade makes for a successful world economy, as if a healthy international free trade were a stable possibility when wage levels are very different in different countries.

The causes of this behavior by America (and less so by Europe) may be diverse. But a contributory cause may possibly be that the established capitalisms view with favor any arisings of local capitalisms elsewhere, that is to say any extension of capitalist methods, even if the profits are made by foreign capitalists, and even if this is at the cost of the profits of the old capitalisms (when the foreign profits are made primarily from American and European consumers, thus taking a large market share away from the old capitalisms). America also refuses to put bars to foreign investment and control in America itself (e.g., in American airlines) partly no doubt because this helps cover the American national debt that has been almost tripled by the Reagan administration, but also apparently as a matter of governmental capitalist policy.

The argument that such market share loss at home is balanced by American and European market opportunities in the new capitalist lands does not hold too well, because the new lands and especially Japan buy little from the old capitalisms; the United States has a long-term large negative balance of trade with Japan. With all this, it is noteworthy that while Japan is a capitalist power in retaining so much profit, it is like the Third World and the old colonies of European capitalism in that it produces primarily for the consumers of the old capitalist countries.

With all this, military and informational technology remains heavily centered in the United States economy, even though America is not trying to exclude Japan from a major position in informational technology.

The joy in the established capitalisms at the prospect of capitalism replacing communism is not only because it opens up new markets, but also because there is ideological satisfaction at the extension of capitalism. The United States government and press, and the international lending banks, insisted on a complete and immediate "free market" for Russia's satellites, and even for Russia itself, as the price for any appreciable economic aid (which for the most part did not come), without regard to the possibility that so quick and massive a change might be catastrophic for those countries or even impossible. Indeed, the unrelenting opposition of America and Western Europe to Russian and Chinese (and Cuban and other) Communism, especially to the pre–World-War II Soviet Union which had posed no military threat at that time, was presumably not only out of a fear that communism might some day replace capitalism, but also out of a refusal to let such large areas of the world be closed to the extension of the capitalist system. (The thaw in respect to Communist China came as the possibilities of doing business with China began to be apparent.)

In any case it would appear that the major determinant of the current foreign policy of the United States is, after the spin-off from domestic policy (including profits for American companies), the universalization of capitalism. Since the retreat of Gorbachev's Soviet Union there is no problem of military security. The only world interest of American capitalism is, then, to keep many third world countries as economic colonies, and to develop a local capitalist structure in various non-capitalist countries, even if they thereby escape from colonial status.

The extension of capitalist method into a large number of national capitalist economies is of a piece with the post-national and post-local-culture tendencies and events of the established capitalisms, such as the shrugging off of nationalism noted above for the multinational corporations. These trends appear in various ways in the current history of capitalism. Where previous empires had used conquered lands for tax and military purposes, with limited influence of the colonies on the home country, the colonialism of expanding 19th century capitalism created in the home population an occupation of administrators and military personnel stationed in the colonies and a growing presence of colonial people living and studying in the home country, thus bringing some of the colonies' world into the home country. This latter presence became much larger precisely with the ending of explicit colonial control, as late capitalism from the mid-20th century on found use for a low paid largely unskilled population brought from the colonies into the home country: West Indians and Pakistani in England, Algerians in France, Puerto Ricans and Mexicans and Filipinos in the United States. Countries without colonies took in comparable populations: Turks and Yugoslavs in West Germany, Portuguese in several European countries. In this way, large foreign more-or-less underclass populations became part of the capitalist countries, reducing the cultural specificity of the big capitalist cities.

Whereas the capitalist countries of the early 1900's expected their immigrants to assimilate, as in the popular notion of the American "melting pot," the current institutions and mainstream big business are far more tolerant than are the American and West European populations toward non-assimilating immigrant communities such as the Algerians in France and the Pakistani in England, or the Hispanics in the United States. Current mainstream capitalism also tolerates certain non-mainstream (mostly, minority) communities, such as the black and feminist and homosexual movements. In contrast, the extreme right of the 1980's, which tries to turn the clock back from the preceding moderate capitalism, also tries to restore the purer community ways and family "values" against the minority movements and the immigrant communities and more generally against the empowerment of the individual (e.g., in the anti-abortion fight). Thatcher wanted no structure in society except family (explicitly) and business (implicitly).

Specificity of national cultures stands to be compromised also by the European Community, which has been promoted for decades by the top capitalists of the West European countries, who expect to gain much from the united European market and from the likely weakening of the not so readily unitable distinct working classes of the individual countries. In this connection one might note the recent reduction of regionalism in United States capitalism. Whereas for the first three-quarters of the 20th century there were differences in cultural-political character and in economic interests between the regional capitalisms of Chicago, of Texas, and of California as against New England-New York, the differences have taken a back seat to a resurgent national conservatism from the beginning of the Reagan years. In all of these developments one can see a muting of national and regional characters and interests under the drive of an evermore purely profit-minded universalization of capitalism.

5.1.4 The Physical Environment

Perhaps the major blow to capitalist decision-making is coming from a direction which fifty years ago no one had expected: the environment.

In the first place, capitalism's use of its technology is damaging human ecology in a way that is becoming increasingly obvious and unignorable: pollution, nuclear waste, global warming, ozone depletion, soil and forest depletion (with other damages that may make agribusiness and its chemical base no longer very profitable), health dangers from food additives, and the like.

Secondly, the world's population growth, accelerated by medical advances in populations (especially Third World) that are retarded economically and socially, has reached the point of taxing available production.

Third, the unreasoned, unplanned, unreviewed, and essentially wasteful technology of capitalism is threatening to deplete the usable material and energy resources of the planet (petroleum, rain forests, plant and animal species, etc.).

Business cannot, by its structure, consider these matters. Its decisions are essentially short-range (to reach a maximum available profit in least time), and its bottom line criterion cannot deal with these problems (most restrictions on wastefulness and most attempts at alternative energy involve an immediate cost against profits). The day-to-day decisions of business disregard or circumvent most environmental considerations and hide their environmental damage. Within capitalism, even the governments, which might be expected to deal with such long-range problems, delay consideration of environmental problems as long as possible.

Even the language of resources hides the damage that modern technology does to them. Thus, somewhat as Columbus did not so much discover America as invade it (in the Indians' words), so the oil and mineral companies do not merely discover oil and minerals but dissipate them.

What makes these considerations the crucial threats to capitalism is, first, that the magnitude of capitalism's use of the planet is beginning to confront the finite magnitude of the planet, and, second, that manipulation, artifice, and military power, which can save rulers from their ruled population, are of no avail here.

5.1.5 Decline in Productional Knowledge

One of the important long-range changes that seems to have begun in late capitalism is the decline in research and development of new ideas and methods in areas related to production for consumption. Such changes can be visible only over generations, because the knowledge and research directions that students in each generation acquire continues through their lifetime. But as one observes the situation in detail, one can see evidence of change and factors that indicate greater future change.

First, new productional knowledge is not needed for the major methods of accumulating wealth today; wealth is achieved today mostly by financial and political manipulation. Nor is new productional knowledge needed for the major profit-makings and business expansions today; they are achieved mostly by market manipulation. Even in manufacture, serious technological innovation is today not of major importance, and less so in the growing service sector. Advances that have productional applications often fail to find support from business sources, many of which — aside from a few industries such as pharmaceuticals — prefer to wait until the development is completed (if ever) and profits are immediate. The great technological field that is developing currently is in information and communication systems — computer software, microprocessors, robotics, vast computer and intercomputer systems, telephone and television networks and interactive provisions, satellite control and utilization, high-tech weapons, and many specific applications such as smart cards and smart bombs. This development may constitute a major component in much future production, and a major factor in the strength and character of regional economies. It is at present the one major promise of new strength and expansion for capitalist production. And perhaps not surprisingly it is the one field of technology in which the United States, which may be losing its central importance in manufacture and possibly even in agriculture, remains the outstanding center.

Second, the bulk of government support for science is devoted to military research and development. While this includes work in various sciences, especially in computers and astronomy and materials science (within physical chemistry), the lion's share of funds goes to weaponry. There is some spinoff from military research to knowledge that can improve people's standard of living, but not much; and the direction of thought is very different.

Furthermore, the increased importance of business and government funds in university research means that the directions that hold no interest for them will not get much funding, and are even discouraged by university administrations which prefer and sometimes require that every researcher bring in outside funding. The direction of research is even more skewed by the fact that many successful or "highly visible" scientists become science entrepreneurs even while at the university, or head business-oriented institutes affiliated with the university, and aim their own work and especially the work of their students at issues of interest to business. While this may bring advances in science and technology, it is too limited in its range and leaves little room for major and independent innovation.

The one field without military or primarily profit-making value that is highly funded — by government, foundations, and wealthy individuals — is medical research, which has such immediate importance to human life, including the lives of the ruling groups themselves. Even here there are the personal interests of big capitalists, as in the Texas cardiac research centers supported by wealthy oilmen.

Aside from lack of research support, the science occupations today suffer from the fact that within the middle class the higher incomes today are not made there but rather in business and service professions — economics, law, accounting, medical care and dentistry. Hence students in the capitalist countries are to an increasing extent not in science. Many students in science, and many hospital practitioners, are from third world countries, and the Asian or Asian-American students who form a large part of the science student body in American universities enter these subjects and work hard at them from a tradition and career orientation unrelated to the late capitalism of today. There was a flurry of science students in America immediately after the Soviet Sputnik satellite, but it soon died down.

One other recent development militates against advances in science today. This is the tendency toward teamwork science, which is often unavoidable in engineering development but not necessarily so in "pure" science. The recent push toward large centrally administered science projects, in which one chief decision-maker (often a "famous" person with his own private ambitions) controls a large or even country-wide effort, or in which a small number of selected centers each with hierarchical planning and control get the bulk of research support, does not promise to be successful. Such top-down organization is inescapable when the top administrator is a scientist working with or for a business. This has led to pressures for particular results, and an increase in fraud and in hidden agendas. Such organization is modeled on what — for better or worse — is the rule in government and in corporations; but it is anathema to research and scientific advance. It is hard to believe that fruitful science will flourish in such conditions.

More generally, the great bulk of the population in the old capitalist countries grows into, and lives in, a culture which disfavors intellectual inquiry and a scientific attitude. It is a culture in which children and adults spend much time passively before the television screen, where the competition for profits (from commercials) leads to a race for maximum audience by means of a flashing jumble of contentless two-second images, and in which ubiquitous entertainment — almost always mindless and of no consequence — has become a daily need of social life. It is also a culture in which dishonesty reigns, whether in the ever-present advertising whose content is generally false (or false by being irrelevant), or in the election campaigns where the big business interests of the political parties have to be hidden from the voting public, or in the news media where the meaning of events and issues is either unmentioned, or confused by "infotainment" or else misrepresented in order to avoid arousing opposition to the existing economic and political powers.

For all these reasons, one has to consider the possibility that advances in knowledge, even such as are related to improvements in consumption, will decrease in late capitalism. This situation would have a deleterious effect on the standard of living of the population. Fed by the current stage of decision-making's distance from production, it would reduce one of the greatest sources of capitalism's acceptance by the population.

5.1.6 Opposition from Below

Sharp struggles of industrial and farm workers against the wages and working conditions imposed by the growing industrial capitalism were common throughout the 1800's and into the mid-1900's. Characteristically, the employers adamantly rejected worker demands; but from the 1870's on employers and government made more and more accommodations with the workers, perhaps because the growth of the industrial infrastructure and technology made it possible for them to afford it while still making satisfactory profits. This accommodation constituted a new flexibility of capitalism, and has yielded many improvements in wages, hours, working conditions, standard of living, and recognition of unions and of the right to strike. From the Great Depression of 1929 into the early 1970's, this development culminated in major advances and safety nets for workers, minorities, and the poor: the Keynesian policies, the New Deal in the United States (and later, civil and minority rights), the welfare state of Sweden ("capitalism with a human face"), and major welfare programs such as the Beveridge Report (initiated by Churchill's Tory Government) and National Health Service in England, and widespread unemployment and social security benefits on the Continent. These steps, from the 30's on, may have been taken partly out of fear that communism would otherwise win the workers over; and they involved a considerable relinquishing of economic decision-making into the hands of government.

The betterment in workers' standard of living led to a reduction in bitterness and radicalism on the part of workers, which in turn decreased the militancy of the unions. This last was due partly to the attitudes of top union executives who sought for themselves the incomes and status of the business executives with whom they dealt, and who destroyed union democracy. And it was due in part to the businessmen's co-opting the thus deranged unions.

Meanwhile, the ability of workers to defend their interests was being compromised by the competition from such different low-waged capitalisms as Korea and Brazil, and by the ability of American and European corporations to move their plants to ultra low-wage areas, such as the Pacific Rim and Mexico. With the reduction of manufacture, especially in the United States and England, the employed skilled blue-collar working class became considerably smaller, and those who remained employed (weakened by the existence of an unemployed underclass) had less clout for fighting back on wages and working conditions.

For the big industrial employers, especially in America and England, this situation, including the depoliticalization and weakening of the working class, provided the opportunity to reverse the labor gains of the last half-century, and also to reverse the welfare state, the civil rights advances, and the relinquishing of decision status into the hands of government. In many companies, especially those taken over by corporate raiders (e.g., in the Frank

Lorenzo airlines), this appeared (roughly from the early 1970's) as a new militancy against their workers ("zap labor"), using strike breaking and stonewalling techniques. In politics, this approach appeared at first as ultra-right movements (and to some extent the young-conservatism of the yuppies), which were opposed by mainstream conservatism (cf. the bitter dislike between New England-New York capitalists and the western right-wing Republicans, and Edward Heath's bitter opposition to Margaret Thatcher — and the Thacherites' bitter opposition to Heath). However, from the late 1970's and on, the ultra-right won out over the old conservatives, and was then found by the business world to be quite useful (cf. the "teflon" treatment of Reagan by mainstream businessmen and media, and the only thinly concealed Thatcherism of the once staid journal *The Economist*).

At present, labor is very much on the defensive, forced in many cases to yield concessions in wages and work conditions, with union contracts cancelled by court approved bankruptcies staged for the purpose, and with strikes lost. Average real wage is falling; governments are right wing or ultra right; unemployment is increasing (masked in part by increase in part-time work and in the lower-wage service sector), and manufacture is decreasing. Many unemployed become unemployable because there are no jobs or because their skills are now irrelevant; some become homeless. Gradually they become part of a redundant underclass, peopled also by minorities and no longer needed foreign unskilled workers. In effect the underclass is outside capitalist society and is kept alive only by poverty-level welfare. This is the notorious excluded third of the "two-thirds society."

5.1.7 Limits to Capitalism

The preceding sections have indicated that capitalism is undergoing large-scale changes, which may present major difficulties for it. Many of these threaten to bring capitalist decision-making to the limit of its ability to operate. There has always been a cycle of business crises in which parts of the economy become unable to find profitability and so have to suspend making the decisions which trigger production; this situation has so far led to business events that retrieve profitability, whence the cycle. The massive crisis of 1929 was overcome only by Keynesian means plus the Second World War, and such events may or may not ensure the prevention or overcoming of any future massive crisis.

Other developments in capitalism may reach inescapable limits. First are the limits of expansion. Expansion of profit-making into more and more areas of people's lives may reach a point where so little opportunity is left as effectively to close this avenue. There may also be virtual limits to finding opportunities for financial manipulation. Since all of these are objectively intervenings between decision-making and the production or service decided thereby, there may in effect be a limit on how much intervening the traffic will bear. Market manipulation may also prove to be limited, so that companies may reach a point where appreciable increase in sales is no longer possible. Also, some of the major recent governmental aids to capitalism are not readily repeatable: Reagan's weaponry budget, etc., which caused almost a tripling of the national debt; Thatcher's economic success, at a cost of overharvesting the North Sea oil-fields; the massive American bailout of the Savings and Loan corruption. And recourse to major or world war (often a crisis solution) is more or less excluded now by the dangers of atomic weapons.

As to the geographic expansion of the old capitalisms, or the growth of capitalisms in new countries, this is clearly limited by the finiteness of the globe.

Then there are the limits of the earth's available resources, even if we throw in the moon and perhaps a bit of Mars. The waste of resources by capitalist competitive production, which can hardly be controlled within the methods of business decision-making, is bringing into the foreseeable future an end to the availability of some of the crucial resources. And pollution and ecological change will sooner or later approach levels that cannot support modern life.

The lack of negative feedback to expansion and to misuse of the earth gives the capitalist decision method no way of avoiding the approach to these limits. Also, the chaotic structure of capitalist decision-making, as well as its indirectness, hobble any attempt to use awareness and planning to forestall crisis.

The polarization of society with the two extremes of a productionally ever-more irrelevant privileged power group as against a large underclass may cost capitalism the wide popular acceptance it now enjoys. Capitalism may then have cause to fear a political confrontation with an embittered working class or underclass such as it feared in the early ideological heyday of Soviet communism. A much milder lack of popular support may form against multinational companies whose home country base seems to them now to be expendable. We may see a bit of this in the near future when the large companies of the European Community rush to manufacture in whatever country is cheapest, and to replace whatever local production disturbs their market opportunities. Neither the population of their original home, nor that of the countries into which they encroach, may be motivated to support them if such support is someday needed.

The creation of new capitalisms, such as Japan, may be accompanied by a certain decline in the old capitalisms. The new try harder, and go to the trouble of making user-friendly products; and they rely on product innovation more than on market manipulation. They have already shown a capacity to win profits away from the old capitalist countries, which now constitute their crucial market. If the old capitalisms gradually fall into a secondary position, a new separation may be created, with basic science and military power remaining at least for a time with the old capitalisms, while production and capital accumulation together with its economic power concentrate in the new capitalisms. Later, the new may also graduate to manipulatory and non-user-friendly methods, but their economic hegemony may remain.

In all of these changes, some most likely and others reasonably possible, the old capitalisms face problems that they will not be able to resolve in the present form of capitalism, despite its present supremacy.

5.2 RELINQUISHING OF DECISION-MAKING

Ruling groups are not likely to develop self-restraint, even when faced with massive difficulties, because such actions would in most cases entail some loss in control and advantage for the people instituting the self-restraint, while the gains would come to the ruling group as a whole some time in the future. Social systems are therefore normally seen to be moving inexorably through their "destiny," without being able to avail themselves of foresight. Nevertheless, the capitalism of the 20th century has been able to accept various restrictions on its functioning, which have in some respects the effect of a stabilizing negative feedback. This flexibility came not out of any feedback mechanism created by capitalist functioning itself, but out of adjustments to forces outside the capitalist decision mechanism. Thus, from early on, employees tried to organize unions or to go on strike, with bitter opposition from employers (and government). As technology became more intricately interwoven and as plants became more massive, employers stood to gain from a more orderly body of workers, and a certain small measure of self-government and initiative by workers (in unions, strikes, etc.) came to be tolerated, and later in part coopted by the employers. Somewhat similarly, faced with continuing clashes of interest between regions, between industries, and between big and small business, and faced with social problems that were beyond what big business could or would treat (down most recently to costly health care for its employees), business grudgingly accepted intervention and management by government. These flexibilities may have been fostered by the chaotic structure of capitalism; communist regimes did not adjust and remained with a more disorderly and uncooperative body of workers. In any case, the flexibilities helped capitalism go on, but almost always capitalism lost some of its economic initiative and control and decision power (though not its political and social power).

In his *Civilization and Capitalism*,[4] Fernand Braudel says "The market economy ... had created an opposition, counterforces both above and below itself." Here we will consider how the space above (or behind) and below capitalism has indeed been used partly in opposition to capitalism but partly also as a relinquishing by capitalism of parts of its profit-based decision-making to a space 'behind' and 'below.'

5.2.1 To "Behind" the Capitalist Advance

The systemic problems and limits noted above are not dealt with by capitalism in any adequate way, and cannot be. The criterion that defines capitalism determines only the individual business decisions of each enterprise; and the competitive environment ensures that this criterion be the overriding determinant, since any deflection by other considerations may leave the businessman behind in the competition. Furthermore, the chaotic membership in the set of business players makes it difficult for any sustained joint effort by the capitalist class as a whole (though it has not precluded capitalism's having a clearcut direction of development). The unrestricted entry into business activity and depar-

---

4. Fernand Braudel, *Civilization and Capitalism. 15th - 18th Century, v.1, The Structures of Everyday Life*, translated from the French, revised by Stan Reynolds, (New York: Harper and Row, 1981).

ture from it (e.g., by business failure), and the constant necessity to calculate risk and to meet competition, decrease the ability of businessmen to control as a body the decision-making of all individual enterprises. Capitalism cannot plan and execute steps that require effective across-the-board cooperation. It does not even have the information and records of all relevant business actions, such as might be needed to decide and enforce concerted activity.

Finally, as has been noted, capitalism has no thoroughgoing negative feedback to keep its systemic problems in check automatically, without concerted intentional actions by whole industries or the whole class.

Given such situations, businessmen have often turned to the government for help, as noted in Ch. 3.5. In the early periods such help consisted in licenses to do commerce (especially abroad) or to produce particular goods, supplying infrastructure for industry, and protection for "property" interests against employees, and the like. As concentration and expansion created giant business concerns, government tended to aid them in particular and to cover their failures. In time big business became not only a social equal (and even senior partner) of top government personnel, but also the source of high-salary sinecures for retiring government and military leaders.

From the late 1800's, governments in capitalist countries found that in addition to all this help they also had to carry out activities or enact laws that directed the production of goods and services, or affected the way business produced these. Such actions were required either for the advancement or salvaging of profitability, or for the basic unmet needs of the population and the country as a whole. The business community in some cases desired these activities but in other cases accepted them only grudgingly or even opposed them. This included direct production of industrial infrastructure by the government, e.g., the railroads of Europe, automobile roads, and dams, but also country-wide economic steps which determined the wage levels of workers, the price levels of basic foods, the money flow, and the like. In later times, it also included tackling tasks that fall within the activities of the business world, but which business finds unprofitable (e.g., cleanup of chemical and nuclear waste, or the risk-reducing insuring of bank deposits, or bailouts of massive failing companies or industries). There are also governmental economic activities, outside the scope of business, that deal with the needs of the country and its population, such as decisions as to what is taxed and how much, and what care (if any) is given to the poor or to the people who are not employed (and so are outside the business loop). Some of the latter is also done by people directly, outside of governmental channels, as in the case of charity. At one time some businesses in England sponsored poorhouses.

In very many of the economic activities of government, the economic interests and power of capitalism are enhanced, while the decision-making activities of capitalism are left intact and not affected. However, in some of the governmental actions of the later period, actions both small and large, the scope of certain capitalist decision-makings is reduced, though the power of capitalism is retained or even salvaged. The existence of the latter type of government decision on production constitutes a bypass for capitalist decision-making. That is, in situations where capitalist decision-making cannot be carried out, either because the required profitability is lacking (i.e., there is no way to expect a profit from making the given decision) or because a necessary economic step is beyond the scope of the chaotic structure of the business world, government will step in and make decisions, as a byproduct of which capitalist decision-making can continue or be resumed. Business also uses government as a quick way to advance its interests. For example, the large and aggressive lending institutions in America (Savings and Loans, banks, insurance companies) have promoted government regulations that helped them achieve great growth quickly, often at the expense of smaller companies. In some cases they seek not to remove government regulation so much as to change it in their favor. They also use government for various specialized services, such as assuming the burden of bad loans. In all this the special interests of big business groups are served, but not by profit-calculating methods. Thus the scope of governmental direct decision methods is increased.

From the point of view of capitalist power, the bypass is an incident. It enhances or restores capitalism's power and ability to operate after some business failure. But from the point of view of capitalist decision-making, the bypasses constitute temporary or permanent reductions, and replacements by a different type of decision-making carried out with different criteria by a different (no matter how friendly) social institution. The decision activities that ultimately determine production and consumption in the society are to this extent changed. This has importance because sooner or later and in one way or another a change in who makes the decisions, and how, will generate a change in the power relations of the society. The decision-maker will eventually wield the power.

That this transfer of decision power is not trivial is seen in the resurgence of the ultra-right hard-line capitalism that used Reagan and Thatcher. The hard-liners demanded a return to an imaginary pure market situation, with laissez-faire and monetarism and reduction of the activities and the economic intervention of government. The formerly popular Keynesianism was for them as bad a word as "liberal." During the 1980's these regimes did not reduce government activity; Reagan's government grew in size as had its predecessors, and government expenditures, notably military, grew tremendously at the cost of a vast increase in the national debt. But the activity of government changed at that time from regulatory decisions on business and decisions on burdens that were beyond the scope of business (e.g., welfare) toward activities that simply helped or facilitated business decision-making (hence, profit) by easier conditions for profit and for expansion, lower business taxes, obstructions to worker opposition, public resource give-aways to private concerns, removal of society-wide obligations such as disposal of industrial waste, and especially massive high-profit purchases of weaponry.

The actions of these governments became in this respect temporarily more nearly like the actions of governments in the middle period of capitalism about a century earlier — except that capitalism was then in its major period of industrial expansion, which it is not now. Indeed, it had been this productional expansion, with its enrichment of various sectors of society, that left room for a more or less government-supported accommodation toward higher standards of living for the workers. This is also not the case now.

Hard-line capitalism could manage its economic program today only in the wake of the preceding improvement in workers' lives, and under cover of the resulting acceptance of capitalism by the bulk of workers. But this accumulated political capital of capitalism will be expended if the advances in standard of living that had fostered this acceptance are not maintained. Indeed, neither the Reagan nor the Thatcher regimes were able to eliminate completely or largely the social services that government had found it necessary to take on during the preceding years. Some Tory backbenchers had suggested that Labor should not fight Thatcher so bitterly, since upon her retirement the Conservative Party would of course return to its traditional (more Heath-like) character. But as the Reagan regime saddled America with a vast national debt that would prevent a return to the large social programs of the government, so Thatcher sought to destroy existing institutional forms so as to leave profit-making as the only channel for societal activities. There would indeed be a return to mainstream conservatism after them, but in a more backward and less stable environment, more nearly similar to earlier capitalism.

Business tries to put off the resolution of its problems not only by the hard-line attack on government encroachment as above, but also by denying the problems and delaying any action to resolve them, with the ultra-right governments participating in these business resolves. Businessmen have hardly modified their decisions at all by any effective measures against pollution, depletion, job loss and impoverishment among their workers. There is a joke, if joke it be, that the energy industry will go along with coal, oil, and nuclear energy, since they own or can own the requisite mines and installations, but they deny the harnessability of solar energy since they cannot own the sun. The putting off of long-term solutions and the lack of any practice in adjusting capitalist decision-making to the new exigencies mean that when the new problems can no longer be evaded the entry of government, both national and local, into decision-making will be more immediate, more massive, and more non-capitalist in its methods.

One must also recognize that despite the essential capitalist assumptions and functions of the governments of capitalist lands, these governments have on many recent occasions found it necessary to limit capitalist powers and to extend the powers and welfare of the "common man." In the post-depression New Deal in America, for example, the government did not only reinstate jobs for the workers but also enacted the Wagner Act, which gave labor important legal rights. And while governments participate in many secret acts of interest to the conservative forces, as the American government did in the Polk assassination in Greece after World War II, they may also pass such laws as the Freedom of Information Act in America, which enabled people to uncover what the government had done — something that companies cannot in general be forced to do.

In this way, bits of capitalist decision-making are being relinquished piecemeal to the government, which then makes its decisions without a profit criterion. As long as there is any profit to be made out of anything, capitalist decision-making continues to expand and move forward. But as noted in Ch. 1, capitalist decision-making is thus seen to be not an ocean covering more of people's lives and more of the globe, but a wave moving forward and leaving behind it major economic problems to be treated by government in non-capitalist ways.

5.2.2 To Below Capitalism

Somewhat as the profit basis and the multiplicity of enterprises make it difficult for capitalism to meet inescapable needs of production and of the population, which are then left to be met by the not profit-based and more centralized government acting "behind business," so in a different way these properties of capitalism may make some production in the capitalist countries sufficiently unprofitable or inconvenient so that it can be left (especially if it is humanly indispensable) to decision-making that is not profit-based and less burdened by administration, carried out under employee [more specifically: worker] control acting "below business." This may be expected not only because of the greater profitability for capitalism in third world manufacture, and in financial activity instead of manufacture, but also because of great rises in environmental costs, and the frequent shifts in profitability as between industries and between companies. For example, it may well be that many big companies will back out of increasingly low-profit agribusiness, leaving much of the industry to smaller, family or cooperative, farms which will be much more attentive to their own land. Such backing-out may take place even if the company is still viable, with customers, etc., but simply is not sufficiently profitable. Bankruptcies, bank closings, and asset or company sales may provide opportunities to employees who would otherwise be laid off, or to unemployed workers threatened (by the decrease of manufacture) with descent into the underclass.

This opening for employees is possible because, given the chaotic feature of capitalism, the lack of conditions necessary for business action will for the most part be piecemeal (especially shifts due to environmental changes), striking at the relative profitability of some companies and industries before others. Also because the same chaotic feature permits anyone to start or buy a company if he can put together the capital. It may be that in some situations the creditors (including the lending banks) and the customers may prefer that the employees buy the company than have it closed, although in many cases banks and others who are involved may oppose employee purchase for ideological reasons.

There are important reasons why employees can make a living out of a plant or service that is making little or no profit. They do not need to profit over and above the employee wages, or to pay the overblown executive salaries. In a depressed period they can operate at a loss, taking home less than their previous take-home pay, whereas a business owner would have to close or else lose his money. They can be expected to have far more responsibility and incentive to innovate in the workplace, pay more attention to the plant and to the product, maintain better and more user-oriented quality, than is the case in ordinary businesses today. These are among the features which are used to explain the current success of Japanese business.[5] Employee-owned enterprises may thus prove viable even within capitalism, and may become more efficient. They would presumably have smaller production units (note that the massive factories of late capitalism may often have been more a reflection of massive management than of efficiency). They would presumably also be less wasteful, and tend to somewhat different and more pragmatic technologies and energy sources.

All this holds on the premise that employee-owners can develop ways to retain the employee-owned character. They would in most cases have to hire business managers, but not at exorbitant salaries (which cannot be really required for the skills involved). The managers would function in constant interaction with the employee owners' representatives (who of course should be term appointees and should be rotated, effectively answerable to the membership). The owners would have to avoid taking on nonshare-owning employees, because that would soon reduce the advantage that employee owners have over capitalist companies.

Ideas and attempts of this type have arisen at many times and places since the late 1800's, and earlier. The fact that most of them have not long survived does not argue against their possible

---

5. The Yamazaki Machinery Company is the largest firm in the Japanese machine tool industry and probably the largest such firm in the world. When demand for machine tools fell sharply during the early 1980's, the management calculated that a 15 percent reduction in wages and salaries was necessary to adjust to the world-wide market drop. Alternative strategies were considered. At a meeting of all employees with management it was agreed that everyone would stay on the job and take a 15 percent pay cut for the duration of the market slump. Afterward the management would treat the money withheld as though it were a loan to be repaid when business improved. Similar practices have been reported for other Japanese firms.

survival in the future, because we are now speaking not of an idea for its own sake but of a possible response of tomorrow's businesses to massive unprofitability and to a further decline of manufacture in the old capitalist lands.

5.3 THE SUCCESSOR TO CAPITALISM

The litany of capitalism's changes and problems should not be taken to suggest that a crisis of capitalism is around the corner. Capitalism in America is still highly productive, and can afford to throw a trillion dollars with equanimity to the Savings and Loan businessmen. It continues to hold the loyalty of a large part of the population of the old capitalist lands, and the admiration of many people in communist and third world countries. Nevertheless, many serious difficulties are developing, the most inexorable being pollution and the depletion of the environment which supports human life. It has been seen that the ultimate response of capitalist decision-making to inexorable problems is to relinquish its decision-making to forms behind it and perhaps also below it.

These two relinquishings have opposite political effects. That to the government, behind business, is clearly attested; and if it becomes large enough to take primacy over capitalist decision-making, it would lead ultimately to a stable non-expanding economy, in all likelihood ruled oligarchically and dictatorially, possibly with some capitalists remaining as a rich rentier class.

The supposition that this would be its political character, as also the supposition below as to the character of an economy of employee ownership, is based on the general observation that at least in modern societies the ways the production-decisions are made have a major effect on social political character of the society, with the makers of decisions being important wielders of power (Ch. 6.8).

The supposition of an eventual roughly stable economy is based on the judgment that an economy which is expanding relative to the size of the population (and expanding at a rate sufficient to provide palpable profits) cannot go on forever in a world whose finiteness is beginning to close in on us.

There are two possible avenues to approximate stability within the general social controls of today's capitalist society.

One is a reining in of profit maximization, carried out by the present kind of capitalist decision-makers or their successors. While this is at odds with the competitive profit-making criterion of capitalism and with its history, it is a possibility that cannot be discounted. It is true that people's social behavior fits into a structure not because they are aware of following that structure, but because their habitual ways and modifications based on self-interest had over time come to constitute that structure. But awareness of historical processes and future dangers has not been available before the present period. Although people have generally chosen to disregard such warnings they may be able to take it into account when the danger to them becomes clear and present. Thus, wars in the capitalist past have seemed to be an unavoidable product of the need of national economies to expand or compete; but when the danger of nuclear warfare became obvious, the capitalists found ways of meeting their needs without nuclear wars. In this vein, it is conceivable that as profit-making becomes barely or only spottily available, businessmen may finally notice the handwriting on the wall, and find ways to freeze their activities and gains. There are a few small hints that such restraint is possible. One is the support that modern mainstream capitalism provides to the welfare state, recognizing the need for a permanent non-capitalist cost (ultimately against profits) to stave off social collapse. This is seen in Scandinavia, in the Beveridge Report's promise of protection "from the cradle to the grave" and in the social-security provisions of virtually all the old capitalist lands, which even the Reaganite and Thatcherite extremists were unable to reverse. Another hint of restraint may be garnered from the fact that capitalism has not so far moved to the oft-predicted state of "monopoly capitalism." For whatever specific reasons, the U.S. automobile industry, which was approaching a two-company monopoly, allowed its home market to escape monopoly via European and then Asian imports. And the giant telephone monopoly of AT&T in the U.S. was broken up in some measure at the company's own instance, in order to free it to compete (so far unsuccessfully) in the computer market with IBM. These, of course, are but straws, and not necessarily straws in the wind. In any case, such a development to a virtually non-expanding business economy would involve a deep alteration in business practices and purposes, for the sake of salvaging part of the business class and its more superficial ways.

The other possible avenue to a stable economy controlled by a ruling group would come from government effectively replacing businessmen as operator of the economy. This could happen by means of a "fascist" coup, at the imminent collapse of business decision-making, or after such a collapse. Or, conceivably it could come through some more gradual transition. Such a transition is conceivable because the economic power-wielders who have grown up as a new factor inside the mechanism of late capitalism are the top echelons in major corporation managements, the military, and the government. Their ability to grow within the competitive and expansionist capitalist system is based in part on their own ability to expand their sphere of action. They can replace capitalist decision-making at one point or another because their own activities are not entirely tied to profit maximization. When and if profits are harder to come by, these new decision-makers can continue to act using more direct criteria (not primarily profit-based) for making economic decisions, within their scope in the economy. Even if they are in the habit of trying to expand, their basis for deciding (where their ultimate criterion is simply the retention of their privileged position) can if necessary be followed without such expanding. Thus, in circumstances where expansion becomes less and less possible, their economic activities can continue in a non-expanding economy.

In contrast, the relinquishing to the employees, "below" business, if it takes place and continues to an influential extent, would create the decision-model of a stable cooperative economy whose political expression would very possibly be more nearly democratic and reasonably humane.

Neither of the relinquishings, certainly not relinquishing to the employees, would of itself change the political form of society. But it would represent an available economic alternative on the basis of which the profit-based decision activities could be remodeled at a time when profit-making comes into massive crisis, or when it can no longer satisfy people's needs as well as the available alternative does. The thought to which one is led by all these considerations is that the successor to capitalism will not be democratic or more humane unless the employee-owned and controlled (largely cooperative) alternative to capitalist ownership and control has spread successfully to a sufficient number of enterprises as to constitute a visible and demonstrably viable alternative. It is not, then, that any widespread employee ownership and the like are certain to arise or certain to bring about a better society, but that they appear to be necessary precursors for a humane successor to come about.

CHAPTER 6

How Capitalism Began

6.1 LEARNING FROM THE PAST

One attitude in historiography holds that each social event differs so uniquely from others that no general lesson can be learned from it. Another holds that one can extract general laws of history or of social change from a broad survey of many historical situations and events. Between these two there is the view, followed here, that in considering the analysis of a given historical situation, or the possible outcomes of our own society, one can learn something, mutatis mutandis, from a detailed analysis of structure and forces in other social situations that are sufficiently close in time or similar in conditions to the situation we are considering.

This view is consistent with much of modern materialist analysis of society, including the historical materialism of Marx, which held more specifically that social situations could be analyzed only in respect to their particular conditions and forces. It also accords with the modern historiographic view that what is relevant is not lists of major events and leaders, but anthropological information about the lives and feelings of the "common people" — and also of the Nomenklatura of each society. This kind of information is presented by historians such as those of the Annales school in France.[1]

---

1. Cf. the work of Lucien Febvre and Marc Bloch. Peter Burke, ed., *A New Kind of History from the writings of Febvre* (London: Routledge and Kegan Paul, 1973).

Before considering which new systems may be able to make a beginning in the present socio-economic situation, therefore, we survey here briefly the beginnings of capitalism itself, and how it became the dominant social system in its area. The relevance of this history to the late capitalist and possible post-capitalist periods lies in two considerations. First, far as the West Europe of the 14th to 17th centuries is from us today, it is nevertheless closer than any other beginning of an economic system (not counting the special case of Soviet Communism). Second, the socio-economic order that began then is basically the one in which we are still living. And, as will be argued in section 4 below, enough remains of the original structure of capitalism so that the climate for any new beginnings within it resembles somewhat the climate which it created around itself during its own beginnings some 600 years ago.

In surveying the beginnings of capitalism, it will be seen that new ways of making decisions which make goods available (by commerce or by production) led both to increased and altered production and also to new relative positions among those involved. It will also be seen that these changes led to changes in social relations and in attitudes and ultimately to new political power. We can ask what past processes and forces led to all this, and we can seek to distinguish any ongoing ones that can have comparable effect in the foreseeable future. Of course, changes in such large and complex structures as modern society are not predictable. But neither are they arbitrary; they are limited to the processes and forces that exist in the current conditions, and to the range of possible outcomes of these processes.

6.2 Developments that Constituted First Steps Toward Capitalist Decision-Making

Changes, especially large changes, in technology and economic arrangements and social ways do not occur as a matter of course in all societies in all times. Many societies, especially in earlier times, changed little if at all over centuries. Such changes as would lead to capitalism did not occur in China or in Japan at times when some of their conditions were not so different from those of medieval Europe.[2] In Western Europe, however, from the

---

2. Joseph Needham, *The Grand Titration* (Toronto: University of Toronto Press, 1969); and the abridgement of his famous *Science and Civilization in China*, in C. A. Ronan, *The Shorter Science and Civilization in China* (Cambridge: Cambridge University Press, 1978, 1981).

11th or 12th century and on, various changes coincided or supported each other in a way that permitted economic activities that eventually led to capitalism.[3]

The later medieval environment, within which capitalist activities arose, had manorial lords who owned or controlled sizeable agricultural areas, on which serfs or tenant peasants farmed, with tithes and military and other duties owed by them to the lord, who in turn owed his tenants (in principle, not always in practice) protection and various material services such as winter storage of grain. The rulers of political entities — kings, counts, archbishops — had autocratic power, and finances based on taxation, licenses and the like, all justified by a claim to the divine right of kings. By most accounts, the peasants lived a miserable life, ill-fed, ill-clothed, ill-housed.[4] At various times, in various parts of Europe, there were revolts of the peasants which, however, came to naught even in the rare case of being momentarily successful [5]: the peasants had no alternative but to return home to their previous condition. For the most part the opposition of the peasants was expressed in various private ways,[6] in songs and stories with secret political references and the like — all of which had no hope of effecting any change in their condition. The latter part of this period, especially from the 12th century on, saw a gradual productional and economic development.[7]

The factors leading to the development of a new — capitalist — form of society, in Europe but not elsewhere, have been widely discussed; but by the nature of their uniqueness they cannot be weighed and unequivocally distinguished.[8] It has been suggested that a determining factor was the course of change in the agrarian arrangements themselves, rather than only in commerce and the

---

3. *The Cambridge Economic History of Europe*, edited by M. M. Postan and H. J. Habakkuk (Cambridge: Cambridge University Press,1965).

4. Fernand Braudel, *The Structure of Everyday Life*, vol. 1 of *Civilization and Capitalism* (Paris: Colin, 1979).

5. M. Mollat and Philippe Wolff, *The Popular Revolutions of the Late Middle Ages* (London: Allen & Unwin, 1973).

6. J. C. Scott, *The Weapons of the Weak: Everyday Forms of Peasant Resistance* (New Haven: Yale University Press,1985).

7. Eric Hobsbawm, ed., *Precapitalist Economic Formations* (New York: International Publishers, 1964); B. Hindess and P. Hirst, *Precapitalist Modes of Production* (London: Routledge and Kegan Paul, 1975).

8. R. J. Holton, *The Transition from Feudalism to Capitalism* (New York: St. Martin's Press, 1985).

cities.[9] It has also been suggested that the feudal economy and system were winding down of their own, independent of the rise of capitalist activities.[10] For our purposes it is sufficient to trace the course of the new economic activities, to see how they developed into a new system, without trying to resolve the historical precursors.

There was a growth in agricultural product, at various periods from then on, due partly to the slow accumulation of technology.[11] This aided the growth of towns, a development that would have been impossible without agricultural surplus. In parts of Europe, especially in the German and Italian areas where the local states were not well developed, some of these towns became semi-autonomous — and indeed were not merged into whole countries until later in the 19th century. These privileged towns largely governed themselves, and so were able to foster the activities and interests of the merchants and craftsmen who were their main citizens.[12]

Various factors contributed to the growth of commerce, especially overseas (the occasional travelers from Europe to the Orient, the technology of larger ships), and of money lending (to nobles and kings, and later to merchants, this despite the biblical prohibition against usury — so much for the effect of religious values). These activities led to accumulations of money in the hands of merchants and lenders. In particular, overseas commerce produced large profits over short periods. The large profits came from exchanging low-cost European products (cloth, baubles, etc.) for gold and perfume and the like, which could be sold to the nobility and others who had little to do with their wealth except spend it on luxurious consumables; and the profits were realized over a short period when the ship reached home safely.

These accumulations of urban wealth differed from the wealth of kings and the nobility. The wealth of kings and nobles came from taxes and royal privileges and the like; from land ownership

9. T. H. Aston and C. H. E. Philipon, eds., *The Brenner Debate* (Cambridge: Cambridge University Press, 1985).

10. Philippe Wolff, *Automne du Moyen Ages ou Printemps des Temps Nouveaux?* (Paris: Aubier 1986); R. S. Lopez, *The Commercial Revolution of the Middle Ages 950-1350* (Englewood Cliffs, N.J.: Prentice Hall, 1971).

11. Jean Gimpel, *The Medieval Machine* (New York: Holt, 1976).

12. H A Miskimin, H. Herlihy, A.L. Udovitch, eds., *The Medieval City* (New Haven: Yale University Press, 1977); L. Mumford, *The City in History* (New York: Harcourt Brace, 1961); F. Rorig, *The Medieval Town* (Berkeley, Cal.: University of California Press, 1969); J. C. Russell, *Medieval Regions and their Cities* (Bloomington, Ind.: Indiana University Press, 1972); E. A. Gutkind, *International History of City Development* (New York: Free Press, 1964-72).

(tithes and tenant labor); or from the special offices in the royal household or in other public statuses. None of these could be repeated or increased without limit, so that this wealth was in no small part spent on luxury. In contrast, the accumulation of wealth in the towns came largely from lending, buying and selling, or other money-based activities: it was profit on money. Here in principle there was no limit. The additional money gotten as profit could now be used to obtain more profit, so long as opportunities (niches) to put the money to use could be found. There was thus the possibility, one might say invitation or pressure, to "keep the money working." With this pressure to use one's wealth for getting more wealth, new activities or new forms of existing activities were developed. For example, some production was moved from the baronial lands to the towns: mills were built in the towns, much more convenient for the townspeople than having the grain they bought ground in the landlords' mills. There were also developments in the ways profits could be made. Businessmen began giving money to farmers to enable them to pasture more sheep, the income from which was shared by the farmer and the businessman. More generally, by the side of ordinary loans, some lenders began to insure the borrowers (merchants, landlords) against loss in their money activities, with the question coming to be just which parties bear the losses and who shares the profits. A further step was that of businessmen investing their money directly in ventures of others (merchants, entrepreneurs, agriculturists).

In all these activities, which developed over centuries in various West European areas, we do not have a pre-set direction, or a growth of local activities toward a structure that could have been named or imagined before this growth occurred. Rather, there was a growing, though small, part of the population engaged in economic activities that were in each case only marginally different from that which their predecessors had done before. Except that slowly developing new conditions made it possible to carry out such activities more widely and to greater gain. That this history looks as though it were following a direction is due to the continuation of the new conditions and the positive feedback of the activities themselves. The particular results and ways of acting that developed out of these continuing local changes we now see, ex post facto, as a direction. The possibility of direction is given by the constancy of the motive force: every economic act is done for self-interest, for the actor's gain.

One new condition was the greater use of money in exchange, which facilitated purely economic activities. That is, as against the common older situation of people selling the relatively smaller amount of product that they themselves produced, or of people buying a particular kind of product for sale mostly to a limited pool of customers. In the towns there were now more cases of people whose occupation consisted in having an accumulation of money which they could use for various economic transactions, no longer limited to one social type. In other social forms, such as the feudal society within which these monetary activities were growing, economic behavior was often mixed with social features. The craftsman often had satisfaction in his work and in his product; the shopkeeper was a neighbor of his customers; the peasant and his landlord could have various services and social contacts, not always inimical; and people engaged in a barter transaction often had other connections as well. In such circumstances, decisions could not but reflect several, possibly dissimilar, considerations. However, in the more purely and uniformly monetary form that was now growing, the economic objective of having an advantageous outcome from the transaction took on the shape of a precise aim: to come out of the transaction with more money than one had before, namely with profit.

Another new condition was the expansion of consumption and of economic activity. This meant not only that more was being consumed (luxuries for the rich, but also at times more food and varied clothing for craftsmen and peasants), but also that more consumption was going through monetary exchange ("through the market," as in the example above of new mills in the towns). As a result of this expansion, people who had amassed money largely by making profit in lending or selling or other money activities had the opportunity to use their gained money in further economic activities so as to obtain yet more profits. This ability to reinvest has a positive feedback: the more profit was made the more money was then available to invest in making yet more profits. And when some people were able to accumulate large wealth, they had more power to control and manipulate the economic environment — the producers and the buyers as well as the rulers of society — in order to make yet more profit.[13]

---

13. The usual statement about the importance of accumulation of capital is to the effect that capitalism needed large accumulation to give it the initial forward push. The same situation can be described in terms of the ongoing processes (which are blind

For people engaged in transactions and starting with an initial capital, to come out frequently with less money than they had before would have meant not only not to succeed but also to dissipate their initial capital. This pressure solidified the profit motive into a paradigmatic criterion for monetary activity: money is invested only if a profit could be reasonably expected. In investing money, the calculation of profitability is purely economic and monetary, even if the final decision might be modified by additional non-economic factors.

The criterion of profitability was further modified by an additional pressure. The free entry of people into monetary and profit-making activities depended almost solely on their having some initial capital and led to competition. Once there was a niche for profit-making, especially an expandable one, there was a good likelihood that more than one profit-seeker would enter it. In such conditions it became relevant for the businessman to try to maximize his profit, because if other businessmen made more profit than him there was danger that they might be able to crowd him out of the competition. More generally, over the aggregate of all businessmen, the ones making higher profit or operating at a higher rate of profit were more likely to remain in business. Thus in the aggregate and over time the goal became to maximize profit. This applied not only to direct competition for buyers, but in general to a striving among all capitalists for accumulating more capital. The de facto criterion for business activity was thus not simply making profit, but making the maximum profit possible in each situation; though many economic islands could continue to exist, where profits were made without attempts at maximization.

One of the later (dynamical) effects of the maximization goal was the trend to large employment, in expanded manufacturing entities, as a way to increase the employer's profits. Later yet was the trend to concentration of capital, wherein small enterprises were replaced or taken over by larger ones, increasing the profits of the larger capitalists by eliminating the smaller.

The motive forces in the economic activities of the participating individuals thus reveal not a juggernaut of a new economic order pushing its way along, but a more chaotic and complex historical process. The direction and the systematization came from

---

to their future) by saying that the large accumulations of profit from overseas commerce and the like had greater economic success and power, and thus created a particular form of capitalism, the "actually existing" form.

the constancy of the motive force — the individual's desire to gain — as it took shape in the unfolding situations that were due partly to external developments and partly to the positive feedback in the participating individuals' own activities. "Self-organizing system" is much too general and vague a concept to be of any explanatory or even descriptive value here, ranging as it does from attempts in computer heuristics and in cosmology to applications in biological evolution and in language structure. Nevertheless, the history of the economic activities that eventually led to capitalism has more of a self-organizing character than of an orderly realization of an economic model.

What we have described here is how new ways of arranging for the availability of goods were able to begin and to take on established form. These new ways consisted of new criteria — profit — for making decisions on economic activity; and they created a new class of people with wealth and status, and above all with a method for bringing about commerce and production.[14]

6.3 THE DEVELOPMENT OF BUSINESS INTO AN ECONOMIC SYSTEM

We see here that capitalist activities took form and spread not directly within the closed land-based domain of the feudal agricultural economy, but mostly within the more open money-based domain of commerce and money lending in the partly autonomous life of the towns. The spread of these activities was due partly to their filling useful niches — at first largely for the nobility, court, and church — in providing availability of goods and money; partly also to the positive feedback of profit-making, which created capital searching for investment (i.e., for profit); and partly to the weakening of the late feudal system, and the growing dissatisfaction of many peasants with the feudal conditions in which they lived (in contrast to the alternative offered in the cities). This led many peasants to abandon their serfdom for employment in the cities — terrible as the conditions were there too. The dealings with America, which began about midway in the centuries that were leading to an established capitalist system, was a contributing factor in the growth of capitalism toward dominance in Europe. It is not without reason that the American Indians consider Columbus' voyages to constitute not a discovery but

---

14. R. S. Lopez, *The Commercial Revolution of the Middle Ages 950-1350* (Englewood Cliffs, N.J.: Prentice Hall, 1971): "An undeveloped society succeeded in developing itself, mostly by its own efforts" (vii).

an invasion of their continents. Vast resources were taken from America into Europe (together with new foods that became important to Europe's economy). The enslavement of the Indian population — in many cases working them literally to death — was begun by Columbus himself immediately after his first voyage, and was a source of considerable wealth for Europe.

The major new development within capitalism was the move toward industrial production. Commercial and moneylending activities continued throughout the history of capitalism, but by 1600 capitalists in Holland, England and elsewhere were also investing widely in agriculture. Some of this was small scale, for example in providing a farmer (at a time when more people were becoming independent freeholders) with money for an extra sheep to raise; and some was large as in providing the money to drain a Dutch lake in order to gain new land.[15] Going beyond this, there were moves toward investing in cottage handicrafts done by peasant families (which were drawn to such work by difficulties in farm income, due for example from "morcellement" of land or from enclosure of open fields), and in large-scale production such as deepening the coal mines. There was also considerable industrial development aside from agriculture, for example in the German areas from around 1450 (firearms, printing, watches) and in England from about a century later (e.g., in mining equipment). With the development of more complex higher productivity machines, and of power-driven machinery, opportunity and need grew for investment by people with large amounts of money.

New occupations became established: people with capital, making profit from its use; people engaged in production, who got from capitalists some of the money they needed for carrying on or expanding; people who spent part of their time working on equipment or material supplied by capitalists; and finally people whose livelihood came entirely from working in workplaces owned and organized by the capitalists. This developed into a variegated and widespread economic system, with more complex economic institutions such as banks serving it. More and more people were involved in it, the employees (workers, clerks) making their pittances out of it, and the owners their wealth. As the numbers of employees in a plant grew the magnitude of profits grew, and some capitalists became as wealthy as many of the landed nobil-

15. Jan de Vries, *The Dutch Rural Economy in the Golden Age 1500-1700* (New Haven: Yale University Press, 1934).

ity. Their personal power, and more importantly the power of the capitalist sphere, became major factors in the life of the country and in the actions of governments. By the early 1600's in England, Parliament was aiding the interests of businessmen and landowners. By the late 1700's, with strong governmental help, capitalism was the dominant economy in England and in some West European areas.[16] The explosion of technology that began at about this time, which capitalism in large part promoted and which only its relations of production were then able to utilize, made capitalism the reigning economic form of Western Europe.

It should be noted that early on the capitalist activities took on a systemic and even quasi-statist character. By the 1300's, in various European cities, many capitalists were not merely looking for opportunities to "keep their money working," but were actively creating such opportunities, and acting economically and militarily against other groups of capitalists. Mercantile dynasties such as the Fuggers arose. The Hanseatic ports fought the Dutch cities. The Upper German merchants arranged blockades of Venice (in 1418 and 1509). The German up-river cities barred the Flemish down-river port merchants. Kings and local rulers were drawn into the political and military confrontations of the capitalists, because of the incomes the rulers obtained from their own merchants and industrial entrepreneurs.[17] We see here how the fact that there was no natural boundary to the opportunities and to the potential gains, and the fact that capitalism in one city or region could have certain common interests as against those elsewhere, gave the early capitalist activities the dynamic of concerted aggression against competing interest groups. Such dynamics operated in parallel with the long-range dynamics of capitalism to expand. Capitalism thus had an inherent tendency toward becoming a system.

This whole economic development is exceedingly well known, having been investigated and described by a host of economic historians and political thinkers in England, France, Germany, Italy, and elsewhere.[18] It has been summarized here to show that even as fundamental a social property as the standard ways of decisions

16. R. J. White, *The Age of George III* (New York: Doubleday, 1968).

17. J. van Klaveren, *General Economic History 100-1760* (Munich: G. Kieckens, 1969).

18. Adam Smith, *The Wealth of Nations* (London: W. Strahan and T. Cadell, 1776); Fernand Braudel, *The Wheels of Commerce*, vol.2 of *Civilization and Capitalism* (New York: Harper, 1982); the works of R. H. Tawney, Asa Briggs, Christopher Hill, and especially Eric Hobsbawm, among many others.

on production, and as complex a system as capitalism, can arise with a common character and can grow in a more or less consistent direction without having been planned or caused by a pre-existing directing source. Rather, the similarity of initial activities and their persistence in a developmental direction come from the continuing press of circumstances and new opportunities within the economy, as is seen in the beginnings of capitalism. It is true that ideologies and intentions can support a socio-economic development, as was famously argued by Max Weber in the case of Protestantism promoting the work ethic of capitalism (in *The Protestant Ethic and the Spirit of Capitalism*). But Protestant teachings, beginning successfully with Luther and with unsuccessful precursors, for example Huss, came and spread well after the beginnings of capitalist activities, and after the growth of a considerable body of capitalist burghers had provided the initial support without which Luther's movement could hardly have taken off.[19]

6.4 THE DEVELOPMENT OF A CAPITALIST SOCIETY

As capitalist activity and its economic system became established in West Europe, it ushered in a period of criticism and rejection of ideas of the old society's world and a new materialist enlightenment. There were exponents of the new ideas and values, such as Voltaire and the more modern Jean-Jacques Rousseau. There were formulators of the capitalist system: famously Adam Smith and Ricardo, and a great many economists. There were philosophers who combined analysis of capitalism with the new ideas of this enlightenment, from the more conservative Thomas Hobbes to David Hume to the very progressive John Stuart Mill. There were social thinkers such as Montesquieu. And there were political thinkers such as Tom Paine and some of the authors of the Declaration of Independence in America. With all this equipment, capitalism was on the way to political power and to the organizing of the whole of social life piecemeal in Holland and England and by massive revolutionary change in France and in various parts of the Continent.[20]

The new decision-makers on production and their thinkers developed attitudes expressing their form of decision-making (individualism, property, profit, work ethic) and opposing the feu-

---

19. J. W. Gough, *The Rise of the Entrepreneur* (New York: Schocken, 1969).
20. George Rude, *Revolutionary Europe 1783-1815* (London: Collins, 1964).

dal authority and its central church (in Protestantism, and later in the social philosophers). It is clear here that the new economic relations gave rise to new social and cultural attitudes consonant with the interests of the new occupations, especially the interests of the clearest beneficiaries and holders of control in these new relations of production. These groups are always the most active promoters of their interests. These attitudes were initially descriptions and analyses of the new ongoing ways, perhaps more than they were the ideologies of defense and expansion that they eventually became. They not only supported the new economy's growth, but also supported the development of social and ultimately governmental institutions conforming to the new economic relations and specifically to the interests of the power wielders — the decision-makers — in these relations. What is relevant to the societal and political importance of any post-capitalist economic developments is that these attitudes began to develop long before the new economic relations were dominant in the society of the time. An example is noted above in the attitudes of the burghers, who supported Luther's activities in the early 1400's when the importance of capitalist commerce and production was still largely limited to the cities.[21]

The effect of new economic conditions on social attitudes is recognized in all materialist views, especially in so-called economic determinism. Marx's formulation is more specific, holding that the new relations of production give rise to new social and cultural understanding (as "superstructure"). This narrower formulation is satisfied in detail by the development of capitalist society. However, for a discussion of the possible course of a postcapitalist society it is not necessary to state a general law here. The experience of capitalism is sufficiently close sociologically and historically to the Western world of today that we can assume that as early capitalism brought in individualism, democracy (of its particular type), new attitudes in religion and art, so there is a comparable possibility that any development of more democratic relations in deciding and arranging production will foster early on the development of more democratic social attitudes and political pressures.

As the capitalist economy became dominant, its ramification and standardization of the occupations and institutions peculiar to it amounted to a new social system. And its views and ideologies

---

21. Raymond de Roover and Julius Kirshner, eds. *Business, Banking, and Economic Thought in Late Medieval and Early Modern Europe* (Chicago: University of Chicago Press, 1974).

pressed for political power, which came either piecemeal or, in conflation with mass upheavals, by revolution.

In sum: capitalism replaced feudalism in stages and without initial political movements or central political leaders. It succeeded by satisfying — no matter how poorly — some wants unfilled in feudalism. In doing so, it developed its economic ways, its productional advantages, and its social and cultural attitudes along the way, gradually eroding those of feudalism and of royal prerogatives.

6.5 THE ENVIRONMENT THAT CAPITALISM PRESENTS TO POST-CAPITALIST DECISION-MAKING

The crucial consideration here is that capitalist society is not entirely closed to alternative ways of deciding and arranging production. The varied activities which originally led to capitalism have left their open entry mark upon the system. The new capitalist ways of arranging the availability of goods and money had originally developed within sporadic economic niches unfilled by feudal economics. Each enterprise was free to start and to survive as best it could and to some extent this situation has remained to this day. Capitalism has not changed internally into an organized top-down "monopoly capitalism" capable of excluding all outside initiatives. In the mixed economies of various European countries, business remains autonomous within its large domain, and is not just a planned sector of a state productional system: this was also the case in the various fascist regimes. Within the old capitalisms, enterprises may still be started by anyone who can put together enough money, and they have a chance to survive if they manage to make a profit. The particular internal structure of an enterprise does not have to be a decisive factor in its ability to operate within the market. But when the internal structure of an enterprise is sharply different from the business norm it may arouse ideological opposition that could greatly limit its prospects of success. The more governmentally intertwined new capitalisms, as in Japan, are less open to alternative or ideologically unwelcome kinds of enterprise — or to new businessmen outside the inner circle.

Furthermore, the specific conditions that any potentially post-capitalist activities face are not the capitalist system in the abstract, but the particular economic and political forms of capitalism at the time that various social forces may be led toward such potentially post-capitalist activities. The profit-maximizing dynamics of capitalism, and its dynamical trend toward distancing decision from production, leave many unfilled openings for new arrangements of production, as will be noted below and detailed in Ch.7. Furthermore, the basic legalism of capitalism — ownership of productive property as a basis of control — is not at present clear-cut and monolithic. In the corporate structure of the 20th century, control is in the hands of a self-perpetuating management, while the "owners" are a fluctuating spread of stockholders almost always unable to exert control. When companies assign some of their shares to the titular ownership of their workers, who can then vote their shares, a grey area is created between owning and being employed.[22]

There is also a potential fluidity between owning and control in the power of vast investment funds were they ever to adopt economic and political agendas of their own (as could happen for the great pension funds). Even the absoluteness of law, which is important because so much of the law in capitalist countries is an empowerment of capitalist relations and structures, has been weakened in America by the pressures of the populace upon Congress and the Supreme Court to the point of reversing laws and court decisions. It is also weakened in principle by the Nuremberg decisions after World War II concerning the individual's responsibility for having followed unjust laws.

The principle of open entry to new production, and the possibilities for participating in the control of existing production, could be eliminated if the successor to today's capitalism were a central power, arising either from capitalists' relinquishing to the government or from a military overthrow. But in the current situation it is not impossible for the successor to develop out of internally novel enterprises — novel in being self-governed by their workers — growing piecemeal within the capitalist market. Such a successor would, by its very origins, be based on open entry for new enterprises. Capitalism can see such novel enterprises as "group-subsistence" drop-outs from the economic mainstream, or otherwise irrelevant to the operation and expansion of capitalism. It may also see the establishment of such enterprises as a relinquishing by capitalism of less profitable production domains or otherwise less interesting to capitalist activity today.

22. Such grey areas were rife in the early days of capitalism, before "employees" were massed, as in the cottage industries and entrepreneur's investing in the production of a farmer or craftsman. Somewhat similarly, one can ask whether the giver or receiver of a mortgage owns the mortgaged house; this is resolved by the ability of the mortgager to take over the house if the "owner" does not maintain his payments, and to recoup his loan with only the residue going to the "owner."

However, the openings for new enterprises are just openings — possible niches that capitalist activity is not rushing to fill. Whether and how these openings are filled, and if by other than purely capitalist enterprises then by what kind, is a different question, to be decided by other pressures in the social economy.

Social and economic innovations are not easily come by. Niches are not filled innovatively merely out of a dislike for existing ways, but only if they cannot be filled in the usual ways, and if the innovation promises its participants an advantage immediately or for the near future. With this, we have to ask who can be the innovators, especially in matters of productional decision-making.

This brings us to a major systemic difference between the beginnings of capitalism "within" feudalism and the possible beginnings of self-governed production "within" capitalism. The beginnings are different in that the earliest capitalist activities were outside the feudal economy proper and provided a complement to it — and only later became an outside competitor in economy and politics. In contrast, it has been argued, any beginnings of self-governed production would have to be made by the workers in immediate confrontation with capitalism.

But, this last is not quite correct. The historical labor movement has indeed been in direct opposition to the employer. Being primarily an adversary inside the capitalists' world, the labor movement could go only as far as reform within the capitalists' world; and anything beyond that could be achieved not by the use of workers' productive power but only by the deus ex machina of force — a revolution — even if triggered in the workplace by a workers' general strike.

However, any self-governed enterprises would be structurally not in opposition to the employer, but rather only in competition with capitalist producers in the same industry — the standard relation in capitalism. Long-term confrontation with capitalism might come up later when the self-governing system would be well along in development, just as the confrontation between capitalism and feudalism became serious only when the capitalist system was well along. We thus see three somewhat different transitional situations: Whereas capitalism was an outside complement and competitor to feudalism, the labor struggle has been an opponent inside capitalism, while self-governed production would constitute competition (and to some extent a complement) inside capitalism.

One might ask in what way the beginnings of self-governed production could complement capitalism. First, it could provide livelihoods to people for whom capitalism cannot provide gainful work. Second, it is argued in Ch.7 that there are many needed or potentially useful products and services that capitalism does not provide because these goods are not sufficiently profitable or because the control of capital is concentrated in few firms. Also many employees lose their jobs as a result of profit-directed capitalist considerations (such as mergers or cheaper labor abroad). Third, a better "quality of life" should be considered to be an incentive. In the latter part of the Middle Ages there was in many parts of Europe a growing flow of individuals from the feudal peasantry into the towns. There was a saying "Town air sets a man free." These dropouts from serfdom provided the work force who accepted employment, unpleasant and ill-paid as it was, because that was the only way they could stay in the town. Later, from ca. 1600 in England, actions taken by landlords, capitalists and government combined to force people into becoming workers, and to impoverish them so that they would accept employment under any terms. The growing phenomenon of dropouts, would-be dropouts, and enforced joblessness (even in the educated occupations) is visible in much of the capitalist area today. On the one hand, job loss today may force people to consider self-help and cooperative forms of production. On the other hand, secondary advantages in the quality of life may attract those who tire of the increasingly arduous and meaningless rat-race of modern capitalism. The freer air of economically serious cooperatives or employee-owned companies, in contrast to the conditions in capitalist employment, is obvious to anyone who has actually worked in them, despite the many problems and troubles that arise there too.

It might be argued that in capitalism a new elite replaced an old one, whereas in the case of self-governed production it would be the producers themselves replacing the old elite, and this would be novel to history. But the fact that power was transferred in the past from elite to elite is not an essential feature of social change, but only a matter of the various historic conditions. In the past it was only elites that had new economic or military capabilities to offer. What is relevant in the development of new social economic systems is not that the new decision-makers be an elite but that the new be able to fill important unfilled needs. If self-governed production can produce under conditions when capitalism cannot, or can do it more acceptably for the population, it can be an historical successor.

It is in this sense that Marx and Engels were able to speak of "scientific socialism," [23] namely, that if and when the people who together carry out the actual production and distribution of goods and services become able to do their work in a self-governing way, free of the control of others, they would be developing a new decision system dependent on no ruling elite. The collectivity of the decision power would come from the fact that all participants are needed together in the work. The absence of outside control by an elite follows from the fact that current business actions are increasingly distant from all that is relevant to the production itself, and can at some stage be replaced by decision-making that deals with the resources and the consumers without the interposition of the special criteria of business.

There have been attempts to start cooperative or communal (collective) enterprises for ideological purposes, whether religious or political. In Ch. 7 below, we discuss the purely economic grounds for starting such enterprises. They are to be found in the economic needs of sectors of the population which are not adequately met by capitalist enterprises or by government.

It will be seen in Ch. 7 that we may expect some pressures on workers and on consumers toward cooperative or group-subsistence production of goods and services, in geographic or productional areas where business is not providing these. There may also be means of production (such as solar energy) which business is not tapping but which cooperative groups can. The opportunity to escape the conditions of employment or to find employment by joining or forming such enterprises may be attractive once cooperative or jointly-owned enterprises become viable and known; and the success of some would encourage further attempts. In this way a piecemeal and local economic development, within capitalist society, of new ways of making decisions on production characterized by various forms of control from below is a possibility, paralleling in some respects the piecemeal growth of capitalism. As in the case of capitalism, we could expect such a development to encourage, early on, the growth of new cultural and political attitudes conforming to this mode of control from below.

---

23. Friedrich Engels, *Socialism: Utopian and Scientific* (New York: International Publishers, 1939). Originally part of Herr Eugen Duhring's *Revolution in Science* ("*Anti-Duhring*") (Leipzig, 1878).

6.6   POSSIBLE FIRST STEPS TOWARD COOPERATIVE DECISION-MAKING

(1) *Steps Toward Workers' Voice in Decisions.* Having surveyed in 6.2 how capitalist decision-making arose, it may be possible now to picture how cooperative decision-making might arise in the situation outlined in 6.5. While the growth of capitalism was sparked by entrepreneurial profits as a new decision system, the industrialization to which it led created an additional and oppositional factor in production: the assembling of workers operating together either in parallel or in series. Initially, this was merely a matter of having several or even many workers instead of one, operating under arrangements made in detail by the entrepreneur. With the growth and standardization of industry, the actions of businessmen became less prominent in the workplace, and the teaming of co-workers more standardized and essential. In this situation the co-workers constituted a factor in the arrangements of production, with group attitudes to their work and with growing "customs and practices" established among themselves in respect to how they worked and how they joined in working. This was in effect a contribution to the social and managerial "relations of production," somewhat as the early capitalists employed people in order to make a profit gradually constituted a new contribution to the relations of production (compared with what had existed in the medieval towns between merchants and their helpers or between craftsmen and their apprentices). During the nineteenth century, incipient forms of organization and decision related to production developed among the workers: unions, strikes, solidarity, seniority as a way of allocating privilege among the individual workers, and also concerted demands of the workers as a group upon the bosses. In the wake of this workplace development the workers became increasingly distinct in social and economic — and later political — attitudes and understandings.[24]

---

24. The common view of workers is that they are entirely controlled and directed by the employer and the straw boss, and can express only bitterness or opposition but no independent initiative. However, the detailed picture of the shop floor, and of worker demands shows more initiative and more independent ways and desires on the part of workers. For the later period a comparable discussion on the "labor process" is to be found in the works cited in Ch.7 fns. 20, 21, 26. But the same trend of workers' independent steps toward decision-making about their own work can be discerned from the early decades of workers being assembled in large plants.

This whole development has some parallels in the development of profit-making employment and of competition, first commercial and later also industrial, from being a growing new way to arrange for production (by investing for profit) to becoming a direct factor in deciding production (by providing the materials and machines, and employing labor). With attendant new economic interests came new social and political attitudes.

As in the case of the beginnings of capitalist profitmaking and employing, new activities are in their time just minor developments out of existing types of activity. When the Luddites of the early 1800's destroyed machinery, or when the masses protested against landowners and government as in the Chartist movement of the mid 1800's, cooperative solidarity by like-minded individuals in like economic situations was necessary in order to create a public effect, but it was not a new contribution to the arrangements of production; in some cases the solidarity had to be clandestine, given the suppression of the Luddites and the illegality of unions in England before 1824. However, when the workers in a workplace made wage or work-condition demands upon the employer, or formed a union, or went on strike over such issues, they were not merely expressing their attitude or pressing their wishes, but were entering the decision process over their work.

At first these activities constituted only a weak veto power over the employer's decisions, but in the collective bargaining process which developed out of this later on, the workers initiated proposals and negotiated outcomes over a certain domain of decisions. The workers' voice in these matters remained weak and encased within the overall power of the employer, but their action nevertheless constituted a first step toward a new contribution to the occupational relations in production. In doing all this the solidarity of the workers — facilitated by their being assembled in one workplace — is not just a matter of the strength of their action, as is the case in public (street) activity (though the latter may have helped the former). Rather, solidarity was the essence of the workplace action, because a few like-minded workers could not constitute a new decision element but only the great bulk of the workers in the workplace could by agreeing on what they want.[25]

---

25. Cf. for example, John Elster, *Ulysses and the Sirens* (Cambridge:Cambridge University Press, 1979).

The workers of the 19th century and after are therefore not like the peasants who could only rise in rebellion but could not organize any replacement for the ruling feudal system, since they could not in general present any alternative organized arrangement for production and consumption.

Later, as the workers' contribution to the decision process became more established, certain steps in the decision process passed into the workers' hands, and such criteria as seniority were developed to enable the workers to allocate preference among themselves when such allocation had to be made. It should be understood that seniority is not merely a particular criterion established by the workers. In effect it is for them comparable to legality: that is, it is a name for workers' deciding allocation among themselves. Seniority is not just a matter of length of time at work. For example one has to decide what "seniority" to assign for a worker who left the job and then returned. And one can decide that having a larger family shall count as additional seniority.

However, the workers' arrangements and decisions noted above are encapsulated within the bosses' decisions, and are thus of secondary importance with respect to production as a whole. The domain of the workers' decision input is too circumscribed so that it does not give them the economic standing from which to develop independent economic and political views. However, if in the future workers can push into becoming, in various productional areas, major independent participants — by the side of the bosses — in production decisions, or if they become the owners or controllers of their own workplace, their actions would then lead them to develop new decision arrangements on production.

Such self-governed production would thus constitute a next stage of the labor movement, in that it would advance the employees of a plant farther into their own decision-making, beyond the initial steps in this direction which have been taken in the historic labor movement. It is then that non-capitalists could be expected to develop into a new and different social and political force. The fact that the enterprises in which workers share real control or ownership would continue to operate within the market does not vitiate their essential difference from capitalist society. It is not the market structure but the ability of businessmen to decide production and consumption that creates the character of capitalist society. Even though they would have to operate within a capitalist financial environment — of bank loans, possibly a minority of shares sold to the public — it does not vitiate their potential for new socio-economic effects, as long as the essential managerial direction comes from the participants in production (with at most a small minority of exclusions such as recent joiners) and as long as the managers operate within such direction.

(2) *Steps Toward a New Society.* In the case of early capitalism we saw several stages that resulted in new production and new decision criteria on production and, following soon on the heels of this, new economic and social attitudes and a new outlook upon the world. In the case of the massed workers of the 19th and 20th centuries we have seen in (1) above small economic steps, chiefly concerning the conditions in the workplace and the details of work arrangements. With this there have come a continuing sequence of social and cultural developments, in the social organization of the workers and in the outlook of the workers and of the thinkers associated with them.

There was a major labor movement in various forms throughout the industrial world, focused first around specific issues of the workplace but later around the whole socio-economic position of the workers. The labor movement was primarily engaged in fighting anti-labor actions of the bosses and the government,[26] but it also built organizational frameworks for the workers' activities and lives, and developed institutions and a body of professionals to provide productional and economic information and social ideas for labor's struggles.[27] Workers' organizations were also able to mount large class-based efforts such as the various political parties (Labour, Social Democratic, Socialist), or the English General Strike of 1926 and the spontaneous French one of 1968.[28]

The attitudes that came with the protests and demands of labor had an effect in the general culture. In John Stuart Mill, who wrote in the middle of the 19th century and thus in the early years

---

26. G. D. H. Cole, *A Short History of the British Working Class Movement 1789-1947* (London: George Allen and Unwin, 1948); E. P. Thompson, *The Making of the English Working Class* (New York: Pantheon, 1964).

27. For example in the work of Sidney and Beatrice Webb, The Fabian Society in England, Raymond Postgate and many others.

28. Scott Nearing, *The British General Strike* (New York: Vanguard 1926); A. J. Cook, *The Nine Days* (London: London Cooperative Printing Society, 1926); Hamilton Fyfe, *Behind the Scenes of the General Strike* (London: Labour Publishing Co., 1926); J. Blancherie, M. Lefebvre, B. Bacquet, B. Bodin, J.-L. Bresson, P. Delage, C. Lefebvre, *Les événements de mai/juin 1968 vu à travers cent entreprises* (Paris: Centre National d'Information pour la Productivité des Entreprises, 1968); *La grève generalisée en France* (Mai Juin 1968), ICO (Informations Correspondance Ouvrières), Supplement 72 Paris: 1968.

of labor's organized voice, we see a combination of the philosopher of capitalism together with the humanist values of labor looking beyond capitalism.[29] The values of capitalism became in part defensive in the face of the more advanced values of the labor movement. Thus the early capitalists found no need to apologize for their enrichment and indeed their aggressive greed. They justified their activities by appeal to the Protestant Ethic and the cult of hard work, or in the goal of keeping one's money working. In contrast, A. A. Berle and Gardiner Means, in their *The Modern Corporation and Private Property*, present the capitalist apologia more defensively: "The socially beneficent results to be derived from the protection of property are supposed to arise not from the wealth itself but from the efforts to acquire wealth" (p. 340).

Opposition to the evils of the ruling system became a continuing and many-sided activity in the European world. Radicalism became an education and an ideal. There was an Anarchist tradition whose criticism was in part moral and cultural.[30] It found followers especially in areas where workers were not massed in large plants, as among the Swiss watch-makers and later among the Catalonian workers before and during the Spanish Civil War. There were also labor movement militants for whom the advancement of workers and the opposition to capitalism was a way of life.[31] There were various special schools of thought, such as the Syndicalism of Sorel,[32] and many ideas and proposals on social change such as Guild Socialism in England.[33]

In all of this development the great push came from Marxism. Marx presented his work as a theory of capitalism together with an effort to change or replace it.[34] This combination can be made more comparable to other intellectual efforts if we observe that the work was a theory of the transition from capitalism. Marx in

29. See especially his *On Liberty*.

30. As in the works of Alexander Herzen, Mikhail Bakunin, P. J. Proudhon, P. A. Kropotkin, and Alexander Berkman.

31. E.g., Scott Lasch, *The Militant Worker: Class and Radicalism in France and America* (London: Heineman, 1984).

32. Georges Sorel, *Reflections on Violence* (Glencoe, Ill.: Free Press, 1950); (*Reflexions sur la violence* (Paris: Riviere, 1971); and *La décomposition du marxisme* (Paris: Presses Universitaires de France, 1982); Wayne Thorpe, *The Workers Themselves: Revolutionary Syndicalism and International Labor 1913-23*, International Institute of Social History (Amsterdam: Dordrecht, Kluwer, 1989).

33. G. D. H. Cole, *Guild Socialism Restated* (London: Parsons, 1920).

34. See Karl Marx, *Capital*, and his various shorter writings on history and the class struggle; Franz Mehring, *Karl Marx* (New York, Covici Friede 1935); Tom Bottomore, *A Dictionary of Marxist Thought* (Cambridge, Mass.: Harvard University Press 1983).

describing capitalism analyzed it in terms that could make it comparable to other economic systems (hence also to a successor system), that is to say, not in its own unique primitives of profit and commodities for the market, but in terms of the social relations of production — e.g., which social groups decide, on what basis, and which social groups produce, on what terms. This is his sociologizing of economics.[35] The status of various sectors of society in respect to production could then be investigated within the changing technology and dynamics of capitalism. Here Marx saw that the growing ability of the massed workers in industry would eventually enable them to dispense with control by the capitalist criteria for deciding production. This was his Scientific Socialism. The effort to change capitalism was thus an intentional participation — an intervention — in the analyzed course of history as given in this theory of the transition from capitalism.[36]

The power of Marx's analysis of capitalism and of social processes, and the fact that its analysis of the transition made it a handbook of intervention in that transition, made Marx's work a watershed not only in the workers' movement but also in the thinking about economy, society, and human values. The political activism that followed Marx had a complex history — the Social Democratic parties that became rather ineffectually reformist, the revolutions in not fully-capitalist countries (which did not accord with Marx's conditions for the transition), the failure of the principled political left to achieve any large following in the capitalist countries. The diversity of paths taken was due in part to the lack of clarity in understanding the conditions for transition and the processes involved. Marx's own work was so early in the development of the workers' movement that he could not see either how workers could develop their decision potential in the workplace rather than just spill over into street protest and revolutionary or parliamentary action, nor how the dynamics of capitalism would take capitalist control proper ever farther away from the workplace.

Meanwhile, the ideas of Marx on society, class control, and values led to a flowering of social and cultural critique comparable to the materialist enlightenment ushered in by capitalism (6.4). There were many historical studies which profited from this sophistication, such as Arthur Rosenberg's *The Birth of the Ger-*

---

35. Cf. Karl Korsch, *Karl Marx* (New York: Wiley, 1938).
36. Cf. Paul Mattick, *Marxism, Last Refuge of the Bourgeoisie?* (New York: Sharpe, 1983).

man Republic,[37] and V. Gordon Childe's *Man Makes Himself* for pre-history.[38] There were a great many studies in sociology, politics and philosophy that used the ideas and methods of class analysis, and much important work in this spirit in literary criticism, art history, and analysis of culture. More generally, these ideas and values have been entering into the broad public awareness, somewhat as the ideas and values of early capitalism entered into public awareness in the 17th and 18th centuries.

(3) *Prospects.* In 6.5 it was noted that the openings for self-governing decision-making in production would be sporadic and piecemeal. This is important for the political character of these new arrangements for several reasons.

First, the development of ways for deciding production based on control from below underlies moves toward a more egalitarian society. Such an economic innovation cannot be imposed over a whole society in one massive and sudden act. Hence we have to consider the possible arising of such economic forms within the existing economy, and locally in individual enterprises rather than at one blow.

Second, whatever massive and sudden political events may take place on the way to basic economic and social changes, the participants in history cannot foresee their timing or circumstances or immediate issues. Hence the participants can prepare for these events only in general terms, which are only partially helpful to any desired egalitarian outcome. Thus the actions that can be attempted with foresight before or between the massive events are in general local and piecemeal, whether they be economic or social-cultural.

Third, the large historical events are too massive and complex, especially given the variegated occupational and ethnic populations in each large country today, to be controllable by any social group (such as the industrial workers, let alone more specialized or ideological subgroups of the population). People with an egalitarian agenda cannot simply try to prepare for historical turning-points; they have to do what is possible constructively and locally now to strengthen the infrastructure that would support their case when historical events take shape.

For these reasons we consider here primarily the possibilities for encapsulated economic developments within the present soci-

---

37. Oxford University Press, 1931.
38. London: Watts, 1936, and New York: New American Library-Penguin, 1951.

ety and market, as a necessary though quite possibly not sufficient contribution to the development of a more humane society. It must be stressed that economic developments do not remain purely economic. As capitalism brought many cultural and social — and ultimately political — changes along with its development, we may expect successful cooperative enterprises to have comparable effects. In addition, and crucially, there are the economic and political oppositions that capitalism arouses in those sectors of the population which it necessarily victimizes. These have been analyzed into structures of social change in the important historical writings of Eric Hobsbawm, George Rude, Fernand Braudel, and a host of other economic and social historians in the various West European countries. There is also the recent and less historically focused grass-roots trend of private social activism on various social, moral, and cultural issues, mostly in the United States. Although overtly tangential to the development of new ways in deciding production, this movement shares the piecemeal, local approach, and the independent, innovative self-help method.

These economic, social, and political developments have the inherent possibility of being mutually supportive, as successful new relations of production breed new social attitudes, while the new social attitudes justify and support the productional relations. The importance of the new decision-makings on production to social change is brought out by the following consideration: It was not the peasant revolts but rather capitalism that replaced feudalism. And capitalism did this not by confrontation — which was the only vehicle available to the peasants — and not by competing with feudalism but by creating external yet useful production, and doing so in the towns partly away from direct immersion in the feudal structure.

To this discussion of the possible development of more egalitarian relations of production we have to add that there are other possible successors to capitalism, moving in the opposite direction, toward greater rather than lesser control from above. There are various forms which such a centralized successor might take. One is the "Leninist" communist regime which despite its pro-workers statements has created dictatorial economic and social conditions in which the workers do not control their work and in which civil rights and freedom to dissent are lacking. The economic collapse of the Soviet regime, and its rejection by the population including the workers, as also the difficulties of other such communist regimes, makes this a doubtful direction of post-capitalist development.

Another possible form is a frozen monopolistic capitalist oligarchy, stabilized by surrendering profit maximization and by reducing profit almost to a shadow while retaining the privileges of a capitalist caste. A third possible successor is a fascist-style government directly controlling production and the lives and attitudes of the population. This may be the most likely successor, given that the difficulties of capitalism lead so often to the relinquishing of decision over production and consumption into the hands of government. In thinking of the possible egalitarian development, we therefore have to think not in absolute terms of how it can progress, but in relative terms of how its course can be pitted against the course of change in the opposite direction.

CHAPTER 7

Self-Governed Production

7.1 DEMOCRACY IN PRODUCTION

We have seen that when in difficulties the transactors of business can cede various domains of decision-making to government, and possibly in some cases to the participants in the work of production. We now consider in what ways the latter relinquishing — to non-capitalist enterprises — may actually take place, in the present and foreseeable capitalist world. We are referring here to enterprises in which the control and direction of the productional work rest with its participants, who of course must come to terms with all the other factors necessary to the production — chiefly suppliers and consumers. The characteristic difference here from capitalism is that these enterprises do not employ people in order to maximize a profit from their work. For profit-maximization in industry one cannot make much profit out of one's own manufacturing activity. For a businessman to profit from his employees' work, it is essential that the decision power over the employees' work be reserved as far as possible to management alone, since any decision power in the hands of the employees would reduce profit by increasing their wages or at the cost of improving their working conditions.

7.2 Ideologically Driven Innovations in Production Relations

Over the last hundred and fifty years or so there have been various ideas formulated about self-governing group production, and various attempts to carry out such ideas. All the attempts were made in particular historical circumstances. This does not render them irrelevant to the present discussion. It has been seen that the independent enterprise structure of capitalism permits various innovations to emerge in local attempts, on the basis of local needs, rather than as a comprehensive new system imposed on the whole society in one moment.

For convenience, self-governing innovations will be considered here under three headings: collectivist communes, cooperatives that do not (or rarely) employ workers who do not share adequately in the profits, and complete or partial workers' control of their workplace. It will be seen that the innovations that have relevance to social history are not merely utopian suggestions but work arrangements that answer serious economic needs for their participants.

7.2.1 Collectives

Communes in which the members share production and income, and much of their social life, have existed at various times since long before capitalism, in many cases formed on religious grounds and following religious social precepts and preceptors. Many of these, including ones in the 1800's in America, ended with the departure of the charismatic leader; a few such as the Hutterites continue to this day but with economic and social controls decided by a parent organization. The major movement of communes with an economic and ideologically socialist purpose were the famous Owenite colonies founded mostly in America by the radical English industrialist Robert Owen in the 1820's, some of which lasted into the 20th century. The 1960's movement of "dropping out" of bourgeois society also sprouted ideological communes which for the most part did not last long.

However, the one serious success of the communes — in its spirit and in its economic viability — is the Kibbutz movement in what is now Israel. The crucial difference between this and the previous communes is that the Kibbutzim were formed as a pragmatic solution to the immediate needs of their participants, although they used the ideas of socialist and communalist thinkers in Europe. The Kibbutzim were formed in the early years of the 20th century by Jewish refugees from Eastern Europe, who came to then Ottoman Palestine and found that those who had preceded them, and had acquired land with the aid of Jewish philanthropists would not give them work; local Arab agricultural labor was cheaper than what the European newcomers could live on. Having no other source of livelihood, groups of these immigrants managed to obtain tracts of land from institutions aiding this Jewish migration and settled thereon to prepare it for farming and to farm it collectively. Coming at a time of economic development by the general Jewish immigration there, the Kibbutzim had little competition from private agriculture and were economically successful. (Later on, the addition of Kibbutz industries was also successful). The standard of living of the members rose over three generations from the frugal life of a pioneer to comfortable middle-class levels.

Each Kibbutz, with a population usually between two hundred and two thousand, is a separate self-governed economic and social entity. There is a weekly meeting of the membership to decide budget, major expenditures, public activities and special personal interests. There are annual elections of officials (centralizers, managers), all carefully rotated, so as to provide administrators for the various production branches, consumption needs and social arrangements. Each production branch operates largely as a democracy, with differences of opinion ventilated in scheduled conversations or meetings. Decisions regarding the level of effort and expenditure to put into a particular aspect of production are made by the elected economic committees and the membership meetings. Each Kibbutz tries not only to earn a profit (for its members' subsistence) but also to diversify against slumps in one product or another, and to have work available for all its members (e.g., the older ones, or ones with special interests). Each member can gravitate toward the type of production that suits him, although the Kibbutz committees and meeting can pull a member out of his work for a period elsewhere if needed. The work hours expected from each member decline with age, and past a certain age a member can decide whether he or she wants to stop working.

In consumption, the Kibbutz provides equal housing (graded by age) and all other consumption needs from its own manufacture or purchase, and an equal annual individual income for individual purchases outside, all by a budget decided in the membership

meeting. In the pioneering period there was little individual purchasing or commodity choice, but this has changed. The Kibbutz
assumes responsibility for all needs of its members, including
travel needs for special interests or for visits to relatives abroad,
and including all medical expenses. It also conducts a public social
and cultural life, with schools, courses and discussions, concerts,
recreation, care of the grounds, and the like. Typically, the main
meals are taken in the central dining hall. Originally children were
brought up in age-group children's homes though in very close
contact with the parents. This is now being replaced in many Kibbutzim in favor of having children live with their parents.

Membership in a Kibbutz is open to anyone who wishes to join
and who is accepted by vote at the members' meeting, usually
after the candidate has worked for some months in the Kibbutz
conditions. The great majority, but not all, are Jewish. The children who grow up in the Kibbutz are accepted almost automatically, provided they announce at some point that they want to
become members. Originally almost all Kibbutz children stayed.
Now with the decline of Kibbutz elan (on which more below) and
with the attractions of urban life outside, more than half leave for
Israeli cities or go abroad. For any member who wishes to leave,
the Kibbutz provides severance pay that depends on years of membership. If a Kibbutz child or member who has left asks to return,
the Kibbutz meeting almost always accepts them. Every Kibbutz
has around it a considerable circle of ex-members and friends.

Although independent in their decision-making and activities,
the Kibbutzim are grouped into two federations, one social-demo-
cratic in outlook and the other leftist (at least originally), which
provide contact and mutual aid among Kibbutzim, clearing-
houses for information and financial problems, and central purchasing and marketing aids. There are over 250 Kibbutzim in
Israel with a total population of over 100,000.[1]

Kibbutz principles preclude the employment of outside labor.
However, when more people were needed in Kibbutz industries

1. Haim Darin-Drabkin, *The Other Society* (New York: Harcourt, Brace &
World,1963); Leon Dan, *The Kibbutz: A New Way of Life* (Oxford: Pergamon Press
1969); Reuven Cohen, *The Kibbutz Settlement, Principles and Processes* (Tel-Aviv:
Hakibbutz Hameuchad, 1972); Menachem Rosner and Alexander Avnat, *Democracy.
Equality and Change: The Kibbutz and Social Theory* (Darby, Pa.: Norwood Editions,
1982); Menachem Rosner et al., *The Second Generation: Continuity and Change in the
Kibbutz* (New York: Greenwood Press, 1990).

and agriculture than were willing to become Kibbutz members, Kibbutzim began to hire outside workers. When many members objected, the officials made the factories into joint ventures of several Kibbutzim or of the Kibbutz federation. Eventually the memberships voted to eliminate hiring workers for a profit; one Kibbutz withdrew from its federation rather than give up its profitable employment methods.

The Kibbutzim were first formed in the pioneering community of Jewish immigrants to Palestine, where the Labor Party and its umbrella trade union held the loyalty of the great bulk of the population, and where the Kibbutz members were admired as pioneers and as practicing socialists. With the establishment of the State of Israel in 1948, the bringing in of large Jewish communities that had no socialist background, the wars with the Arabs, the rise of living standards both in the Kibbutzim and in the country, the growing militarist, capitalist, business-minded, and religious attitudes in Israel combined to weaken the socialist ideals that were in any case declining in Europe as well, and overwhelmed the special place that the Kibbutzim had enjoyed in the country. Many in the younger generation lost interest in the socialist purposes, even though many of the younger generation remained in the Kibbutz because they liked its economic and social character. Despite these societal changes, the Kibbutz has remained fundamentally true to its original character even though it has less of an explicit political ideology. There is no power elite or bureaucracy in the Kibbutz; and no person or group has power over the production and life of the rest of the population. The atmosphere in a production branch is very different from what it is in a society in which there are bosses. The sense of liberation and underlying equality is palpable. The uncomfortable distance among people that characterizes all societies in which there are major differences in income or in power is not felt in the Kibbutz even though many other social and interpersonal difficulties remain there as elsewhere. The forgetting of many of the political and social values of the original socialist belief has eliminated neither the egalitarian relations of production and consumption nor the atmosphere of a self-governing workplace and of the social relations that go with that.

The Kibbutzim, many of which are now in their third and fourth generation, are an unusual phenomenon which may or may not be able to rise elsewhere. But even though their circumstances were unusual, some general conclusions can be drawn from their success. First, communes or other egalitarian and self-governed productional arrangements are possible and economically viable (even though so many other attempts failed) but only if they can satisfy the economic needs of their participants. Second, the economic and social character of the community or productional unit rests not on its ideology but on the structure of the decision-system and on one's participation in it. Third, a society controlled from the bottom up can avoid the formation of a bureaucracy provided the principle of rotation is guarded jealously. Finally, egalitarianism is not "against human nature" as some have claimed in rationalizing class-ruled societies. No one is uncomfortable in a Kibbutz just because he cannot live better than the others; people with aggressive personalities find other ways of expressing themselves than by trying to control others by economic power. A self-governed economic structure has not been found to violate or miss out on any basic human needs. Quite the contrary, it has provided an easier social atmosphere than is otherwise common. The atmosphere and social climate is quite unlike that of the Soviet kolkhoz, a collective form managed top-down that is often disliked by its own members.

It is not important here to ask whether a collectivist commune can function in larger populations, or whether the whole economy of a country could be composed of Kibbutzim, or in general whether Kibbutz life does not make demands upon its members that most people would not wish to meet. Perhaps Kibbutzim cannot encompass a whole population but the point is only that collectives are viable and can satisfy economic and social structure needs for some — perhaps many — people in certain situations. As has been argued above, the development of new arrangements of production and of social life is a matter of the rising of many forms in many places, not of a single form mandated for everybody and imposed by a ruling group.

7.2.2 Cooperatives

Cooperatives have less of a supra-economic interest, and less of an ancient lineage, than communes. We will consider here producers' and consumers' cooperatives, especially the former where decisions are made by and for the participants — e.g., in the case of farmers, processing cooperatives but not purely marketing cooperatives. We do not consider here the so-called cooperatives that were formed by Russian and Polish communist managers in 1990 as the tool for quick personal enrichment in a collapsing economy, nor in general cooperatives that make profits from employing large numbers of non-members.

There were Owenite cooperatives in England in the 1830's. Later, the organized Rochdale movement specified the criteria that a cooperative (primarily consumers') must satisfy in order to be chartered by it; some Rochdale cooperatives continue to this day. During the Spanish Civil War, Catalonian workers, largely anarchist, created a famous system of producers' cooperatives with an anarchist character.[2] At much the same time in China, Shanghai workers dismantled their factories in the face of the Japanese attack and carried them on their backs to the western areas where they set up the machinery in producers' cooperatives which paid considerable attention to their own needs.[3] In the last years of Franco, when there were many small industrial bankruptcies in a depressed Catalonia, the local government instituted an arrangement whereby the workers of a failing enterprise were lent money to buy the enterprise from the owner (provided the owner retained at most only a small interest in the salvaged company — this so that the owner would not make the arrangement into an easy source for a loan to himself). Many workplaces and jobs were thus saved, and the great majority of the cooperatives were financially successful.

Worker cooperatives, in most cases rather small, exist in various capitalist countries, e.g., in France and in Italy. They have also been established in a number of third world countries such as India, and as a byproduct of land reform laws designed to distribute the land of some of the great estates into the hands of the peasants working that land; so for example in El Salvador.

The great example of cooperatives is the Mondragon Cooperative Group in the Basque area of Spain, begun in 1956 by a priest, Father José Maria Arizmendi-Arrieta, who planned the coopera-

2. Sam Dolgoff, ed., *The Anarchist Collectives: Workers' Self-Management in Spain 1936-39* (Montreal: Black Rose Books, 1991); Gaston Leval, *Ne Franco, Ne Stalin: le collettività anarchiste spagnole nella lotta contro Franco e la reazione Staliniana* (Milano: Instituto Editoriale Italiano, 1952).

3. Ch'eng-Feng Ch'en, *On the Long March with Chairman Mao* (Peking: Foreign Language Press, 1972).

tives and their main institutions, and who influenced people in his impoverished Basque area to establish and support the first cooperatives.[4] By 1990, there were some 20,000 members in about 100 cooperatives of which only three had failed (an unheard-of success ratio). The group consists mostly of industrial cooperatives (some of which manufacture components for others), some agricultural producers' cooperatives and farmers' marketing cooperatives (in which, however, the sales personnel are members on a par with the others), a consumers' (supermarket) cooperative, a building cooperative that constructs housing for the others, a credit-union-like cooperative bank that takes in members' savings and supplies loans and financial services to the cooperatives, a social security organization funded by payroll deduction in the cooperatives which deals with unemployment payments, pensions, and health clinics for cooperative members, and a cooperative of students at a related technical school who work part-time in the producers' cooperatives (this educational cooperative being operated jointly by the teachers, the students, and the cooperatives which provide work).

Each cooperative was a new enterprise rather than a continuation of an existing business that was bought out. Each was organized not only to provide work for its members but also to foster an ideology of egalitarianism and of concern for the needs and cultural advancement of the members and of the neighboring population. The expansion of the cooperatives was all within a small region, and some were built to provide materials and services to the already established cooperatives. With its emphasis on community needs, the general direction was toward building a cooperative society locally. More than half of the people working in the Mondragon area proper are now working in cooperatives. In the course

---

4. Ana Gutierrez Johnson and William Foote Whyte, "The Mondragon System of Worker Production Cooperatives," *Industrial and Labor Relations Review*, Vol. 31, No. 1 (October 1977) 18-30; David P. Ellerman, *The Socialization of Entrepreneurship: The Empresarial Division of the Caja Laboral Popular* (Somerville, Mass.: Industrial Cooperative Association, Inc., 1982); Henk Thomas and Chris Logan, *Mondragon: An Economic Analysis* (London: George Allen & Unwin, 1982); Keith Bradley and Alan Gelb, *Cooperation At Work: The Mondragon Experience* (London: Heinemann Educational, 1983); David P. Ellerman, "Management Planning with Labor as a Fixed Cost" *The Mondragon Annual Business Plan Manual* (Somerville, Mass.: Industrial Cooperative Association, 1984); David P. Ellerman, *The Democratic Worker-Owned Firm: A New Model for the East and the West* (Boston, Mass.: Unwin and Hyman, 1990); William F. Whyte and Kathleen K. Whyte, *Making Mondragon: The Growth and Dynamics of the Worker Cooperative Complex*, 2nd ed. revised (Ithaca, N.Y.: ILR Press, 1991).

of establishing this system, many new arrangements of production and of decision structure and social relations had to be devised, at first by the remarkable founder (who consistently avoided becoming a "leader") and later by the various cooperative managers. They consciously tried to eschew bureaucratic rigidity, but not surprisingly with some failures along the way. Economically, the cooperatives have been successful, enduring periods of stagnation at times when Spain as a whole has been in serious depression.

Instituting new ways of organizing work in the plants was an important productional feature of the cooperatives. At the initiative of some new managers, Mondragon began to investigate new work organization in some forward-looking capitalist enterprises and in various cooperatives, as an alternative to assembly-line methods. Changes were made, especially in new cooperatives, to make work conditions far less onerous. At the same time productivity increased. It is of interest that these new methods had already been developed in corners of the capitalist world (e.g., at a Volvo plant in Sweden), and that the push for the new ways did not originate with the workers themselves.

The key innovations in Mondragon were in the relations between the cooperative and its members.

As to ownership: members do not own shares in the cooperative. Rather, they contribute money to it which is credited to their capital account in it, and which they recover if and when they leave. Interest is paid on this account, in addition to wages for work, but members cannot sell their share to anyone else, in particular not to outsiders. As owners with capital accounts, they elect (with one person - one vote, after an initial attempt to give managers more votes) a governing council to make the decisions on production and to appoint a manager (without rotation among members); the manager may be brought in from outside. No cooperative may have more than 10% of its workers in non-member status; many have few or none. From 1991 and on, as Spain began to enter into the European Community, Spanish industries had to prepare to compete with European industries in general. In this difficult situation some Mondragon cooperatives have been hiring more nonmembers. In addition, the members elect an advisory social council to deal with their personal needs. Wages are graded into unskilled and skilled and managerial levels, with maximum wage differential being 3:1 (later 6:1). In addition, some cooperatives have had individual merit-rating in white-collar jobs but not in blue. All wages were open to scrutiny by the members. New members can be accepted by the cooperative after working for a probationary period. In slack times, members could shift, or with their approval be shifted, temporarily or permanently to another cooperative. In very bad periods people have had to be laid off, in which case the cooperative (through its bank) has paid unemployment benefits.

One test of these structural arrangements came in 1974, when a job-reevaluation procedure instituted by management in the oldest of the cooperatives (founded in 1956) angered many of the workers and erupted into a confrontation with management.

The job evaluation committees had established a grievance procedure through which point scores on individual jobs could be changed, and many were in fact changed. However, no provision had been made for changing the bases of the job evaluation, which had been established through a two-year study and discussion process among committee members.

The leaders of the protest movement sought to place their grievances before the Management Board. The Board ruled that, as specified in the constitution, such matters must be taken up first with the Social Council. Some of the protesters were members of the Social Council, but they had come to the conclusion that this organ was useless as a channel for redress and they insisted upon meeting with the Management Board. When the Management Board stood firm in its refusal to meet with them, the protesters turned to direct action and organized a strike. The strike was very brief and not effective in shutting down production altogether. (It involved both Ulgor plants and 414 members and began June 27; all were back at work by July 4.) The constitution of Ularco distinguishes between sympathy strikes in support of general political positions and strikes in response to internal problems of the firm. The Management Board is free to impose mild if any penalties in the case of a sympathy strike, but expulsion from membership is supposed to be automatic for those provoking a strike in response to internal problems. Accordingly, 17 of the strike leaders were expelled and 397 received lesser penalties. They in turn followed the constitution and got the required one-third of the membership to sign a petition calling for a general membership meeting to consider the revocation of penalties. After several tense and stormy meetings, the membership voted to sustain management's position, and the dismissals were upheld by a vote of about 60 percent of those attending.

While the job evaluation results were sustained by the membership, the strike was obviously a traumatic experience for leaders and followers alike. This experience precipitated a period of re-examination of the structures and processes of governance of the cooperative. The Social Council undertook a self-study aimed to determine how it could become a more effective organ for representing worker problems to management.[5] (Four years later, in 1978, the strike leaders were reinstated.)

That even one such confrontation could develop in a successful and well-meaning cooperative and could lead to such a showdown points to a crucial aspect of social and economic structure. It is true that the structures in a society — the ones that have grown historically or the ones that new social factors push into being — determine how social groups can interrelate. But the ultimate force lies not in the ideal structures but in the real relations among people. When the most valued relations cannot be satisfied within a structure then new structures may have to be formed or a confrontation erupts. Conflicts of interest always exist in places of work. A crucial difference between the conventional business framework and a self-governing workers' decision-system is that the latter evolves ways for resolving internal conflict so as to maintain and extend a self-governing mode of decision-making.

The election of a parallel governing council (basically economic) and social council was a recognition of the possible divergence of people's interests (or the interests of subgroups among them) when they function as owners of an entity and when they function as workers within the entity. As it turned out, the election of parallel councils was not sufficient for the character and intensity of such divergences. The social council was not equal to the governing council in power, and the managers naturally thought primarily in terms of the economic success of the cooperative. The managers did not see all the considerations from the workers' point of view, and they certainly did not recognize the validity of new (noncooperative) ways, such as a strike, to press members' views. The managers demanded, with subsequent approval from the majority, that dissatisfied workers go through channels, through the social council. But the social council was

5. A. Gutierrez Johnson and W. F. Whyte, op. cit.

admittedly too narrow in understanding the new demands and too lacking in power to satisfy those making the demands. One might say that if it was "valid" for the founding members to devise the structures of governing council and advisory social council, it was also "valid" for the insurgents to use an additional new structure, perhaps even a strike. The insurgents may have been wrong in their demands, but the fact that the majority was not with them is not a sufficient answer to them — not in a community which wants to function together without police power. Such communities need ways to come to terms with their minorities more constructively than by majority vote or by threats to involve laws other than the rules of the community.

More generally, no ideally devised structure can create a permanent utopia; it has to be able to consider unexpected problems or even structural innovations from unexpected directions. Specifically in the case of social structures devised for decision-making from below, there has to be feedback from below and room for changes instituted from below. The question is not whether a strike is a fair or reasonable method under the circumstances, but only that the threat of it was an expression from below and should have been negotiated on a par with majority voting, not as something excluded or something inferior to decision by a majority vote.

The strike also showed that the manager of a cooperative, however democratically named, had too strong a voice and initiative as against the workers in it, and that democratic election of a governing council with subsequent decision-making by that council is insufficient counterweight to the permanent (non-rotating) manager which the council itself appoints. When we look at cooperatives as a particular structuring of decision-making, rather than only as a structure of ownership, we see that the distinction of cooperative production from capitalist is not satisfied by avoiding ownership-for-profit alone, but requires that the people who work, instead of the businessmen, appoint and oversee administrators who are in turn accountable to them.

7.2.3 Workers' Councils

Self-governed industrial production was an idea that fitted closely with those trends in European radicalism (such as anti-Bolshevik Marxists, e.g., Rosa Luxemburg and Karl Liebknecht, with antecedents in the syndicalism of Georges Sorel) that framed the issues in terms of the ongoing interests and potentialities of industrial workers beyond the single goal of seizing political power, in particular by means of a party speaking in the name of a generalized proletariat but in actuality ruling over it.[6] In 1917 workers' councils (soviets) arose immediately in St. Petersburg factories after the revolution in Russia, but were soon taken over by Lenin's government, despite its slogan of "All power to the Soviets."[7] In 1918-19 with the fall of the Kaiser's Germany, the workers in Hamburg took over their factories (and in some degree the economy of the city) and ran them for some months by creating workers' councils (Arbeiterräte) in each plant.[8] In the wake of this and of kindred trends, there was a movement for legal and public recognition of such workers' councils (expounded by Karl Korsch and others)[9] and considerable discussion such as in the work of Anton Pannekoek (the Dutch astronomer who together with Rosa Luxemburg rejected Lenin's 1915 Bolshevik program that was later to become the Communist Third International)[10] and of the Council Communist movement (as in the work of Paul Mattick and his journals *Living Marxism* and *New Essays*).

Later there was a scattering of other cases of workers taking over their factories,[11] operating them on their own so long as materials and customers were available: e.g., in Italy in 1920 just before the rise of Mussolini and much later in the French watch factory Lip.[12]

The idea behind workers' councils is of a decision structure, within a plant or larger productional entity, that is free of outside control except for the productionally necessary considerations of materials, technology, consumers, and adequate but not maximal

6. E.g., M. Shipway, *Anti-Parliamentary Communism: The Movement for Workers' Councils in Britain 1917-45* (New York: St. Martin's Press, 1988).

7. M. Brinton, *The Bolsheviks and Workers' Control* (London: Solidarity, 1970); O. Anweiler, *Les Soviets en Russie* (Paris: Galimard, 1972).

8. Peter von Oertzen, *Betriebsräte in der Novemberrevolution* (Berlin: Dietz, 1976).

9. Karl Korsch, "Arbeitzrecht fur Betriebsräte" (1922), 279-502 in *Karl Korsch Gesamt Ausgabe, vol.2 Ratebewegung und Klassenkampf* M. Buckmiller, ed., (Frankfurt am Main: Europaische Verlagsanstalt, 1980); K. Brigl-Matthias, *Das Betriebsrateproblem* (Berlin: de Gruyter, 1926); C. W. Guillebaud, *The Works Councils: A German Experiment in Industrial Democracy* (Cambridge: Cambridge University Press, 1928).

10. Anton Pannekoek, *Workers' Councils* (Melbourne: Southern Advocate for Workers' Councils, 1950); and *Les conseils ouvriers* (Paris: Belibaste, 1974); Serge Bricianer, *Pannekoek et les conseils ouvriers* (Paris: EDI, 1969); Serge Bricianer, *Pannekoek and the Workers' Councils* (St. Louis: Telos Press, 1978).

11. Groupe Noir et Rouge, *Autogestion, état, revolution* (Paris: Le Cercle, 1972).

12. *Mise au Point 2* (Paris: Imprimerie Tautin, 1974).

profitability. No inside power wields control; only by egalitarian democratic participation do all those involved in the production exercise control. Important as this subject is for long-term analysis of possible arrangements of self-governed production, it is not discussed here because there are not enough ongoing processes or pressures, even in local special conditions, to offer any insight at present into how such arrangements may come to be.

7.3 ECONOMIC PROCESSES TOWARD EMPLOYEE SELF-GOVERNING IN PRODUCTION

The events and trends considered below differ from those in 7.2 in that the motive force involved here is more purely the economic interests of employees or employers. Although ideological values have developed among the workers in support of their economic needs, the initial pressure for employees' actions, as also pressures on the employers, derive from their ongoing economic interests, changing with the change of conditions. In 7.8 we will consider the effects of these conditions and actions not only on the immediate advantages and powers of the employees, but also in laying the grounds for later actions by them and achieving later advantages. The argument presented in 7.3 is that workers' decision power over their own work, and more recently their ownership status in their workplace, are advancing, due to ongoing economic interests and social trends.

7.3.1 Workers' Pressure for Economic and Workplace Concessions from the Boss

From before the 19th century and into the present, workers have fought for their livelihood with varying intensity and tenacity. First it was in small (often secret) groupings or individually, often just to destroy the machines that were putting them out of work (Luddites, Captain Swing). As workers came to be increasingly collected into large workplaces, they were enabled to act more collectively for their common interests: wages, work conditions, later the ability to strike rather than just to leave their jobs, the ability to form more or less continuing organizations of their own (trade unions), and the defense of the "customs and practices" of work that they had developed among themselves. This constituted the great labor movement of the 19th and 20th centuries, which has been magnificently described by a host of scholars, such as (for English labor) Sidney and Beatrice Webb, G.D.H. Cole, Eric Hobsbawm, George Rude, and E.P. Thompson.[13]

It is important that this movement, starting with a long period of defeats and with the hounding and executions of many of the activists, was continued and renewed by generations of workers who had no outside traditions of beliefs or institutions to maintain their direction. It is even more important that this movement grew out of a situation in which industrial capitalism found it profitable (hence necessary) to create new structures for production: subdividing the production of a commodity into detailed and rationalized specialized functions, which involved the massing in one workplace of workers engaged in producing something together. This in turn gave the workers the communality of interests and the communication and numbers that enabled them to act together as a force. And what is most important is that the workers were not merely opposing the employer or destroying his property, as individuals had done before, but were developing — within their work situation — common positions on pay and conditions and common ways of working together, criteria for allocating functions and priority among themselves (under the name of "seniority," etc.), and institutions and types of collective action of their own. The struggles and organizations of the mature labor movement were not merely the result of rejection or bitterness over the decision-making ways of the employer: they were also incipient decision-making activities by the workers about their own work.

Employers in general were naturally opposed to high wages (though merchants gained from higher wages to the local working population), better workplace conditions (which cost more), workers thinking for themselves (thus disrupting the employer's control over the shop floor), and worker organizations. Nevertheless, there are indications that by the turn of the century some industrialists found it advantageous to have an economically and socially more stable and somewhat more educated population of employees. True, the advances in wages and workplace conditions, which took place for example in England and the United States at the end of the 19th century and thereafter, came about in the wake of the massive unremitting pressures of strikes, unionization, and shop-floor demands. And the great governmental

---

13. E.g., Eric Hobsbawm and George Rude, *Captain Swing* (London: Norton, 1975); cf. Ch.6 above, fn. 26.

advances in labor rights in the U.S. New Deal came in the wake of the greatest ever blocking of profitability, i.e., of business ability to decide production. However, the post-war welfare state laws in Europe (and in the United States of the 1960's) may have been in part an acceptance by capitalism of the need for a stable and not impoverished working population.

7.3.2 Workers' Pressure for Decision Power

Although the most common issues in labor struggles were wages, workplace conditions and, earlier, hours, there have been more recent pressures for workplace democracy, which mean in effect for workers to have major decision power in internal issues governing their work arrangements. Discussion and movements promoting "industrial democracy" were present from the late 19th century, especially in the industrialized United States, England, and Germany.[14] These matured in, for example, the English Shop Steward movement of the 1910's and 1920's.[15]

At roughly the same time, and in the 1930's, the development of mass workers' organizations and actions and of labor contracts between employees and employers (especially industry-wide), created further pressures and institutions of labor self-government; for example, collective bargaining, labor economists and analysts and organizers employed by the large trade unions, the push for closed union shops and for laws to prohibit strikers from being replaced (after settlement of the strike) by scabs who had been hired during the strike. Many of these provisions were included in the New Deal laws, and some have been weakened during the union decline and the business attack on labor in the 1970's and the 1980's. But what should be noted here is that the continuation and advance of labor activity — the labor struggle — brings in its wake pressures and institutions of labor decision-making in respect to their workplace, which workers then try to establish at the expense of the employer's decision-making over their work. The widespread development of customs and practices in joint work, which workers try to protect against infringement by the boss, is dramatic example of the same process. Work-

---

14. Sidney and Beatrice Webb, *Industrial Democracy* (London: Longmans, Green and Co., 1897).

15. Branko Pribicevic, *The Shop Steward Movement and Workers' Control 1910-1922* (New York: Oxford University Press, 1959); G.D.H. Cole, *Workshop Organization* (Oxford: Oxford University Press, 1923).

place self-government is sufficiently a natural development in the sociology of modern technology that it has been frequently promoted by liberal intellectuals within capitalist society, and not only by the workers directly involved. There have also been explicit recent attempts to extend the machinery of democracy into the workplace.[16]

One may ask how it is that workers can develop bits of self-government, and can fight to maintain them, in the face of the economic and political power of the employer class. To understand this it is of interest to note that very little of this development is to be found among employees who are not closely involved in the actual production. Lower managerial personnel and office workers are less ready to form unions or to strike or to make demands for workplace self-government. It is not that their pay is appreciably higher, or that they are in any substantive way more "middle class" (except in the very attitudes that are here involved). Rather, it may be that the massed interlocking activities of the directly productional employees give them an objective status in the arrangements of production, which they can defend and amplify in ways that suit the workplace and its personnel against the decisions of the employers. In contrast, employees whose activities are more specific to the steps of business decision-making proper have fewer grounds to oppose the ways in which their employers make their business decisions.

Quite a different movement, beginning more recently than the workplace movement, has been the pressure for "worker participation" in company decisions,[17] and more explicitly for worker representation on the boards of their corporations — though to the extent that this has been instituted the worker representatives are usually involved only in workplace issues. Such proposals have

---

16. E.g., E.S. Greenberg, *Workplace Democracy* (Ithaca, N.Y.: Cornell University Press, 1986); D. Zwerdling, *Workplace Democracy* (New York: Harper and Row, 1984); Frank Lindenfeld and Joyce Rothschild-Whitt, *Workplace Democracy and Social Change* (Boston: Porter Sargent, 1982); and see *The International Yearbook of Organizational Democracy: vol. I, Organizational Democracy and Political Processes,* Colin Crouch, ed. (London: John Wiley & Sons, 1983); *International Perspective on Organizational Democracy, vol. II,* Bernhard Wilpert and Arndt Sorge, eds. (New York: John Wiley & Sons, 1984); *The Organizational Practice of Democracy, vol. III,* Robert N. Stern, ed. (New York: John Wiley and Sons, 1985).

17. R. M. Mason, *Participatory and Workplace Democracy* (Carbondale: Southern Illinois University Press, 1982); J. R. Carby-Hall, *Workers' Participation in Europe* (London: Croom Helm, 1977); G. D. H. Cole, *The Case for Industrial Partnership* (London: Macmillan, 1957).

been discussed from time to time, especially in Germany where calls for Betriebsräte (works councils, whose modern status is distinguished from the Arbeiterräte — workers' councils — of 7.2.3 above) appeared from the 1920's and on. Much of this pressure was a deflection from the movement for workers' councils in Weimar Germany before World War II. "Mitbestimmung" ("co-determination") laws for worker representation in company boards were enacted in West Germany after World War II, but to the extent that such representation has been established it has had very little effect on the company behavior or on workplace conditions.[18]

Meanwhile, various types and degrees of self management by workers have been introduced in various circumstances, all within a capitalist environment, or in any case within market relations.[19] Some of these have had the structure of independently operating works councils.[20]

It is perhaps here that one should mention the workers' council structure in communist Yugoslavia, because the councils were encapsulated within the government's economic plan somewhat as the workers' councils mentioned above were encapsulated within the capitalist management.[21] These councils were formed by communist governmental plan, with reference to the revolutionary soviets of Russia (7.2.3). They functioned closely within governmental productional decisions, and were more bureaucratic than is envisioned in the radical ideas of Arbeiterräte. Nevertheless they operated as decision forms by the workers for their workplace. While

18. Goetz Briefs, ed., *Mitbestimmung*, (Stuttgart: Seewald, 1967); A. L. Thimm, *The False Promise of Co-Determination* (Lexington Mass.: Heath, 1980).

19. Christopher C. Gunn, *Worker Self-Management in the USA* (Ithaca, NY: Cornell University Press, 1984); G. D. Garson, *Worker Self-Management in Industry: The West-European Experience* (New York: Praeger, 1977); F. H. Stephen, *The Performance of Labor-Managed Firms* (New York: St. Martin's Press, 1972).

20. A. Sturmthal, *Workers' Councils* (Cambridge, Mass.: Harvard University Press, 1964); A. E. C. Hare, *Works Councils in New Zealand* (Wellington: Victoria University Press, 1943); G. Hunnius, G. D. Garson, J. Case, *Workers' Control* (New York: Random House, 1973).

21. Branko Horvat, *The Political Economy of Socialism* (New York: Sharpe, 1982); E. T. Comisso, *Workers' Control Under Plan and Market* (New Haven: Yale University Press, 1978); Jaroslav Vanek, ed., *Self-Management* (London: Penguin, 1975); H. M. Bachtel, *Worker's Management and Workers' Wages in Yugoslavia* (Ithaca, N.Y.: Cornell University Press, 1973); M. J. Broekmeyer, ed., *Yugoslav Workers' Self-Management* (Dordrecht: Reidel, 1970); Saul Estrin, *Self-Management: Economic Theory and Yugoslav Practice* (Cambridge: Cambridge University Press, 1973); William M. Evan, *Organization Theory* (New York: John Wiley and Sons, 1976), 33-46.

they are unique in many respects, including their magnitude, they perhaps are closer to being, mutatis mutandis, a communist equivalent to the intracapitalist Betriebsräte idea than to anything else.

7.3.3 Business Pressure for Employee Ownership

The most important fact concerning the great expansion since 1975 of employee ownership in the United States is that it was proposed by business people, enacted by governments with no pro-labor stance, and in most cases instituted by companies with no pressure or input from their employees. Despite this or because of it, the suggestion will be made in 7.8 below that it has the greatest promise for self-governed production of all the historical processes surveyed in 7.2 and 7.3.[22]

(1) *Extent.* Employees' ownership of stock in the company in which they work has existed sporadically since the early days of public companies, i.e., companies in which shares could be bought by the public. Many corporations give their executives options to buy their stock, and a few have done so for their other employees. Starting in the late 1960's, Louis Kelso, a businessman who felt that capital was too narrowly held in America, pressed for a system in which companies could contribute to a fund that would buy shares in the company in the name of the employees.[23] Upon leaving the company, the employees would receive from the fund the current value of their shares. Meanwhile the company would use the fund for its investments or other needs. In effect the company was assigning part of its capital to its employees (titularly, but de facto when an employee left), in exchange for certain advantages (in taxation, in accounting practice, presumably in employee loyalty).

Laws giving tax and other benefits for such Employee Share Ownership Plans (ESOP) were passed by Congress on various occasions from 1974 and on. Most ESOPs are formed by the company management, and funded mostly or entirely by the company. ESOPs can also be formed by the employees of a company in order

---

22. In the copious literature on employee ownership and in particular on ESOPs (Employee Share Ownership Plans, below), it may suffice to refer to two major comprehensive accounts: Joseph Blasi and D. L. Kruse, *The New Owners* (New York: Harper Collins, 1991); Corey Rosen and K. M. Young, eds. *Understanding Employee Ownership* (Ithaca, N.Y.: ILR Press, 1991). Most of the statements about ESOPs given in this section are cited from these two books.

23. Louis Kelso, *Democracy and Economic Power: Extending the ESOP's Revolution* (Cambridge, Mass: Ballinger Publication, 1986).

to borrow money for a leveraged buyout of their company (for example in the employee buyout of United Airlines). These plans have spread widely in the United States. Small beginnings of such plans have appeared in England and in a few other countries.

ESOPs were first established in small privately held companies of a few hundred employees each. By 1991 about 11,000 U.S. companies had ESOPs; in almost all of these the ESOPs held over 4% of the shares and so were not an insignificant part of the ownership. About 12 million employees were taking part in these ESOPs. Companies in which the ESOP members owned the majority of the stock ranged from supermarket and hospital chains with tens of thousands of employees to the Avis car rental company with over 13,000, to Weirton Steel Corporation with over 8,000, to Republic Engineered Steels with 5,000, and to other important manufacturing companies. About 40% of the workers who are in ESOPs are in public companies, but the large majority of companies with ESOPs are private and smaller.

In addition to the ESOPs that had been established, there have been many near misses. When the Greyhound Bus Lines, now the only coast-to-coast line in the United States, bought up a competitor by means of a loan and thereafter was unable to maintain payments, it tried to cut costs and was faced by a protracted strike, during which the strikers' union proposed to buy the company. The company managers however controlled 52% of the voting shares and thus warded off the buyout. In 1990, when United Air Lines was in financial straits, the employees with the cooperation of their unions offered to buy it (for $4.38 billion), with the approval of the parent company which owned UAL, and went so far as to get promises of the necessary loans and to get the vice chairman of Chrysler Corporation to head their new company; but the deal fell through at the last minute. In 1994, the deal finally was made. Also in another major airline, TWA, which was bought by a corporate raider on borrowed money (to be repaid thereafter out of company earnings) the resulting financial difficulties led the Machinists' union employees to propose buying the company, but the owner refused. And in 1990, when the *New York Post*, which had long been a money loser, was in danger of being closed, the workers' unions proposed acquiring an ownership stake in the paper in exchange for union concessions on wages. In 1992, when the *New York Daily News* was in difficulties, there were suggestions for workers' concessions in exchange for shares. The idea for employee share ownership or even buyouts is now ready at hand when companies are in difficulties or when jobs are jeopardized.[24]

(2) *Advantages for the Employer.* ESOPs offer many immediate advantages to the employer. The laws allow tax deductibility for company contributions to ESOP funds, and for loans obtained by the ESOP funds (if no more than 1/3 of the shares are owned by high-paid employees). Companies can thus make considerable savings from their contributions to their ESOP or from borrowings from the ESOP (the loans being gradually repaid by the company), since the use of the fund remains at the company's discretion. The ESOP borrowings do not count on the books as debts of the company, an important consideration in public accounting of the company's debt. Companies can borrow through the ESOPs for constructive capital. More frequently they have borrowed to buy their own shares from the public or from current owners in favor of ownership by the ESOP.

Companies can form ESOPs or use their existing ESOPs to fend off hostile takeovers. In the case of public companies, the laws require that the employees be able to vote their titular shares (even though they don't actually own the shares, if the company has borrowed the money for the ESOP and has not yet repaid the loan); hence the company needs the employees to vote against the corporate raider, which would usually be in the employees' interest too. In general, managements favor ESOPs because these have the general effect of entrenching the existing management of a company. Employees generally have a greater interest than do public shareholders in management continuity, and are less likely to vote their shares for a management change.

In many cases management favors an ESOP or other employee-ownership form as an alternative to various other employee advantages: e.g., instead of wage raises or other benefits, in exchange for wage and other concessions on the part of the employees, or as replacement for the company's pension and health funds for the employees. This "restructuring" of wages and benefits means replacing the fixed costs of pension funds or the like (which remain high even if the company later does poorly) for the floating value of company shares (which go down if the company does poorly). And some companies see ESOPs as an alterna-

---

24. Keith Bradley and Alan Gelb, "Employee Buyouts of Troubled Companies," *Harvard Business Review 63* (September - October, 1985), 120-130.

tive to unions; indeed some companies (such as a health-food supermarket chain) have been formed on this basis.

Management interest may also be influenced in the future by the finding that firms with ESOPs generally do better than firms without.[25]

There are many ways in which management can use ESOPs to their own advantage, and to the gross disadvantage of the employees or the public shareholders. An ESOP can be so formulated as to give the executives disproportionately high incomes even to the point of weakening the company, and so as to exclude lower-paid employees from any part of the control. It can be used to load a failing company on its employees, who will be left with worthless shares. There are various other dangers for the employees, some of which can be foreseen and averted by appropriate formulation of the ESOP of each company or of all companies. Such pro-worker formulation is possible because in many cases the company has enough to gain from the ESOP to make it amenable to many of the demands from the workers on the detailed conditions.

(3) *Other Reasons for Establishing an ESOP.* Some 40% of companies with ESOPs have been reported to have formed an ESOP in order (at least in part) to provide additional benefits for the employees, in order to increase their loyalty and attention to the company's work, and perhaps to get them to work harder or more committedly. Some ESOPs have been formed (sometimes with company help) by the employees in order to buy out a plant or entity which the parent company wants to spin off or divest because it is less profitable than its other plants, or because the given plant does not fit into their current or future strategies. Some employee buyouts have taken place when their workplace or company was on the verge of bankruptcy or of being closed (e.g., so as to enable the company to open a replacement plant in low-wage areas such as Mexico).

The major specific pressure other than the directly economic is seen when management forms an ESOP in order to assure continuity of the company (this reported as a factor in about one half of all ESOPs). A common situation is an employee buyout of a retiring owner, or of passive members of the owning family. The owner may prefer to sell to his employees for personal reasons; but laws also make it economically advantageous for him to do so

---

25. Rosen and Young, *op.cit.*, 30.

rather than sell to outsiders, or to close the business and then have to give severance pay to all the employees.

Finally, various governments of formerly communist countries in Europe have considered giving employees shares or ownership of their plants (while retaining a management not controlled by the workers) as a form of privatization. On a small scale this was done for other reasons by the Thatcher government in England in privatizing national property.

(4) *Advantages and Disadvantages to the Employees.* Although companies are usually the major funders of their ESOPs, the employees contribute directly in some cases, and in most cases contribute indirectly by making wage and work condition concessions or forgoing raises and various benefits. They also take on various risks. If the company fails their share may be worthless, though the fact that ESOP companies do better on the average than companies without ESOPs suggests that this risk is not so great. If their pension and health funds are linked in some way to the ESOP, the risk becomes very great, because company weakness or failure would leave them with a smaller or even no retirement income. Whereas company health depends on the ups and downs of business, pension and health funds are in general fixed, usually invested in a mix of stocks; and they are in various ways protected by law. But in contrast to these risks, the workers have certain gains: ESOP companies in general put in more total benefit money (including the ESOP itself) than do non-ESOP companies, and employee income is generally higher there, even aside from the value of the shares. In addition, ESOP companies offer greater job security in respect to arbitrary firing or other personnel changes, though little protection against being laid off in the case of work-force attrition.

As against these risks, U.S. ESOP laws protect employees against some of the above risks, for example by giving certain tax advantages only if no more than 1/3 of the ESOP shares are owned by the high-paid employees, or only if the ESOP owns a majority of the company's shares.

Crucial further protections needed by employees are that pension and health funds be uncoupled from the ESOP and from the company's future health. ESOPs bring so many advantages to the company that employees can well demand that this and other protections or advantages be included in the formulation of their ESOP. For the long term there is a crucial condition that employees should seek in their ESOP structure: that the voting power and share strength be sufficient to give the ESOP employees substantive input in the management of the company — implicitly to the point of being able to affect control and replace management. This last seems to be out of reach as being suicidal for business interests; but as will be noted in 7.3.4 there are factors moving in this direction for the future.

Finally, there is the question of ESOP's relation to unions. Present laws on ESOP formation exclude union members from first year participation on the grounds that they have other benefits in their union contract. Unions distrust ESOPs, in no small part because management in many cases see ESOPs as alternatives to unions. Nevertheless, unions can work with ESOPs, and in the successful buyout of United Airlines the unions were an active and important participant. The relation of ESOP members to workers outside their own company and the alertness to conflicts of interest between them and management, both of which can best be provided by active membership in unions, makes it very important for ESOPs to work with unions, perhaps as special sectors within them. Somewhat similarly the problems that led to the strike of cooperative members against their cooperative in Mondragon (7.2.2) could have been better treated if the cooperative members had also been members of a union with wider-ranging occupational understanding than that of the cooperative members by themselves.

The overall attitude of employees to ownership in their companies is seen in the finding that many workers say they would be willing to forgo wage increases and benefits, or even a month's wages, for participation in the ownership of their company. This desire has been interpreted as due to some not otherwise evidenced capitalist psychology of "owning" for its own sake; but we can say simply that the employees understand that ownership might in some way change their power in respect to their job.

(5) *Buyouts.* In some ESOPs, and in other companies with employee-ownership arrangement, the employees own a majority of the stock. In addition, there are cases where employees buy the whole company at once, especially if the owner is retiring or if the parent company wants to divest itself of a particular plant. In many of these cases the employees have to obtain a loan (to be repaid from future earnings) in addition to putting up money of their own. In contrast to leveraged acquisitions of a company either by corpo-

rate raiders or by the company's own top management, the employees in this case are carrying the cost of the loan themselves, because the money for repayment would otherwise have gone to them. In almost all cases the employees accept an outside management; or, if the managers joined in the employee buyout, the workers accept the managers as controlling the operations of the company.[26] Nevertheless it will be argued in (8) below that the majority ownerships and buyouts are steps on the way to worker control.

(6) *New Cooperative Enterprises*. Much less frequent than employee ownership in existing companies is the founding of new employee-owned enterprises. These differ from producers' cooperatives (7.2.2) primarily in that they are larger and therefore are more heavily dependent upon a professional management distinct from the workers. A description of one rather striking example, a large new bakery in Pittsburgh (Pa.), is given here because it shows the circumstances that can lead to such new enterprises (*New York Times* 1/27/92, p.10, by Michael deCourcy Hinds. Copyright © 1992 by The New York Times Co. Reprinted by permission.):

> ...City Pride [Bakery] is the nation's first start-up of a major manufacturing company intended to be owned in full eventually by its employees, almost all of whom are being hired from welfare rolls and long-term unemployment lines. Many of its workers, who lost their old jobs when the city's last commercial bakery closed in 1989, organized to obtain government loans and private investments to establish the $9 million company...
>
> City Pride is also unusual in its intent to provide jobs to people who need them the most in Pittsburgh. And the bakery plans to offer high school courses, free child care and subsidized lunches to its unionized worker-owners. When a group of City Pride's investors and workers gathered to talk about the company's mission earlier this month, the hotel meeting room overflowed with idealism, spiritual talk and visions of a humanitarian workplace...
>
> There is so much civic pride in this bakery, scheduled to open in March, that it has become a symbol of Pittsburgh's economic resilience... The new bakery may also create a model for other cities struggling to hold onto manufacturing jobs and factories...

26. Rob Paton, *Reluctant Entrepreneurs: The Extent, Achievements, and Significance of Worker Takeovers in Europe*, Milton Keynes (England: Open University Press,1989); A. Hochner, C. S. Granrose, J. Goode, E. Simon and E. Applebaum, *Job-Saving Strategies: Workers' Buyouts and OWL* (Kalamazoo, Mich.: W. E. Upjohn Institute, 1988); J. Logue, J. B. Quilligan, B. S. Weissmann, *Buyout! Employee Ownership as an Alternative to Plant Shutdowns: The Ohio Experience* (Kent, Ohio: Kent Popular Press, 1986).

Dissatisfied with its out-of-state bakeries, Giant Eagle [Supermarkets] has agreed to give its private-label business to City Pride, which promised to provide a wider range of breads at a lower cost. With that commitment, City Pride instantly obtained more than twice as much business as it needed to turn a profit...

The Penn Traffic Company, which has 90 convenience stores and supermarkets in the area, has also agreed to buy City Pride Bread. And over the past year, a volunteer sales force led by the unemployed bakery workers obtained verbal bread orders from hundreds of neighborhood groceries, pizza shops, hospitals, university cafeterias and Pittsburgh's public schools...

City Pride's primary marketing strategy — to provide local supermarkets with fresh bread in the store's own wrapper — fits into two national trends in the food business. Supermarkets are trying to increase profits and build customer loyalty by stocking shelves with more of their own premium, private-label brands...

But while the demand for private-labeled bread is increasing, the wholesale bakery industry is consolidating. The number of commercial bakeries has shrunk from 3,000 in 1972 to fewer than 500 highly automated plants today. With fewer bakeries, serving stores from greater distances, supermarket owners say, the bakery industry is less able to meet the need for custom breads.

Pittsburgh got caught up in the industry consolidation when its sole commercial bakery, Braun Baking, was purchased by Continental Baking Company and later on, in 1984, Continental was bought by Ralston-Purina. Continental has since closed about 20 plants, including Braun.

City, county and state agencies tried to keep the bakery in town and its 110 workers employed by offering Continental a package of benefits, including a low-rent lease on a new factory, reduced utility charges and real estate taxes. The company rejected the offer and now ships bread to Pittsburgh from its bakeries in Columbus and Akron, Ohio.

When the laid-off workers saw that Continental rejected that offer they said, 'Why can't we get the same deal?' and, to some degree, they got it,' said Tom Croft, executive director of the Steel Valley Authority, a local economic development organization that, along with the bakers' union and the city's Urban Redevelopment Authority, coordinated the City Pride project.

The laid-off Braun workers became lobbyists, obtaining public commitments that now total $2.6 million or almost

1/3 of the project's total cost. The largest ones include $500.000 in Federal grants for job training, $1.1 million in state loans and grants and $560,000 in loans from the city and the county...

Before public agencies offered to make significant investments, the workers had to find a management team, develop a business plan and obtain lots of private investment. Church groups, from far and near, were among the earliest to invest, providing a total of $315,000, while more than a dozen business and individual investors, including Pittsburgh's major banks, have invested about $6.5 million.

The bakery will start off with about 100 employees 'including about 40 from the plant that closed — who will own 10% of the business. The number of employees is expected to increase to 300 over the next five years, by which time the workers would be in a position to buy the remainder of the company from the private investors.

(7) *Pension Funds.* At present pension funds are managed by companies for their own employees, or by unions and other managements (for example, for all the workers in an industry). At times they have been grossly mismanaged by companies that left their workers nothing when the company collapsed, by corrupt officials of national unions, and by financial managements. They act no differently from other investment funds; and the employees whose money is in a pension fund have no control over it. Meanwhile pension funds have become among the largest and potentially most powerful investors in America. Some suggestions have already surfaced that the pension funds should not be merely pawns in the strategies of the major manipulators of finance capitalism (some of whom had unloaded their junk bonds onto those pension funds), but should be able to exert influence on what is done with their money. Furthermore, it is not unthinkable that, in the long term, control of the pension funds should move into the hands of effective representatives of the workers whose life pensions constitute those funds. The pension funds could in principle be a massive instrument of employee interests within the machinery of capitalism. The fact that business would not like this does not preclude its coming to be because the logic of ownership argues in favor of such a development. To a large extent business people are imprisoned within the criteria of ownership and profit, which determine their ability to act. They cannot always stop a development just because they fear it politically for the long term.

But such a development seems to be far in the future, and has no serious pressures working for it now.

(8) *The Implications of Ownership.* Ownership is not an explicitly necessary ingredient of the criteria for capitalist decision-making for it consists only in the expectation of profit. Initially and for the most part, the capitalist's money-lending and entrepreneurial investments were made with his own money. But upon occasion he was able to use other people's money given to him for the purpose, or to arrange a combined effort of his money and a farmer's work. Joint stock investments were introduced in the 1600's, with the owners of the shares having no effective control over the operations of the company. Today, the top executives of a large incorporated business enterprise direct its activities toward profit maximization, and get vast incomes out of company earnings — to all intents and purposes what a capitalist owner's relation to the company would be — without necessarily owning any of the company's capital or risking their own money in its losses or bankruptcy.

However, ownership remains the basic legalism of capitalist control over operations. The innovation of the executives' shadow capitalism was effected by reducing share-owners' power to participation in the annual stockholders' meeting. The early corporate raiders tried to operate despite this reduction by campaigning among the stockholders for enough proxies to unseat the management (in favor of themselves) at the annual meeting. In view of the difficulty of doing this, they finally resorted to the underlying power of ownership simply by buying a majority of the shares. Since the raiders in general lacked the money for such a massive action, they did it with loans which were to be repaid from the earnings of the company after they gained control of it.

A much smaller and more recent grey area in ownership is being formed in employee-share ownership and buyouts. The intent here is that the companies continue to be operated by managements, with the employees' ownership, even if a majority, being of no more relevance to decisions than were the public stockholders. However, economic and productional problems for the workers, and differences of interest between managers and workers, are bound to arise in every company. In the usual company structure, the workers can only protest or demand, and have no recourse except to work less well or to use union threats or to strike. But when the workers own a majority of a company (and to a lesser extent when they own a sizeable block of its shares), they can insist on solutions that are more acceptable to them; and in the extreme case can in principle vote out the existing management. Neither management nor the workers think in such terms now, and influencing a management — not to speak of throwing it out — is no simple matter in a company that has to continue operating and earning all the time. Nevertheless, as unsatisfactory situations arise for the workers in an employee-owned company, they are certain eventually to use their ownership power to impose decisions.

In Weirton Steel, when management had to lay off almost 2,000 (out of over 8,000) workers because costs had to be reduced, some of the workers asked "How can we be laid off if we own the company?" and a group organized to find an alternative solution.[27] In Republic Engineered Steels, which had been bought by its 1,000-man managerial staff and its 4,000 hourly workers together in 1990, the managers decided in 1991 that 625 of the workers (worker-owners) would have to be laid off, whereupon the workers instigated other cost cuts which reduced the number that had to be laid off to 105.[28] It can be expected that such entries of the workers into the decision-making normally done by management will develop only sporadically, as the workers find management's ways unsatisfactory. But in such cases the workers will come to use the power that ownership gives them.

In the radical movement it is understood that the power of the workers lies in the fact that they are indispensable to most production — without any regard to ownership. Without in any way reducing this essential status, the trend toward employee ownership gives an additional avenue to workers' control of production, via their ownership. In particular, it creates the conditions for spanning, at first in a scatter of companies, the decisions from direct productional work to larger decision-making over the whole enterprise. This bridging will have to be developed if worker decision-making is to have the scope required for administering a whole enterprise.

7.3.4 Business Moves Toward Accepting Worker Decision-Making

The general attitude of company managers has always been to reject workers' control over the work, or their participation in the

---

27. *Business Week*, September 9, 1991, 40.
28. *New York Times*, November 22, 1991, 24.

direction of the company. Workers generally distrust management, and do not even desire to give it constructive criticism; but to the extent that they do, management in general neither listens nor understands (despite the not infrequent Suggestion Box), not surprisingly as managing and deciding is precisely their function in the company. Nevertheless it is known that workers have many useful opinions about the work process, and that worker input can improve quality and the production process and shop-floor atmosphere, reducing waste and increasing productivity.

In spite of employer opposition and employee reservations, there are some pressures, perhaps increasing, for greater worker decision-power. The constantly rising level of technology and of workers' knowledge, recognition of the limitation of centralized decision methods such as the assembly line ("Taylorism," "Fordism"), and the spread of worker-oriented arrangements in some forward-looking factories, all raise the issue of assigning more decision-making into the hands of the workers.[29]

This issue has become more prominent again in the recent debate on the "labor process" — in effect (from the point of view of the present book) the question whether new relations of production are being developed within capitalism. The earlier radical view was that capitalism throughout its history, and in particular "Taylorism" throughout the 20th century, took control over the labor process, making each worker virtually a robot, following the imperative of the assembly line, the foreman, and all the higher managers behind him — all pre-set by "experts."[30] More recently, investigators of labor have observed that in fact the workers carry out considerable decision-making on their own work — especially recently — and that management may come to realize that it has to come to terms with this trend.[31] In any case, capitalism's con-

---

29. Cf. Lawrence B. Cohen, "Workers and Decision-Making on Production," *Proceedings of the Eight Annual Meeting of the Industrial Relations' Research Association 1955*, 298-312; Seymour Melman, *Decision-Making and Productivity* (Oxford: Basil Blackwell, New York: John Wiley, 1958); Lawrence B. Cohen, "The Structure of Workers' Decision," *Journal of Economic Issues 10*, June 1976, 524-537.

30. Such pre-set planning, which is derided by business people when initiated by Communist central planning ("command economy"), is the ideal of the hierarchical corporation structure. It is also the ideal of governmentally supported "big science" in which a few scientists who are either famous or otherwise favored by the power wielders are supposed to plan and hierarchically control the work of all the lesser scientists under them.

31. Michael Burawoy, *Manufacturing Consent: Change in the Labor Process under Monopoly Capitalism* (Chicago: University of Chicago Press, 1979); also his *The Politics of Production* (London: Verso, 1985); Richard Edwards, *Contested Terrain: The*

trol over the workers has weakened rather than continued unabated. The serfs and peasants in feudalism operated under heavy controls even before capitalism; the extent of their freedom of choice in respect to their detailed activities amounted to little indeed. From the early 1800's to the late 1900's there have been periodic reductions in direct control over the workers, interspersed with attempts by employers to regain some of the lost control. The reduction of control over the workers in the old capitalist countries can be seen when we compare it with labor powerlessness in Japan, and somewhat differently in the Pacific Rim from Korea to Singapore or in Mexico. There not only are wages far lower than, for example, in the West, but also the workers live and work under far more massive discipline.

Some worker empowerment is due to workers own struggle (7.3.1), and some to the needs of modern technology. If we extrapolate from the past record — for all that extrapolation should be used only with the greatest caution — we would expect that workers' decision-making on their own will increase, partly encapsulated within businessmen's control and partly in new enterprises formed on this basis.

As to capitalist management, it is now recognized by many that giant centralized corporations, such as General Motors and IBM, are not — or are no longer — the most successful way of arranging production. The bigness of plants — far beyond the needs of rationalization of production — was in part a reflection of the bigness, hierarchical structure, and control requirements of management, more than a requirement of mass production. Some of the entrenched managements of the largest corporations have become so frozen, and so distant from productional and even marketing realities, that the result has been a sharp decline, as has happened to the automobile and steel industries in the United States.[32] More generally, some people cast doubt on the whole of management in respect to workers,[33] while others think that mod-

---

Transformation of the Workplace in the 20th Century (New York: Basic Books, 1979); Paul Thompson, *The Nature of Work: An Introduction to Debates on the Labor Process* (London: Macmillan, 1983); Andrew Zimbalist, ed., *Case Studies on the Labor Process* (New York: Monthly Review Press, 1979); Craig R. Littler, ed., *The Experience of Work* (Aldershot (England): Gower, 1985).

32. Richard Preston, *American Steel: Hot Metal Men and the Resurrection of the Rust Belt* (Englewood Cliffs, N.J.: Prentice-Hall, 1991).

33. The president of a mid-sized steel company is quoted as saying "You can't 'manage' people. You can bribe them." (*New York Times*, January 14, 1992. Op Ed) — an attitude that may be behind some of the ESOPs.

ern capitalism is being forced to move toward decentralization and toward more room for worker participation in decisions.[34]

A particular new factor in worker decision power is the competition met by industries in the old capitalist countries from Japan and the low-wage third-world areas. Manufacture in the U.S. and England has been reduced, in no small part because of imports from Japan. Many American and European companies have moved their manufacture to the Pacific Rim or Mexico. This is no long-range solution, if for no other reason than that the home working population cannot be totally disregarded. The welfare rolls cannot be doubled or tripled, and the unemployed population cannot be counted upon to remain forever quiescent. One of the few ways out is for American and European companies to pit the education and initiative of their worker population against the low wages and lack of labor organization in Asia and Latin America. Since 1990, General Motors has been trying to do this, perhaps only in a half-hearted fashion, in its new Saturn plant, which gives great freedom to worker initiative and organization. Whether and in what way such changes in workers' decision-power may become interesting or serious, first in the production process and later possibly in company board rooms, it is too early to tell.

When the recognition of workers' decision status is combined with employee ownership, the possibilities and pressures apparently change.[35] At present one third of ESOPs provide for worker participation in workplace decisions, far more than in non-ESOP companies. The record of ESOP so far suggests that neither ownership nor participation-programs separately bring about improvement in plant performance, but the combination of the two does. Worker decision participation in company policy in general, beyond the job issues, is virtually non-existent whether in ESOP companies or in others. Even the voting of shares, which only lays the ground for possible owner participation on general company issues, is disliked by management. In public companies all ESOPs are provided by law with the power to vote their shares, but in private companies only 20% of ESOPs have full share-voting power, and half of the companies said that they would not have formed their ESOPs if it had involved share voting.

---

34. N. J. Piore and C. Sabel, *The Second Industrial Divide* (New York: Basic, 1984).

35. This issue is still unclear. Cf. for example B. J. Toscano, *Property and Participation: Employee Ownership and Workplace Democracy in 3 New England Firms* (New York: Irvington, 1983).

However, it may be impossible to evade the eventual right of ESOP members to vote their titular shares. And the small ESOPs have a good likelihood of growing in time to own larger blocs of their company's shares. When the ESOP bloc is large enough, and certainly when it owns the majority of the shares, it will be impossible to evade the workers' voting of their shares so as to control the company in their own interest — within the possibilities of the company's economic health — and to participate on general company issues.

7.4 SUPPORT WITHIN CAPITALISM FOR STARTING SELF-GOVERNED PRODUCTION

7.4.1 Due to the Open-Entry Structure of Capitalism

First, as indicated in Ch.6, capitalism began in scattered individual enterprises finding unused opportunities to make goods available by commerce or by industry; and it has retained open entry in principle to this day. Although the economic and political power of big business as a whole can greatly reduce the chance of success for enterprises whose character it opposes, big business cannot police or control all economic areas and openings (e.g., in 7.4.2-3). Indeed, business cannot assure the continuity of its own giants. The greatest enterprises, such as the East India Company, finally leave the stage. Major companies go into bankruptcy, such as Pan Am Airlines in 1991 and TWA in 1992. The greatest corporations find it necessary to subdivide into partially independent units, as in the case of General Motors before World War II and IBM in 1991. Few massive capitalist entities, such as the Rockefeller interests or DuPont, continue their prominence past 100 years. There is much movement, with entities entering and dying, growing and decaying. Finally, there are the global dynamical factors: the expansion requirement of profit, the growth of non-productional activity due to arbitrariness of product in business and the growth of capitalist pollution vis-à-vis the size of the earth. All these change the conditions and content of business activity. In part, existing businesses adapt to such changes. But in part, new enterprises arise that are better attuned.

Secondly, the trend toward increased intra-business profit opportunities, and toward finance capitalism in general, ushered in profit levels that cannot readily be matched in industry. The honing of new tactics (e.g., junk bonds) and the developing technology of business (via computers and electronic finance-operations) have freed speculators and investors to move immediately toward maximum profit. As capitalism becomes increasingly a mobile search for the bottom line, the greatest activity will be in finance and a few high-profit areas. Capitalism will not then be equally aggressive in all areas of production — not in those which have lower profitability or are otherwise less attractive to investment (e.g., because of local political instability). In such areas, workers' enterprises may be easier to start because the competition from profit maximizing enterprises may be less and weaker.

In major depressions or even lesser recessions, there may be bankruptcies and business closings which cannot be replaced by new profit-maximizing starts, but may leave room for "subsistence" enterprises to start up. Just as the starting of enterprises in capitalism is individually sporadic, so is the distribution of individual bankruptcies and failures; and the closing of a profit-seeking enterprise does not necessarily mean that a workers' enterprise cannot replace it and survive. Indeed, in future difficult conditions for capitalism, letting unattractive areas of production go largely to subsistence enterprises ("relinquishing to below") may in some cases be less unpalatable or threatening to the business world than nationalization, or even than having a rampant (e.g., "fascist") government organize or take over the ailing industry ("relinquishing behind").

In any case, the in-principle open entry for business starts which had aided the growth of early capitalism makes the introduction of self-managed production more possible within capitalism — certainly more than it would be in the existing communist societies or third world countries.

7.4.2 Areas of Lesser Profitability

Furthermore, some of the areas abandoned by big capital may require more capital or more initial staying power than small business investors can afford, especially if the investors have to pay regular wages during a long incubation period. Such are the selling and the producing of special audience books and recordings, the operation of special audience local radio stations and possibly even television channels, the establishing of scheduled and semi-scheduled taxi, bus, and air transport to currently unserved communities (possibly even rail service, since throughout the United States there exist many rail lines which had been dropped

from service, largely under the pressure of automobile interests).
Some such attempts have been made as cooperatives or as profit
enterprises, and of these many have failed. However, some have
succeeded, such as the left-wing Pacifica radio chain, in many
cases with the help of a movement-like devotion on the part of
consumers for whom it fills a need. Success is possible, but it
requires a pinpointing of consumer niches which ordinary business is passing up. In particular, the audience-size rating system
on which television advertising is based makes it virtually impossible for commercial (profit-maximizing) television to meet the
needs of specialized audiences. In these cases success is promoted
by socially or politically motivated relations between producers
and consumers in the specialized markets.

Opportunities for non-profit starts are more available when the
low-profit areas passed up by much of big business are too important for the population, or for particular sectors of it, to be readily
eliminated. Such was the case in the middle decades of the 20th
century with the coalmines of England, and to a lesser extent in
France and in parts of the United States, before the closings and
nationalizations of mines. Such may still be the case with much
of agriculture in the old capitalist countries, eventually even in
the United States. The despoiling of the soil by chemical agribusiness, and other results of the productional methods of that giant
industry, is making agriculture less profitable in many areas. Such
may also be the case some day with solar energy, which the business world is diligently avoiding.

A current example is the fiasco of the American Savings and
Loan industry, and the pressure to deregulate banking. Governmental actions fostered by financial interests had led to high
interest rates (which the old Savings and Loan companies could
only with difficulty pay out of the old low interest they were
charging). Thereafter the Reagan administration deregulated those
companies so that they could lend at high interest, but only for
high-risk loans (thereby helping financiers unload junk bonds),
with government officials explicitly declaring that the old modest
profit companies should no longer exist — an attitude which
spoke only for the interests of high-flying operators and the
finance-capitalism establishment. Despite the fact that many
high-risk loans defaulted and the industry collapsed, the high-risk
methods were not withdrawn, and the high profits (many achieved
illegally) were largely unrecovered. In the face of this collapse the

banking industry and the government in the United States have been promoting a "reform" of banking by precisely the same methods, not because the banks are unable to function or make a profit but because the bankers insist that current banking is not sufficiently profitable (*New York Times* 2/9/91). In effect, this simply means that capitalists are refusing to carry out these services in the old safe ways because they are not as profitable as the bankers would wish them to be. Hence, if the old services, especially home mortgages, are to be maintained, it will have to be by companies devoted to something other than maximizing profit (as discussed in 7.5).

In general, the deterioration in the "quality of life," which is widely recognized in the old capitalist lands, came about because many products had been altered in ways that are not in the consumer's interest, and many services have been dropped or reduced dramatically — all this not because the old could not be maintained, but because there was more profit in doing otherwise.

7.4.3 *Situations Supporting Self-Governed Production*

There are in capitalist society some economic factors, and some situations that support the establishment of relevant cooperative and employee-owned enterprises. Such are:

(1) *Job Problems:* The constant shifts in business — plant movings, plant closings, mergers — create groups of jobless. The issue becomes sharpest when a particular plant is closing, and the employees face the possibility of buying it, or of starting a comparable plant of their own. More generally, the decline of manufacture in America and England, partly because companies move their production to the third world and partly because of imports from Japan, create a more or less permanently jobless body of workers, engineers, and managerial personnel. As news spreads of former employees organizing to form their own enterprises, one may expect pressures on various groups of these jobless to try to resolve their problem in this same way.

(2) *Community Needs:* Although business pays no attention to the effects of plant closings and mergers on lay-offs and on the communities in which the plants had operated, and although national governments also pay little attention, the communities themselves — the population, the local consumers' businesses, the local institutions such as churches and chambers of commerce, the local and regional governments — can be brought in

their own interest to help such groups as might try to resume production on their own, or to supply goods and services that are not otherwise available to the community.[36] The issue is acute in more-or-less one-company towns or neighborhoods, or when there is a wave of bankruptcies or mergers, or a long-term decline in a major industry (e.g., coal, agriculture, automobiles). Another case is that of ethnically separated or discriminated communities which cannot attract business investment. The Black self-help movement has had a checkered career (including the involvement of Black nationalism); and the new black middle class largely divorces itself from any interest in the extremely poor black multitude. Nevertheless, cooperative self-governed methods could find support and might succeed. As to goods and services unavailable locally for various business reasons (cf. (4) below), prominent examples are fresh foods such as bread (cf. 7.3.3 (6)) and vegetables, or transportation between small towns.

(3) *Products:* There are a great many products and services that people need, or would welcome if available, but are not provided by business for any one or more of several reasons; because they are not sufficiently profitable, or because they endanger current profitable business, or because they have too long a lead time before they can be developed to the point of profitability, or simply because they are too small or labor-intensive or innovative to fit into the business methods of entrenched big managements. Examples are: solar energy, which would interfere with the highly profitable oil corporations; many local needs as in (2) above, which don't fit big business centralized power structure; and many technological innovations such as modern non-chemical agriculture, which would interfere with the chemical industry and with big agribusiness.

Failure to develop many innovations is more pervasive than is commonly realized. In neglecting various productional areas, big business is affected not only by their relatively low profitability but also by businessmen's disinclination to refrain from exploiting old technology while waiting for new technology to develop to the point of profitability, or to commit their resources to a long industrial development. In addition, big business favors the larger and more centralized units of production and commerce, over smaller and less centralized alternative forms. Thus the personal com-

---

36. Jeremy Brecher and Tim Costello, *Building Bridges: The Emerging Grassroots Coalition of Labor and Community* (New York: Monthly Review Press, 1990).

puter did not come from IBM, the giant leader in the industry, but from the private activity of the engineers who devised the Apple computer. Big business' rejection and delays in introducing such new technologies leaves room for small independent enterprises to seek and develop both the unsatisfied markets and the untried new technological possibilities. In some cases the situation clearly invites such independent entries. New enterprises are occasionally started by individuals, in the ordinary profit-making manner and in many cases are eventually bought out by the industry giants. But they can also in principle be started by all the employees involved in an employee-controlled enterprise to carve out a more or less permanent niche of their own in the technology, production, and economy of the society.

(4) *Ecological Concerns:* This issue is so widely discussed these days as to need no detailing here. The magnitude of capitalism's waste and pollution is now such as to threaten the ecology within which modern human life survives. For business, any adjustment based on ecological concerns would be likely to cut into profits. Hence business, and to a lesser extent the various governments, stall; and if they do anything, it is too little. It may be difficult to establish worker-controlled plants that would be ecologically more considerate, because costs might make them non-competitive. Nevertheless some attempts in one field or another might well succeed, and further research might indicate how ecological concerns can be met without great cost increase. In any case, the search for adequate but less than maximal profits together with special sales appeals to concerned consumers might succeed where big business is not even interested in trying. The current growth of "Nature Food" stores is an example.

(5) *Size:* Aside from all the substantive considerations that make big business pass up niches for profitable production, there is also a structural one: big business is too big, too hierarchical, and too set in its ways (by virtue of the self-perpetuating feature of managements) for various products and services. Big technology has been profitable up to a point, but its later massivity was in part independent of the merits of the case. Furthermore, many recent technologic developments make possible a smaller scale than that of big business: solid-state physics and miniaturization, modularity, computerization (not only for production plans and records, but also for specialized markets), complex systems analysis and computer modeling. Various other business developments

also favor smaller productional entities: for example , the "just-in-time" approach wherein factories do not pile up big inventories but produce to fill specific orders and ship directly to the customer as soon as the product is completed. With this, there are human considerations of how people can best fit into production structures (or vice versa),[37] and even considerations of the way division of labor is changing with the changing character of the population and the demands of capitalism.[38] "Small" may be too limited for much of today's technology and population size. The best promise for employee-controlled enterprises may be in mid-size production.

(6) *Business Interests:* Certain business interests open opportunities directly or indirectly for employee control or ownership. Conglomerates and holding companies that want to quit a certain (less profitable) productional field, or to divest themselves of a particular plant (which still makes a profit, or could make it under altered circumstances), or to break up their massive manufacturing system into separately operated or separately owned facilities are such. There are business chains which routinely drop the bottom few earners in their chain even though they remain profitable (with the intention of replacing them by other openings), or which drop an owned company if it cannot reach a preset profit level (in some cases, 15%).

Companies have been known to acquire profitable specialized-market enterprises, and then kill them because of some particular consideration of the acquirer. For example, the last classical-music magazine, which was making a profit, was bought by a magazine corporation and thereafter closed in the interests of a popular-music magazine in which the corporation had greater interest.

In addition, it is conceivable that when a company is about to close in bankruptcy, its creditors and lending banks, or even its suppliers and customers, may prefer to support a buyout by the workers rather than have the company close down.

Finally, employee ownership and participation in control can constitute a business interest, as noted in 7.3.3 (2), e.g., when a company wants to protect itself against unfriendly takeovers or corporate raiders by having (in advance) a sufficient number of its

---

37. Cf. E. F. Schumacher's famous *Small is Beautiful: Economics as if People Mattered* (New York: Harper, 1973).

38. E.g., F. Manske and H. Wolf, eds., "The Future of Industrial Work in Changing Capitalism," *International Journal of Political Economy* 20:4, 1990-91 (New York: M. E. Sharpe).

shares owned by the workers (as in an ESOP arrangement). Thus, when two 32-year-old raiders tried to buy control of a company and told its 73-year-old head, John Justin, that they would eventually win because they would outlive him, the *New York Times* commented (12/26/90) "The tender offer is unlikely to go anywhere soon, if only because Mr. Justin, his board and his managers control 23 percent of the company, while an employee ownership plan holds 16 percent. That makes it almost impossible for the raiders to assemble the two-thirds of the shares they need to complete the deal." In 1991, National Register Corporation tried to counter an unfriendly takeover by AT&T, via an ESOP program for its workers, but was stopped by the court on the grounds that this was being done only to thwart the takeover.

(7) *Governmental Considerations:* One has to remember that not only business but governmental policy too can affect the opportunities for employee-controlled production. While both are undoubtedly opposed in general to this direction of economic change, they may not necessarily always wish or always be able to oppose the individual openings. Although governments in general favor not simply business but specifically big business over small, there are situations in which government is forced to break up an industrial giant, or to protect small concerns from being swallowed up by larger ones (in the U.S., under the little used anti-trust laws). More generally, both business and governments in capitalist countries have lived with a mixed economy, and in some cases with a see-saw of fluctuations between nationalization and privatization. A mixed economy consisting not only of business and government ownership but also of a considerable scatter of employee-controlled or owned companies is not an unacceptable development for business or government to envision. That such a development nevertheless contains the seed for a post-capitalist economy and a more humane society will be suggested in 7.8 below.

7.5 Viability

There are various factors that make for the viability of cooperative enterprises within a foreseeable late capitalism, and some that work against their viability.

7.5.1 Due to the Internal Structure

What is being discussed here is the control of production by all the people directly engaged in it. In such a situation these people would necessarily have a management that is in some effective way under democratic oversight. Relations to other producers (suppliers, or next manufacturing steps) would be controlled by the market or by agreements among all the groups involved. In this structure, the ultimate decision-making power comes from below, from the people involved in each step. As a result, the needs and interests of the workers would presumably be taken into account to the extent possible, with consideration given to the interests of other groups involved, including the ultimate consumers and the ecological interests of the population as a whole. Greater concern for their interests promotes the satisfaction of the work force and its allegiance to the productional goods of the enterprise. When workers are merely employees, removed from the decision process and from the profits, and controlled from above, their apathy and even ill-will toward the production process and the company are not surprising. But when the company and its decisions and its profits are theirs so long as they work there, there is both reason and evidence to expect attentiveness to detail, responsiveness to the problems of production, improvements in procedures, and innovation in the product and in the production process.

Certainly, the Kibbutzim have been viable both economically and socially, for several generations, and have achieved a considerable advance in the standard of living of their members as well as in the "quality of life." The Mondragon complex has been viable and so have many smaller cooperatives in Europe and not a few large cooperative efforts in India and other Third World countries as well. Maintenance of viability, and of the ability to weather politically motivated opposition present problems to self-governed production but are by no means unachievable.

Apologists for capitalism argue that economic unfairness is necessary for the productional success that capitalism has brought, but the argument is not supported by the evidence. Search for new products or cheaper processes may well have fostered capitalist technology and design, but this would hold for employee-controlled companies in the market as well. Causing employees to work harder may have been furthered by threat of wage reduction or firing; but incentives to work and to improve the work, as well as smoothness of teamwork, are hampered rather than fostered by unfairness in the workplace.

Employee control of enterprises is a contribution to job maintenance. Employee-owners would certainly try to stem the drain of manufacture from the old capitalist lands, and to save jobs in the home country. This requires serious, sustained innovation in all aspects of production and enterprise operation, from product design to marketing. All this is needed to enable a combination of high-wage workers, using sophisticated production methods, to produce at low unit cost and price. Conventional business managers with short-term profit perspectives have been reluctant to take this path, and have typically preferred to abandon production, or to transfer operations to currently lower-wage areas.

Maintaining jobs is a natural interest for working people, and would lead them toward openness toward the requirement of long-term planning — as in the industrial planning needed to convert from military to civilian industry,[39] and the regional planning needed to organize new work for coal miners where natural deposits become exhausted.

To save jobs in the face of capitalist competition at home and low-wage competition from the Third World is very difficult. To maintain jobs for all workers is all the more difficult in view of seasonal differences in required staff, occasional contractions of an industry (requiring temporary or permanent layoffs), and the like.

7.5.2 Technological Niche

The natural size of cooperative or employee-controlled enterprises is likely in most cases to be midsize — larger than a company that an individual or partnership can ordinarily establish, but

---

39. The Executive Council of the AFL-CIO has accepted a comprehensive policy aimed at facilitating conversion from a military to civilian economy. On Feb. 20, 1992, the Council declared:

The decline in direct military threats to U.S. national security and the reduction in military spending require an economic conversion program for the transfer of economic resources and workers from military to civilian production. Such a program would insure that those who built the nation's defenses need not suffer in times of peace...

Under the 1990 Economic Conversion legislation, the Defense Department has transferred $50 million to the Department of Commerce for industrial reconversion and $150 million to the Department of Labor for worker adjustment assistance. This is a meager step in the right direction that provides insufficient funds and lacks special conversion features. The existing legislation provides inadequate worker adjustment benefits and specifies no direct plant-level conversion support or requirements.

Conversion planning should provide for:

— A national commission in which labor, industry and government together plan and coordinate conversion related activities.

smaller than what big business tends to attain in its constant attempt to expand and to achieve concentration of capital. For this reason the most natural technology for self-governed enterprises may be different in detail or in character or in size from a small company's capacity or from big business ambitions. As noted in 7.4.3(5), many recent technologic developments favor midsize productional entities. These would in most cases require access to massive central technologies — communication and information systems, technology and science agencies, managerial and marketing aids. However the entity itself could be cooperative internally. It would take an extreme situation for the power wielders in the economy or society to try to deny cooperative entities access to these central technologies. One might say that such dependence nevertheless limits the effects of midsize cooperative efforts: the central bodies would not themselves be cooperative. But that is looking too far ahead: by the time many of the productional entities proper are cooperative, the status and power of self-governed enterprises and also their ability to form some of their own central bodies would resolve some of these problems.

Technology is constantly being modified — innovated, rationalized and simplified, reduced in cost and size and in energy requirements. From time to time whole new technologies for existing products or purposes are introduced; and new technologies open the way to new processes and products and services. Therefore, were a structurally distinct midsize cooperative type of

---

39. (cont.)— Community committees in defense-dependent areas, where labor, management and local leaders can work together to develop conversion plans.

— In-plant Alternative Use Committees to engage labor and management in joint exploration of civilian market possibilities.

— Sufficient advance notice of defense procurement cancellations and cutbacks to allow time to develop alternative use plans.

— Appropriate funds to facilitate the planning process.

The business development program should provide for

— Incentives to help firms convert existing facilities from military to civilian use.

— Plant-level technology and skill assessments to inventory the production potential of defense-related establishments.

— Support for new business ventures.

— Start-up funds for planning, research and development in the form of grants, loans, loan guarantees or tax incentives.

The assistance program for workers should provide for:

— At least six months' advance notice of major layoffs and/or closing of defense plants or military bases.

— At least one week of severance pay for each year of service at the affected establishment or with the employer.

enterprise to develop in particular industries, it would in time be able to use new technologies too large for many private businesses and too small — or small-time — for big business plans. The history of the industrial revolution shows that new ways of production needed to develop new manufacturing opportunities have fostered the innovation of technology; we may expect that the needs of midsize and cooperative or self-directed productional facilities will foster — perhaps among cooperative-minded engineers and scientists — new technologies that will be of particular applicability and utility in such new production entities.

7.5.3 *Reduced Distance Between Decision and Production*

The fact that the ultimate control on decisions would rest at the "bottom" of the productional hierarchy, with the personnel directly involved in production, dismantles one of the damaging dynamical trends of capitalism: the increasing distance and contentual irrelevance of decision-making from the production thereby decided. For one thing, there is direct reduction of distance. The decisions of capitalist corporations are typically made by managers who are not the main or sole owners and who tend to build complex layers of command and bureaucracy between them and the actual production. This is natural since their status and income is in part correlated with the size and complexity of the

---

39. (cont.) — A special federal unemployment system with benefits similar to those provided under the earlier Trade Adjustment Assistance program. This would include at least 26 weeks of additional federal unemployment compensation beyond the first 26 weeks of regular unemployment insurance payments.

— Expansion of training, retraining, relocation and placement programs including adequate funding of the Employment Service to facilitate the conversion process.

— Adequate health insurance protection for displaced workers.

— Early retirement options for workers affected by defense cutbacks to be paid for out of the adjustment fund.

The federal government should provide funds to state and local governments to offset the loss of local taxes and federal impact aid in communities hard-hit by cutbacks at defense plants and military bases.

The AFL-CIO calls upon Congress to enact legislation that provides adequate planning at the national and local level for economic conversion, effective support for business and labor to develop alternative uses of the defense-oriented facilities, and appropriate assistance for workers adversely affected by cuts in military spending.

We urge Congress to allocate a significant share of federal budget savings from defense cutbacks for use in economic conversion planning and assistance.

For bibliography on economic conversion see *The New Economy*, an international periodical on economic conversion and disarmament, from the National Commission for Economic Conversion and Disarmament, Washington, D.C.

bureaucracy under them. In contrast, a decision-system controlled from "below" is best served by a far leaner and more nearly transparent network of channels of control, with fewer hidden interests and inputs and with less room for the accumulation of personal power (or corruption). Also, it is well known that the workers involved in a manufacturing process can make valuable suggestions or improvement, except that they do not normally do this in the employment situation, and are rarely listened to if they do.

For another thing, the interests of the productional personnel favor a commitment to their existing productional facility and to the products that it produces or that with continued attention to modernization, it can be modified to produce. This counters the financial mobility that has developed in finance capitalism, where investment can be switched from one enterprise or industry to another, and it encourages attention to the needs of the particular market available to the given enterprise. More than the market manipulation by contentless advertising, it invites user-oriented product modification, product innovation addressed to market needs and development of market loyalty even to the extent of movement-supported producer-consumer contacts or the like. Such developments have rarely been sought in the stock-market-based and advertising-mediated capitalism of today. It is also very difficult to achieve in today's world, as is seen in the weakness of the special consumer relation sought by the cooperative market movement (e.g., the Rochdale cooperatives in England). Nevertheless special consumer relation is not unknown even in capitalism (e.g., in certain catalog-based marketings) and it presents a little used opportunity to producer controlled companies.

7.5.4 Freedom from Profit Maximization

Attempts to start enterprises do not have to be based on profit maximization. In principle what is necessary is only the availability of capital, know-how, and contacts or plans for input (materials and workers) and output (markets), and the expectation of enough profit to cover operation, loan-repayment and reinvestment (technological and market maintenance and improvements). The characteristic search for profit maximization comes from the dynamics of capitalist accumulation, from competitive pressure, and from the race for economic and social power. Without the need to maximize profit, there may be opportunities for enterprises to operate with less than the maximum profit-level of the given industry, and there may be specialized avenues for maintaining market share with only moderate rather than maximal expansion.

For an enterprise to fit in principle into the capitalist world, all that is essential is that its buying and selling go through the market or at least have the ability to do so even if in fact there are various fixed arrangements such as barter and captive consumers.

Businesses, especially local ones, can succeed without profit maximization. When a chain habitually closes its lowest-profit locations, generally the outlets that it closes had been succeeding and making a profit, only not as much profit as the other locations. When the Tribune Company in Chicago, which owned the *New York Daily News*, was trying to close that paper in 1991, the paper was in general making a profit of some 5% according to its ex-editor; but, he said, the company required that each of its papers turn in a 15% profit. When the Reagan government was trying to close down the small Savings and Loan banks, it found a small successful bank in Vermont — by no means the only one of its kind — which had taken no risks (such as buying junk bonds) to raise its income, but had modestly carried on its local business successfully. The government officials then tried to force each such local bank to merge with big speculators "because it is too small." The prevailing commercial mark-up in America is currently 40%, and in some areas closer to 100%; there is little question that a business can survive with lower profit.

In current financial practice, the demands of profit maximization impose limitations on business functioning. In publicly-traded companies, management has to watch its profit standing, since even a few quarters of low profit and low stock prices can bring the corporate raiders down on them; this hobbles any plan that involves lower current profits for the sake of higher later profits. Among stockholders, the race for high profit and fear of loss make them unable to withstand the junk bond-based offers of the raiders, even though the resulting indebtedness of the company may cripple or bankrupt it. In contrast, a company at least 51% owned by its employees can legally preclude sale of its majority to outsiders, and can plan its activities without these restrictions. Furthermore, profit is a manipulable concept, for example, the sums routed to the executives are not counted as profit. Typically management tries to minimize production costs, but tends to escalate its own administrative costs. Annual income of top managers — salary, bonuses, stock-options — in the largest U.S. companies can approach $100 million.[40]

If we ask what constitutes enough profit, as distinct from maximal profit, it clearly has to cover an acceptable standard of living for the employees, all the costs of equipment and marketing, including loan repayment, plus enough for periodic improvements, innovations and renovation in production processes, product, and even in further distribution and marketing. Indeed, the employees can in difficult times accept lower than average industry wage, somewhat as employees are explicitly willing to defer raises or other gains in favor of saving their jobs or of receiving stock in their company.

Escape from the imperative of profit maximization carries a number of possible advantages for the enterprise. Such an enterprise must develop alternative strengths in order to survive the competition of higher-profit capitalist enterprises. These strengths may include avoidance of the overblown incomes of top managers, leanness of the administration, clarity of the line of command (which is often intentionally obscured, and complicated, in capitalist corporations), and avoidance of the worst excesses of the "corporate structure" with its Byzantine office politics, sycophantism, and the struggle for personal power within the company. These strengths would also include the allegiance of the workers, attention to consumer needs, and the drive to build consumer loyalty instead of relying on advertising cachet. In normal business times, toward which most business calculations are directed, all of these alternative methods may not be so valuable to a company as the methods that modern businesses actually use. But in major depressions and economic crises, and even in times of major readjustments such as may be forced upon the economy by ecological changes, these alternative means of operating may enable the survival of cooperative enterprises at a time when the wasted costs and the irrelevant activities engaged in by big business today would lead to major disruptions and failures.

7.5.5 Difficulties

There are problems other than profitability. In many instances a profitable company has been forced to the wall by a more powerful competitor who wants to eliminate it. Or an industrial giant,

---

40. Cf. Graef Crystal, *In Search of Excess: The Overcompensation of American Executives* (New York: W. W. Norton, 1991).

or a corporate raider armed with junk bonds, can offer the owners or stockowners of a company enough money to make them sell it. A possible defense against this tactic would be an arrangement whereby a majority of a cooperative's shares are held permanently by the cooperative itself, unsellable by the cooperative members except back to the cooperative, and unsellable by the cooperative to any outside person or entity. Local and midsize enterprises can try to avoid such dangers. The same fluidity of capital that enables a midsize company to try to become larger has made much of capital fly toward the big time and toward financial manipulation. One may try to stay out of the way by knowing how to get the support of one's geographic or market area.

The difficulties of establishing and maintaining self-governed enterprises in a profit-maximizing environment are vast. In addition, there is the lack of tradition and experience in how to create and conduct such enterprises, and the lack of existing social supports such as communal or special-interest consumer groups. Finally, there will be political difficulties, since some business interests will oppose such enterprises as threats to capitalism. Such opposition is a heavy burden for self-governed enterprises to bear, and can destroy many of them. However, it may not be lethal to the whole development toward self-governed production, for there are many situations in which business would accept it (e.g., in buyouts that are convenient for companies or communities, 7.3.3-4), or would tolerate it as providing subsistence for parts of the population. The experience, networks and even managerial and financial support institutions that these protected cooperatives bring forth can help in forming and maintaining other cooperatives that might otherwise have been more vulnerable to opposition from competitors, bankers and government agencies.

Nevertheless, the profit-maximizing of capitalism is itself caught in a dilemma, for the kind of enterprises which are natural to it do not constitute a stable system. Products are made out of resources, and resources are limited. The more profit business makes, the less room there will be eventually for making future profits. Furthermore, the more capitalism succeeds in blocking workers' opposition the more it makes socio-economic conditions unsatisfactory to large parts of the population. On the other hand, the more flexible it is in conceding certain victories to the workers, the more it enables the economic and political infrastructure of an eventual noncapitalist system to develop. And if particular areas of production essential to the population become too low in profitability to attract adequate investment, the business world will not be able to oppose in dog-in-the-manger fashion the growth of quasi-non-profit forms whether governmental, private, or cooperative. In some situations private efforts may be too weak, and government may be either too ineffective or too threatening to capitalism, so that the business world might find that relinquishing an area of production to producer-controlled cooperatives was the lesser evil.

For this reason, the movement toward producer-controlled production does not necessarily have to be confrontational against capitalism, but may proceed up to an appreciable extent within the flexibility and the give that capitalism has occasionally shown, both because of its loose structure and because of its periodic difficulties. It is true that the flexibilities of capitalism arise for the most part only when business needs them for survival or advancement, and that business would try to limit this retreat, by using capitalism for profits and allowing "socialism" for losses only. Nevertheless, these "socialist," i.e., self-governed, methods can thereby take root in some areas of production. Any appreciable success can be expected only as the difficulties and inadequacies of capitalism pile up to an extent well beyond their present levels — witness the long history of non-capitalist attempts that have failed or have held out only with great effort. The early preparations for cooperative developments cannot, however, wait for capitalist crises but have to begin long in advance.

It has to be recognized that in some respects the character of producer-controlled enterprises resembles the market-governed status of middle capitalism (though not of course to its internal structure) more closely than it does that of capitalism today. However, not all the changes toward a corporate world and market manipulation work to strengthen capitalist productivity and popular acceptance. In certain respects a turn to earlier more entrepreneurial forms, which is impossible for mainstream capitalism because of its forward dynamics, may prove stronger productionally and politically.

7.6 GROWTH

We have seen that existing and expected conditions in capitalism permit the start-up and survival of some participant-controlled production. Not every enterprise will necessarily succeed,

but the question is whether enough of these attempts will succeed, and enough new ones will be started, to make such production arrangements an increasingly large part of the available economic options. In Ch.6 it was seen that the initial spread of capitalist activities (before they came to be promoted by governmental
action) was supported by their supplying additional goods (at first
for the rich, but later also to some extent for the urban craftsmen
and others) and by the gains to their participants (primarily to the
entrepreneurs, but to some extent also to the peasants who sought
work in the towns so as to escape serfdom). In the case of participant-controlled production, we have noted goods and services and
protection against joblessness and bad work conditions that the
pursuit of profit maximization fails to supply while a more moderate "subsistence" profit level could. We have now to consider
whether the pressures that lead to cooperative attempts will continue, and how successfully the new kinds of enterprises would
satisfy them.

The fundamental status of profit maximization in business
decisions, and the dynamical directions of profit-making and of
distance between decision and production, are all unchangeable
within capitalist structure — short of the creation of some new
kind of only nominally capitalist governmental system. In the
specific case of employee ownership there is evidence that the
business pressures to move in this direction will be continuing.[41]

As to how adequately participant control satisfies these pressures, its purely economic viability for its own members has been
considered in 7.5. However, if its example is to spread, the participant-controlled enterprises will have to retain their character and
not slip into bureaucratic control, or into a two-tier employment
arrangement exploiting additional workers by the side of the original members (7.7). Such backsliding would decrease the difference
between participant control and ordinary business control of
enterprises, and would reduce the attractiveness of participant
control as a solution to employees' job problems. In addition to
direct job gains, participant control opens the door to other social
advantages not at all natural to business. When the ultimate
deciders of an enterprise's action are also the population of that
enterprise, it is natural for the enterprise to attend to many population needs that are irrelevant to business management and
would constitute additional costs against its profit maximization.

---

41. Joseph Blasi and Douglas Kruse, *The New Owners* (New York: Harper Business, 1991), 243.

These include avoiding layoffs to the maximal extent possible (e.g., by first cutting all other marginal costs, or by spreading the work reduction over the whole force), joint housing schemes, child care especially for women members, technical and general education, personal financial aid, user-oriented health and pension arrangements. To this can be added training in managerial tasks and in the company's particular activities, so as to build a pool of members who can rotate in managerial posts or in management oversight committees. Many of these services have indeed been organized in many participant-controlled enterprises, including the Kibbutzim and the Mondragon complex, various successful factory complexes in the Soviet Union, and various Third World cooperatives — not to mention the plans for the Pittsburgh bakery cooperative described in 7.3.3(6).

The comments above apply to individual enterprises, and to their relevance and attractiveness as models for future opportunities. Once there are enough self-governed enterprises of one kind or another in a region or within an industry, the success of the enterprises and the spread of their model can be furthered by networking among the enterprises and by the establishment of support institutions; this is seen to a high degree in the Kibbutzim and in Mondragon. The establishment of such inter-enterprise structures occurred to some extent in the development of capitalism, at least in the formation of financial institutions (which were themselves profit-making enterprises). This was an understandable process, since the individualist and unorganized form of capitalist activities did not in itself provide for any inter-enterprise links or supports. However in the case of capitalism it was a slow and not very natural development because of the competitive and individualistic economic motivations. In contrast, self-governed production is based on cooperation rather than competition, and naturally invites inter-enterprise supports. The need for networking is as great among cooperatives as among the early capitalist activities, because the self-governed enterprises would also be starting independently and locally, as did the capitalist enterprises. The networking does not necessarily involve outside control, or the subsuming of local decisions under central bodies; it can be federative and democratic. The like is seen in the non-controlling networks that grow among independent grassroots groups in the United States, in respect to their activist and educational activities. The networks can facilitate and clarify the contacts of a plant to its suppliers and to its customers, thus helping to organize and to direct many decisions that have to be taken in the essential activities of the plant.

It would not be surprising if such new ways for outside contacts turn out to be more rational, less costly, less wasteful, less effort-consuming, and more effective than the present capitalist modes, where all relations between differently owned enterprises in a long chain of intermediate components to an ultimate product must go through the productionally arbitrary calculations of intermediate profit-maximizing decision-procedures.

The network can also guide relations of a plant to any participant-controlled competitors or other related production groups, enabling them to cooperate on common interests and to avoid mutually destructive conflict.[42] There can even be arrangements among them for borrowing workers or inventory, or for finding temporary work for laid-off members, or other cooperations that strengthen now one, now another. And a sufficiently large number of participant-controlled enterprises can together create a wide variety of valuable joint institutions: banks, pension funds, health-care providers, information banks, managerial and other courses, research into appropriate production methods, work design, niches available within the existing economy, marketing methods and loyal customer environments.

Beyond networking, there is one other development that can help self-governed production to get started and to succeed, and also help it to maintain its participant-controlled character. This is a social or political movement, which could clarify many things: awareness and understanding of the reasons for productional self-government as a resolution for current economic problems, motivation for workers to use the productional power that they have, and finally the human and social values created and expressed by productional democracy. The possibilities for such a movement may exist in segments of the grassroots movement of today (particularly in the United States), though many grassroots groups may be quite business-oriented in outlook and would not support participant-controlled production. By the same token, there are undoubtedly many workers who enter an employee ownership situation for their immediate needs while having no part of

---

42. Among gypsy fortune tellers it is understood that one does not open a store within a given number of blocks of any other gypsy fortune teller.

any broader, and especially non-mainstream, attitudes or ideas. In any case, the speed of participant-controlled production cannot be part of any specific movement, much less follow any political party or organized external leadership, for it can grow and succeed only as a response to the economic and social needs of the people engaged in production, whoever and whatever they may be. Nevertheless, a general climate of opinion, and a movement or set of movements that sympathizes with productional self-government, can provide ideas and values of greatest importance to this emerging development.

It is also important that productional self-government not be estranged from the labor union movement, but rather cooperate with it wherever possible, and be seen as a sister development. This is so not only because business might seek to set the two against each other in order to weaken both, but also because late capitalism may witness a long "mixed" period in which part of production is in business employment and part in self-government with occasional moves from the former to the latter; any estrangement between unions and employee ownership would confuse such transitions.

In presenting the considerations that indicate the possibility for self-governed production within capitalism, no attempt is made here to formulate a "theory" or general picture of how this development will occur, much less how cooperative production can be organized and can function within capitalism and after. It is clear from past experience that no one can predict or usefully plan the future of society. All we can do is suggest with some evidence or support that the conditions of today's and tomorrow's capitalism make it possible for participant-controlled enterprises to meet the needs of some people, and so to become established and to grow.

7.7 PRESERVING THE PARTICIPANT CHARACTER

Experience has shown that many well-intentioned cooperative enterprises gradually lost their economic and social self-decisioned character, although some, such as the Kibbutzim, have preserved the essential structure and character through several generations. With the loss of democratic decision-making structured from the bottom upward, these enterprises lose their status and value as alternatives to capitalism. It is therefore not as a matter of ideological purity but rather of their practical value to social change that one must consider the preservation of their character as a producers' democracy.

(1) *Management.* The most immediate danger, because of the enterprise's immersion in the capitalist world, is the passage of de facto control into the hands of business managers. The decisions on buying and selling, and on loans and tax considerations are so crucial to viability and so central in the business world that new employee-owners are likely to find themselves captive to the decisions made by the business administrators whom they hire. The first harm is simply that decision powers and initiative are taken out of the workers' hands. But another harm is that the personal (occupational) interests of the business managers may be at variance with those of the workers who have bought or formed the company. Furthermore, even representatives of the workers elected to oversee the business professionals may find common cause (personally or occupationally) with them, and may develop positions of de facto power for themselves which would nullify much of the intended workers' control.

The problem is much more pressing in large employee-owned plants such as the steel companies mentioned in 7.3.3 (8). Managements hired by worker-owners often make no attempt to find new ways of operating (made possible by the new status of the workers) that would circumvent lay-offs as the first answer to hard times: e.g., new ways to cut costs or to raise productivity or to improve the product. Even if the workers are required to hire a management acceptable to the lenders from whom they get their initial loans, the new owners can set up active committees to track the actions management is considering, and to solicit alternative proposals from the workers themselves where desirable.

There are also problems with the details of ESOP or buyout plans, such as limit the future power of the workers and the permanence of worker ownership. For example, in the case of Republic Engineered Steels, the 4,000 hourly workers and the 1,000 managerial employees each put up the same sum, $4,000, to buy 10% of the company (borrowing the rest), but the shares were distributed among all employees according to their pay. Obviously it would be best if the workers can see to it that the formulation of the initial contract gives them greater power and rights in management. Workers have considerable leverage in these matters, for their sacrifices are crucial to the buyout. In Weirton, the workers, through their union, accepted an initial 20% wage cut and 6-year wage freeze, with later sacrifices when plant modernization was required. But even if a better initial contract is impossible, the worker-owners can unilaterally form committees and internal organizations that would give them more information, more input, and in effect more control over their company's decisions.

A different case of worker ownership without managerial control is the proposal, floated after the Soviet collapse in some formerly Communist countries, of giving ownership shares in the state-owned factories to the public at large or even to the workers in the factory, while leaving management entirely independent of these nominal owners, to be appointed by some public authority and in effect self-perpetuating. Here the worker-owners would have to fight for control over management; otherwise they would gain nothing as against capitalist employment or Communist state ownership.

(2) *Hiring Non-Members.* The most important structural danger, however, is not management but the tendency to hire non-member workers who do not participate in the control of the enterprise. This may seem to be unavoidable when temporary or long-term extra hands are needed. The inconvenience of fitting temporary people into the democratic control system, and the attractiveness of making profit out of them as businessmen make profits out of their employees, may encourage profit-making considerations at the expense of non-member employees to color the decision-making of the members. Such two-tier systems in income and decision participation not only are anathema to the value of the enterprise as an alternative to capitalist structure, but also sooner or later abrogate the advantages that these enterprises can possess over capitalist concerns in times of economic stress and in the long run. They result in the loss of work force solidarity, and of allegiance and work commitment in many of the workers. These divisive effects are well understood by workers in business enterprises, who have opposed the creation of such two-tiered wage systems by their employers.

The issue of the shifting number of workers needed at various times can be met in various ways. One way, well developed in the Kibbutzim, is to diversify the production of a cooperative work force so that slack in one product is expected to be taken up in another product. It is a kind of rationalization of production. It is quite different from diversification in capitalist conglomerates. The rationalization that was developed in industrial capitalism was designed to make maximal use of the work force in a given productional program, whereas here the problem is how to combine several productional programs in order to find more or less constant work for a given work force. A related way of meeting the problem is to shift workers among several different worker-controlled enterprises in the same region.

However, the basic approach to the problem of external employees in an employee-controlled company is the definition of membership or of decision-participation. From a capitalist viewpoint, an employee-controlled company is seen as just another kind of private partnership, with each worker owning a share of the company. This is indeed what government regulations might see in such a cooperative. In Barcelona when the government wanted to salvage companies that were going bankrupt (shortly before and after Franco's death), it lent money to the workers to buy out the owners by buying shares, with each worker repaying the loan from his later earnings in the company. Such an arrangement raises the question of what a worker does with his share when he leaves the group, or dies, and how new workers enter the group.

In contrast, the enterprise can be organized in terms of control rather than ownership, with share-owners receiving profit but not voting power. Then the plant and its good will may belong to the government or to the group (possibly ceded to it by the government) but not to its individual members. The founding members would share decision-making and profits (after reinvestment needs) and would elect or accept new members as needed — temporary or permanent — sharing profits and decision-making with them for as long as they are in the group. Voting would presumably be one-person one-vote, in any case not by number of shares held. Part of the profits would be set aside to repay any investment by the founding members, while the rest would be shared among all workers whether founding or new. The group might protect itself against temporary members who may lack commitment to the group's needs by delaying a new worker's decision-participation until that person has been in the group for a certain period. Even so, many problems remain: For example, does democratic participation in decision-making permit a majority to vote down the special interests of a productional or ideological minority? What sub-units can vote their local preferences? How do component or independent groups compromise their differences?

The share system leaves room for non-voting shares to be sold even to non-members, thus giving the worker-owners access to additional investment funds. In some cases this may be economically necessary for the company. This possibility is not foreclosed in the decision-participation system if the group sells non-voting shares yielding dividends at a percentage of profits, as an explicit way of borrowing money.

(3) *Bureaucracy*. One last danger has to be mentioned. Members who are elected to business and administrative positions in the group may succumb even after short periods in office to the many openings for corruption, e.g., from suppliers or customers. Or they may prove grossly inefficient in their tasks. Or they may simply create a semi-permanent internal organization under their suzerainty. This problem has arisen often in cooperatives and in the economic institutions of labor unions, where the vagueness of accountability and profit-requirements frees them from controls such as business imposes upon executives.

Against all these dangers there may be various structural defenses. Elected and appointed posts may be rotated, members trained so as to maintain a pool of possible executives, watch-dog committees created to monitor all in positions of power and sources of potential corruption, ombudsmen appointed for complaints and whistleblowers; accountability and provision for recall may be established for all officials (which requires constant information and facilities for instruction on the problems of the enterprise), and income differentials may be limited (if any) among different kinds of work, including business and leadership functions. In addition to such structural considerations, there is an important ideological factor: Preservation of the cooperative character would be strengthened if the members of cooperatives and the supporting community around them understand the criterion of democratic decision-making from below, and if they draw upon a social movement aimed at escaping the deleterious effects of contemporary capitalism and at building an economic and social alternative to it.

The crucial point here is that a structure of actively maintained decision-making from below — which implies no non-member workers — seems to preclude the formation and operation of bureaucracy, and even to a large extent its associated corruption. This has been seen over several generations in all of the Kibbutzim, whose internal affairs have remained clear of bureaucracy — as against the State of Israel which within a few years of its birth had in place a typical entrenched bureaucracy. In contrast the inter-Kibbutz plants, which were maintained by some Kibbutzim and included hired workers as well as Kibbutz member workers, exhibited instances of corruption among their Kibbutz-member administrators, as did some of the large economic and political institutions formed by all the Kibbutzim together. At the extreme of this spectrum are the large institutions and productional enterprises operated by the great labor unions and labor parties, such as in Israel and in Germany of the early 1900's. They became wholly bureaucratic and in many cases corrupt.

Discussion of organizational structure has generally concluded that the problem of bureaucracy is inescapable: in corporations and large business organizations, in the labor movement, within governments, and in the wholly bureaucratic Communist governmental and productional system.[43] But an operative control structure from below may be an essential ingredient for avoiding it.

The preservation of the control-from-below character of non-profit enterprises within capitalism is, almost paradoxically, aided by the fact that opportunities to create them are only sporadic. If such enterprises could be established by a master plan or central ideological organization there would always be danger of the leaders taking steps that conflict with control from below or with the current needs of the people, all in order to strengthen the organization or to reach an expected later good; but such manipulatory indirectness will in many cases lead to failure of the enterprises or of their control-from-below character. In contrast, when each attempt has to prove its efficacy and its control-from-below character in order to hold its own within the existing society by offering a better environment for production or for living than business is offering, then each attempt has to be nonregressive and directly to the good for the people involved. The aggregate of attempts is accretional and cumulative and is comparable to the "do no harm" principle of medical treatment.

In all these problems touching the success or character of non-profit production, the methods and strategies have to be tried out

---

43. Robert Michels, *Political Parties* (London: Jarrolds and Sons, 1915), *Zur Soziologie des Parteiwesen in den modernem Demokratie* (Leipzig, 1911); Max Weber, *Wirtschaft und Gesellschaft, Grundriss der Sozialokonomik* (Tübingen: Mohr, 1955).

in real cases within the present society, and not just thought out in theory while waiting for political change.[44]

7.8 RELEVANCE TO SOCIAL CHANGE

We have seen small ongoing pressures toward increased workplace decision-making by workers, and larger pressures toward workers' partial or complete ownership of their workplace. All these developments are taking place within the business world, mostly with no post-capitalist intent. In particular, employee ownership does not in itself encourage leftist attitudes,[45] and may even encourage the worker-owners' hiring of additional non-owning workers. However, what is important here is not the immediate attitude or political stance, but the long-range interests and power that are bred by the new decision-making and ownership statuses. The mere fact that the ownership of a plant is not scattered among many people in the public but is assembled in the hands of the plant's own workers creates not only a new power but also new associated interests. In *The New Owners* (p. 235), Joseph Blasi and Douglas Kruse report a statement by an ESOP investment banker, Adam Blumenthal: "Under early industrial law, workers had no serious employment rights, but when management assembled them physically under conditions of mass production this created de facto power when they organized. This turned into the union movement. Similarly, under early employee benefit plan law, workers also had few rights, but their ownership interests are now assembled by management in such a way that their de facto power will unavoidably organize."

As noted in 7.3.3(8), the relation between ownership and control is ineradicable because it is systemic. But systemic timeless relations between abstracts are only names for real-life time-ordered relations between events or between people. When the Weirton workers bought their company in 1984, it was as a way of saving their jobs, rather than with any search for new managerial principles. But when their management tried to lay off some of the workers, they could hardly escape the realization that they as owners could seek other ways of reacting to the work attrition.

---

44. Cf. J. Habermas, *The Theory of Communicative Action* (Boston: Beacon 1984); Russell Hardin, *Collective Action* (Baltimore, Md.: Johns Hopkins University Press, 1982); Mancur Olson, *The Logic of Collective Action* (Cambridge, Mass.: Harvard University Press, 1965).

45. Cf. E. S. Greenberg, *Workplace Democracy* (Ithaca, N.Y.: Cornell University Press, 1986).

However, such new applications of the power which inheres in their ownership does not arise immediately and automatically, but out of new difficulties that come from time to time.

The fact that these developments take place within capitalism bears the promise of their being able to continue in current conditions, as against being merely an accidental and not necessarily repeatable "dropping out" from the existing economy. The fact that business, or present society, occasionally finds them useful in one way or another does not mean that these developments cannot grow beyond capitalism. In the early days of capitalism, the kings and rich landlords were the first source of the profits that enabled the merchants to accumulate capital and to become economic powers beyond what the old power wielders had bargained for — and this not even because the rulers could not have fitted out their own merchant vessels. Somewhat similarly, businessmen assign stock to their workers because they gain from doing so, even though in the long run the workers may accumulate workplace control beyond what the businessmen bargained for.

The developments discussed in this chapter turn our attention to matters of social change, and in particular change toward a more humane and equitable society, to the workplace, and specifically to the productional workers.

The workers are relevant here — for all that they are fewer and less well organized than they recently were — because it is they who are essential to new employee-owned or employee-governed production. The workers in a plant can hire managers and still have a new type of enterprise which might be viable in conditions that present difficulties to capitalism. But if the managers buy out a company, as has recently been done not infrequently on a leveraged basis, and then hire workers, we simply have another capitalist enterprise with the same character and problems as the others. Worker buyouts can conceivably keep enterprises going during capitalist crises (7.5,4)[46]; but management buyouts can do no better than other companies, and in some cases saddle the company with so much debt (to pay for their buyout) that it falters or fails.

The increase in workers' decision power and ownership is not a massive single program that any group can seek to institute as a decisive social event. It is an accretive development in response to continuing pressures of the kind surveyed in 7.3-4.[47]

---

46. Jean Matouk, *La gauche peut sauver l'entreprise* (Paris: Ramsay, 1977).
47. Cf. the innovative discussion in Daniel Mothe, *L'autogestion goutte à goutte* (Paris: le Centurion, 1980).

If there is a considerable growth, perhaps in periods of capitalist difficulties, in self-governed enterprises and their networks, there is no reason to expect a steady growth until they cover the economy, or a growth up to some massive upheaval which would then reorganize the whole economy along their lines. New developments, especially ones that sooner or later run afoul of established powers, do not happen so smoothly. If anything, we can expect a period of mixed economy — capitalist, governmental, and self-governed all co-existing, possibly with various economic or productional or regional specializations. All may deal with each other through a market mechanism, although alternatives to the open market, such as barter and quota agreements, could develop — some of these exist all the time.[48] As has been noted, business powers may have no interest in undercutting certain self-governed enterprises, especially the smaller "subsistence" cooperatives in economic areas that are less profitable. But in addition, when capitalism goes through its periodic depressions, the government may not be able to avoid some responsibility for the population and may have to help self-governed enterprises for the jobless and for unfilled consumption needs. How the economic structure would develop beyond this stage is too far from the present for any educated guesses.

From the point of view of what this economic development means for the character of social life, the crucial point is that the way production is controlled has a major effect upon attitudes toward work and society in the people involved (6.4), and upon their readiness to stand up for their attitudes. This without denying other major influences such as those of history and ongoing culture. Furthermore, the changes in social climate do not wait for some massive overthrow of the power structure but begin to be felt in the social and economic environs of the new productional arrangements. It is particularly important that changes in workplace control may gradually create new ways of deciding and arranging production. Whereas the corporation structure clouded the difference between ownership and management, employee ownership (even if not majority) clouds the difference between the owner and the worker, the employer and the employee, between

---

48. Alec Nove, *The Economics of Feasible Socialism* (London: Allen and Unwin, 1983); Branko Horvat, *The Political Economy of Socialism* (New York: Sharpe, 1982); Leland G. Stauber, *A New Program for Democratic Socialism: Lessons from the Market- Planning Experience in Austria* (Carbondale,Ill.: Four Willows Press, 1987).

profit made out of the means of production (workplace control) and livelihood gained out of one's own work. So, any appreciable growth in workers' decision-making in the workplace would cloud the difference between the employer's power to decide and the employee's requirement to follow decisions about his work made by others.[49]

As for the network structures that can be expected to grow among self-governed enterprises, they may develop new appropriate types of arrangements (such as boardroom-type consensus as against majority-vs.-minority votes, and federative as against hierarchical associations) and appropriate institutions (such as pools of permanently or temporarily available engineering or managerial personnel sympathetic to productional self-government). Such ongoing new arrangements and structures would be a great aid to the spread and maintenance of productional self-government, and would go far toward changing the economic and social — and even political — climate well before any question arises of an "end" to the capitalist economic system or of a change in the whole power structure.

If self-governed enterprises are established within capitalist society, sporadically wherever opportunities arise much as the capitalist entrepreneurs themselves began, and then form networks of their own among themselves, there is little question but what they and their networks would continue permanently non-centralized, as even capitalism managed to remain despite its dynamics of concentration. This would be a great assurance of economic democracy, initiative and independence, in contrast to what we might expect even if a possible future well-meaning government would institute from above a system of self-governed production.

The economic-social structure that would naturally develop around participant-controlled enterprises would thus be on a basis of self-government from below federated upward so as to relate one group's self-government to that of other groups with which it is economically or socially involved. Such a structure is not hospitable to control from above, or to disregard of the interests of

---

49. These and all the other byproducts of changes in decision-making and in ownership are among the "objective conditions" for social change as described in Marxism: in effect, that the employer's contribution to production be dispensable in that it can increasingly be supplied by the workers themselves. The political importance of workplace changes is stressed here not as a convenient locale for public political action, but as a source for the production control and therewith social-control outlooks which are more explicit and more fundamental factors in social action than any general anti-status-quo attitudes in the public as such.

affected groups. It thus avoids many of the evils that are due to control from above, even if such control is well meaning. Aside from this, an infrastructure of participant-controlled enterprises would seem to avoid some of the byproducts of capitalism damaging to humans. They would not produce great accumulations of personal wealth — which enable a few individuals to have enormous influence in public institutions — because any large profits would have to be shared among all the workers in the company. Presumably, they would not create massive corporate power, such as grows in capitalism under the pressure of profit maximization and capital accumulation, because the workers in large participant-controlled enterprises would have little to gain from such great concentrations of economic power; those who provide the main pressures in this dynamics of aggrandizement are the managers with their multi-million incomes and personal power, and the wealthy shareholders (who hold the great bulk of shares) who can shift their money from company to company in search of highest yield. Furthermore, the extremes of unproductive financial manipulation, such as leveraged mergers and buy-outs, would not be promoted by worker-owners. After all, they cannot as a group gain much from such activity and might lose much by burdening their company with massive debts, whereas an individual financial entrepreneur today can gain vast amounts even if the company he acquires is thereby bankrupted.

APPENDIX:

On Employee Ownership

We return to the statement in 7.3.3 that employee ownership is the most promising current development in this respect. The main reason for saying so is that while employee ownership does not directly lead to self-government, it creates the grounds for the employees to move in that direction within the foreseeable future. The status of ownership is fundamental to the criteria that determine business ability to act, and fundamental in the legalisms of capitalist governments. It is the bottom line of power to control, as managements of public companies, comfortably entrenched behind the impotence of the annual share-owners' meeting, found when corporate raiders bought up the stock with no more than the company's own future earnings as collateral. True, one sees in the ESOPs no drive toward control, and even the explicit employee-initiated buyouts as at Weirton generally leave managements in place to continue de facto control of the company's activities.

Concentrating employees' ownership within the company in which they work creates new possibilities in the control of production by clouding, with legal force, the basic capitalist distinction between owning and working, between employer and employee, between a businessman's making profit and an employee being the person by whose work the profit is made.

So much for the potential in employee ownership. What makes it important among all the other productional self-government movements, many of which are far more clearheaded and interesting, is simply that there is at least for the present more pressure within business, and somewhat greater readiness among employees, to move along this path.

Employee ownership has its limitations in respect to productional self-government. It does not go — in its pressures or in its horizons — beyond one plant or one company. But it broadens employee horizons to encompass explicitly the whole plant or company, and to deal pragmatically with issues of management; it invites their becoming more competent to deal with the full range of plant issues. If organizations and clearing houses for ESOPs come into existence and if ESOPs develop close cooperation with unions and with their community or customers, the relevance of ESOPs could reach farther.

A final issue is related to political culture. It has been argued that ESOPs promote the capitalist values of ownership in contrast to class-consciousness of workers against owners (as indeed is the case in some companies that form ESOPs for this purpose). However, first, the capitalist value is not ownership but rather profit from ownership or from other sources, and ESOPs are capitalists only if they make appreciable amounts of profit from nonmember workers. Second, ESOPs create the grounds for a situation in one plant at a time which is comparable to the situation that those promoting class-consciousness want to see reached in all plants: self-government by all participants in a productional enterprise. There are two differences between the ESOP approach and class-consciousness. One difference is that the broad ideology of class-consciousness contributes to a new cultural outlook and political understanding; but such general outlooks can also develop piecemeal from many people being in similar situations, as among the burghers before the rise of the Reformation and later the capitalist thinkers. The other difference is that class-consciousness deals directly with the idea of large productional reorganization of the whole society; but large reorganizations do not have to come in one large event — indeed they more often accrue piecemeal from many small events of people meeting similar problems with similar knowledge and social equipment.

The close relation of the economic structure of a society to its political power structure, and ultimately to its social culture, is seen in a broad range of complex societies. It is particularly clear in the case of capitalism if for no other reason than that we know its history in detail, and that the economic structure of capitalism grew gradually and was accompanied — not always smoothly — by the growth of the political power of capitalism. This growth culminated in what may be called the capitalist governments, in which the interests and methods of capitalism are incorporated in the concepts and principles and laws of the government. In the case of the communist regimes (if we do not count here the risible use of "socialist" and "communist" for such regimes as that of Mengistu in Ethiopia), the new communist governments instituted new economic structures, even though their power was not initially based upon the economic structure (i.e., upon an appropriate economic ruling class).

In many societies, one can see that the source of economic power is the ultimate decision or veto power on the productional activities of others, a power which rests in some societies on birth (aristocracy, caste) or occupational position (e.g., in feudalism), but which in business rested on a particular method, namely paying for goods or for work and then selling the product for more than it cost. In each society the people who have the final power of decision on social production generally use this power to provide themselves with better-than-average living conditions. They also try to protect their privileges, and the decision- system on which these are based, by promoting among the underprivileged, the victims of their own privileges, such social attitudes and such institutions as justify or defend the existing system. This their power and importance enables them to do, over time. One may conjecture that in a society of decision-making by the producers themselves, which would not have a distinct power class (elite), the social attitudes that justify a power-wielding class would not be promoted. There might be no one with special interests to promote attitudes favorable to decision-making from below, but such specific ideology may not be needed when there are no particular occupations whose members as such are underprivileged and are the victims of any elite's privileges.

It is the control from above by an "elite" that establishes the victimization of people in underprivileged occupations and its attendant inhumanity; and it is the promotion of attitudes to make the people accept these conditions as being natural or inescapable that fills those cultures with dishonesty. In capitalism, the chief conditions which promote the inhumanity and dishonesty are, first, employment — that most people cannot work (produce, earn a living) except by working under an employer, with the employer making the major decisions as to what they produce in what conditions and for what wages, and with the employees having little power and little choice vis-à-vis the employer — and, second, wealth — largely in the hands of the employers and which helps them control many of the institutions and attitudes that affect people's lives.

Any direct ("reformist") attempt to lessen the inhumanity and dishonesty of elite-ruled societies can have only limited effect, because the power of the elite is retained as long as they retain their economic base. Only the growth of other arrangements of production and consumption where the essential decision-making is not restricted to a special privileged occupation or class can have the promise of a better social and political culture. This is so not because such new arrangements would assure a more humane society but because they do not block it. Such economic arrangements are thus a necessary, though not sufficient condition for the improvement of society.

As was observed at various points in the preceding discussion, such new arrangements of production cannot be made suddenly or by fiat, but have to grow and prove themselves within the experienced world of that generation (and country) which is faced with the need to create fundamental new productional arrangements and institutions. This means: first, that we do not expect them to be instituted from the ground up by a new government after the political power of the existing elite has been brought to an end; and second, that the new arrangements are of a kind that can grow within the conditions of the existing society, and can provide a better life to the people involved.

Within the technologic capitalism of today, such new arrangements cannot be simply a return to individual production and barter or the like; they can only be a mix of various production arrangements, chief of which would be groups of workers controlling their own production and consumption in a network with others doing the same. To call such arrangements "self-exploitation" and simply "a different form of capitalism" does not make them exploitation in the sense of capitalist employment, and does not create the basis for victimization that the capitalist employment structure does.

The growth of producer-controlled production requires: First, that the enterprises be more than merely expressions of the ideas of a number of individuals, but a novel way for particular people to succeed economically in the place and time in which they live (e.g., by ESOP-controlled plants); and second, that they develop appropriate special arrangements with others of their type, and with suppliers and finance sources, and with customers. (Examples of such medium-scale developments are the Kibbutzim in Israel and the Mondragon cooperatives in Spain.)

There is little question that it would be most advantageous to them to fit in with other cooperative enterprises and with social movements and consumer interests standing to gain from the spread of cooperative production. Productional enterprises will have to deal with each other — for resources, for materials, for parts, for further processing, for sharing markets, for sharing knowledge, for joining in developments too large or wide-ranging for single enterprises, and for other joint needs (including political self-protection). Non-profit companies will have to deal primarily with the regular profit-seeking businesses. But as the non-profit sector grows it will be useful or even necessary for the enterprises to develop new and more appropriate ways of interacting with each other. It would not be surprising if such new ways turn out to be more rational, less costly and less wasteful and less effort-consuming, and more effective than the present capitalist modes, where all relations between differently owned enterprises in a large productional process have to go through the productionally arbitrary calculations of intermediate profit-maximizing decision-procedures. The potential for more effective inter-plant and producer-consumer relations outside capitalism is not negated by the sorry record of Communist regimes, where interplant arrangements were as unproductive and corrupt as were the intra-plant arrangements (not to mention the total inadequacy of meeting consumer needs). In any case, the development of ways for dealings among non-profit plants is essential if non-profit production is to become a serious contender for society-wide arrangements of production. The over 200 Kibbutzim in Israel, each controlled by its own worker-members, have found it necessary and possible to create a complex productional, economic, and social network which greatly enhances their viability, and amounts in some respects to a voluntary state within the country, sometimes quite different from the rest of the society.

The growth, networking, and movement-development is not furthered by forming an overall hierarchy, and perhaps not even a single overall federative organization. For it is essential for worker-controlled production that active and effective control from below be maintained in all respects. Any activity that lacks control from below will restrict representativeness and innovation, and sooner or later invite corruption.

CHAPTER 8

In the Aftermath of Soviet Communism

8.1 POLITICAL STRUCTURE

The discussion so far has not considered the Communist regimes except in passing. However, their present state and the collapse of the flagship Soviet regime throw light on issues of the present discussion — not only on the general processes of modern social change, but also to some extent on the directions of change from capitalism. From the complex course of this collapse, and the vast subject of the Communist regimes as a whole, we extract here a few considerations relevant to our issues.

The Communist regimes, while using the rhetoric and the theory of the capitalist working class ferment, were established in countries that were only in part capitalist (Russia, China, Cuba, Vietnam). Perhaps because there was no sufficient working class, Lenin and later Mao and the other leaders offered a revolution not by the working class but by a vanguard party of (more precisely, for) that class. In China, Mao's revolution was necessarily "for" the massive peasant class (more than the working class), aside from being also in effect a national war of liberation from the Japanese invasion. While the concepts of a vanguard party and of temporary "dictatorship of the proletariat" had been developed within the tradition of Marxist politics, the application made by Lenin and the other Leninist leaders went far beyond the Marxist intent. As is well known, there were opponents within the left to Lenin's policies both before and after the Revolution: before, from the Russian Menshevik Marxists[1] and Rosa Luxemburg[2] and Anton Pannekoek[3] (in the Zimmerwald Conference of 1915 out of which the Bolshevik's Third International grew); after, from anarchists and the Kronstadt sailors, neither of whom had originally been committed opponents.[4] Later, there was ideological opposition from various anti-Bolshevik communist groups in the west.[5]

In the wake of the middle-class revolution against the Czar, the Kerensky government was overthrown by Lenin's Bolshevik party under the promise of "All power to the Soviets" — workers' councils created to control their workplace. Immediately thereafter, Lenin centralized all productional control, suppressing any power of the Soviets,[6] and instituted economic policies (especially in regard to peasant production) which he was forced to rescind, after a major famine, in favor of a moderate New Economic Policy.[7] While it is idle to speculate whether Russia would have developed differently had Lenin not died early, or had it been possible to prevent Stalin's becoming a dictator, one has to recognize that the policies and actions of Stalin, including the physical elimination of opponents from whatever direction, had precedents in Lenin's regime. China and other later Communist regimes showed the same properties of centralized economic planning, some of which failed disastrously, with drastic moves to correct the undesired results (including, e.g., Mao's Cultural Revolution), and with no opposition or independent views permitted from left or from right.

---

1. L. H. Haimson, *The Mensheviks: From the Revolution of 1917 to the Second World War* (Chicago: University of Chicago, 1974); L. Martov, *The State and the Socialist Revolution* (New York: International Review, 1938).

2. Rosa Luxemburg, *The Russian Revolution* (Ann Arbor, Mich.: Ann Arbor Paperbacks, University of Michigan Press, 1961); *Die Russiche Revolution*, ed. by Paul Levi (Hamburg: F. Oetinger, 1948).

3. A. Smart, *Pannekoek and Gorter's Marxism* (London: Pluto, 1978).

4. Paul Avrich, *Kronstadt 1921* (Princeton, N.J.: Princeton University Press, 1970); Isaac Deutscher, *The Prophet Armed: Trotsky 1879-1921* (New York: Oxford University Press, 1954); Anton Ciliga, *The Russian Enigma* (London: The Labour Book Service, 1940).

5. E.g., Paul Mattick, *Anti-Bolshevik Communism* (London: Merlin and New York: Sharpe, 1978).

6. "Groupe Noir et Rouge, *Autogestion, État, Revolution* (Paris: Le Cercle, 1972); C. Sirianni, *Workers' Control and Socialist Democracy: The Soviet Experience* (London: Verso and New Left Books, 1982); M. Brinton, *The Bolsheviks and Workers' Control. 1917-1921* (London: Solidarity, 1970).

7. Arthur Rosenberg, *A History of Bolshevism* (Oxford: Oxford University Press, 1934); E. H. Carr, *The Bolshevik Revolution 1917-23* (New York: Macmillan, 1951-53).

Those who wished for change from the evils of class-ruled societies (and from the particular evils of the Czars, Chiang-Kai-Shek, Batista, Somoza, and the others), and those who felt that the Marxist analysis had much truth and human promise, may regret that the revolutions made in the name of Marxism and human betterment came out as they did. But one must not only recognize what indeed took place, but also try to learn why it took place.[8]

8.2 ECONOMIC POLICIES

In production control, the Russian regime (and in varying degrees the other Communist governments) replaced private profit-making and the market by new arrangements that were patterned on the "central office" structure of management used in the larger, multi-division American firms. But they were planned from above, and many of them worked very poorly. Among the earliest moves of Lenin and later Stalin were attempts to replace individual peasant agriculture by higher-technology agricultural collectives (in particular the deeply disliked Kolkhoz system) controlled ultimately by the government. The collectivization met massive opposition, not only from the richer peasants, which led to farmers' killing off their livestock and to widespread famine; the planners had to retreat from parts of their program.[9]

In the total economy, central production managing created a detailed chain of command from the top down to the individual workplaces. The top management offices were naturally not up to the task (no one could be), and the bureaucratic system that mediated the chain of command quickly froze into an unresponsive obstructive bureaucracy. The managers appointed to the workplaces — especially in the lower priority, civilian enterprises — developed their own irregular ways of acquiring materials and equipment for their plants and exaggerating their plants' production. Not only were plants poorly and inefficiently managed, with time lost because of lack of materials or of breakdowns in antiquated equipment, but also because the quality of the products

---

8. Hopes are not sufficient for history. The prominent American social critic Lincoln Steffens said, upon returning from a visit to the early Soviet Russia, "I have seen the future and it works." But it didn't work, and it turned out not to be the future. Bertrand Russell, who visited the Soviet Union in the spring of 1920, was prescient in his appraisal of Bolshevism as a failure. See his *Bolshevism: Practice and Theory* (New York: Harcourt, Brace and Howe, 1920)

9. Cf. Lynne Viola, *The Best Sons of the Fatherland: Workers in the Vanguard of Soviet Collectivization* (New York: Oxford University Press, 1987).

became very poor since the managers' reports to the planners — often quite false — were concerned primarily with the quantity produced as required by the plan and rarely with quality — except in the priority military industries.[10]

The workers were given a major gain in the assurance that there would be virtually no unemployment. However, the way the economic plan and the managers' interests worked out in practice led to wasteful use of the work force, with unneeded workers cluttering many of the factories. The poor performance of the plants led to a poor economy with low incomes over-all: according to the saying of the workers, "We pretend to work, and they pretend to pay us."

The over-all result was low production and low quality in what was produced, as well as widespread corruption in the state managerial bureaucracy. In addition, distribution was very poorly organized, neither parts and materials to the plants nor finished goods to the consumers were successfully delivered. The system of rationing was egalitarian for most of the population (not counting the bureaucracy who were provided special privileges), but in the face of scarcity and low quality it created new hardships — of long queues for food and other necessities, and encouraged elaborate private arrangements for people to get needed supplies. People's real incomes were improved by the low rent and cheap bread, but even this had some unexpected byproducts, as when people fed their pigs the bread that was cheaper than feed.[11]

In all, the command system succeeded in industrializing the Soviet Union[12] (and in varying degrees the other Communist countries), at great human cost but hardly greater than the cost exacted from people during the original industrialization of the capitalist countries. It also succeeded in military production, bringing the Soviet Union — a country with little prior infrastructure though rich in resources — close though never quite equal to the military level of the West. But it failed later, not surprisingly, in consumer production, which had become a more pressing issue in the Soviet Union after the main industrialization stopped at about the time of Stalin's death, when the people's desire for some improvement in their life became more prominent.

---

10. Joseph Berliner, *Factory and Manager in the USSR* (Cambridge, Mass.: Harvard University Press, 1957).

11. Alec Nove, *The Soviet Economic System* (London: Allen & Unwin, 1986).

12. Although the various five-year plans were never fulfilled, early Soviet Russia had outstanding growth in GNP, especially during the 1930's.

In considering Communist failures and successes, judgments can only be comparative (in respect to capitalism), the more so that the political effect today is based on Communist citizens' comparing their lot with that of capitalist citizens. We therefore cannot leave this subject without noting that the capitalist record is not as much better as some might think. Capitalist industrialization was famously inhumane to its own population, and even more to the colonies it later invaded. Capitalist production is wasteful of the lives and well-being of its workers and of the earth's resources. The chicanery and intrigues at the executive level of corporations, the behavior of the big corporations and the government toward the population, the political irrelevance and scandalousness of the massive finance capitalism, the low quality and low durability of modern goods, the falsity of advertising, all make a story whose difference from the Soviet Union is perhaps more in style and degree than in kind. Even the amount of usable civilian production, which is certainly much greater in the major capitalist countries, has less human meaning when one takes into account its distribution. The Communist working class, middle class, and even the ruling groups all have had less than their counterparts in capitalism; but the increasingly large underclass of capitalism is excluded from consumption in a way that was not seen in the Communist areas — apart from their forced labor populations.

The economic pattern, set first in the Soviet Union, was repeated with various modifications in China, in Vietnam (where a more "reformist" leader maintained a mixed economy in the South), and in most other Communist regimes, all with varying degrees of difficulty or failure.

8.3 Social Policies

In their early years, most Communist regimes made large improvements in the life of their "working class" population — workers, the poor, in some cases also the peasants. This was clearly the case in the Soviet Union and China, in Cuba and Nicaragua, but hardly in North Korea and not at all under the Khmer Rouge of Cambodia. While there were big advances in literacy, opportunity for education, equality of women, and the dropping of some restrictive social traditions, the structure of the command economy left no room for liberalization in such matters as consumer choice, and the structure of the party dictatorship left no room for civil liberties. Nevertheless, we can see, more clearly during the collapse of Soviet Communism than while it was in full voice, that some of the major values of the Revolution's rhetoric — or should we say the radical ethic — have stayed with many of the workers. These values include opposition to wealth and to enrichment and to all large differences in income, dislike of the competitive spirit and of capitalism, revulsion at corruption and at the fake cooperatives made recently by some Communist plant managers; and a strong sense of solidarity and civic responsibility. These have apparently become part of the expectation and the understanding of life among many working-class people.

Western observers have claimed that this is simply the indoctrination by the Communist propaganda machine. It would be more nearly correct to say that the workers picked out of the rhetoric what they could use in the ongoing conditions. In contrast, the Communist rhetoric of Soviets, of workers' councils controlling the workplace, did not have visible presence for Soviet workers, as the Soviet managerial arrangement of production broke down after August 1991.[13]

More generally, the workers to a man are reported to despise the Communist system under which they lived, and they show no residual influence from the party cells that operated in each plant. Thus, it is not just rhetoric ("propaganda") that explains the tenacity of some Communist attitudes. One might then think that it is rather the realities of social life that are mirrored in these attitudes. But the "intellectuals," and managers and would be middle-class elements (many of whom lived in much the same realities) appear

---

13. For this reason it is all the more striking that by May 1990 at Novokuznetsk, the First Congress of Independent Workers' Movements and Organizations declared that

"... management of state and collective enterprises should be carried out by bodies of people elected by the workers and staff themselves...."

In 1991 a Moscow Information Center (Alexander Buzgalin, *Trechprudny Pereulok of d. 6 kv. 46 Moscow 100301*) published "Looking for Alternative to Stalinism and Liberalism," and "Left and Working Movements in the Ex-USSR" (1992). Also in 1992 from A. Buzgalin et al (eds.), "Economy as a Democracy."

Earlier, the *Current Digest of the Soviet Press #30* (1989), brings excerpts from "Sozialisticheskava Industrig, July 30" (1989):

"DONETSK STRIKERS WANTED TO RUN MINES BUT LET SPECIALISTS RETAIN RESPONSIBILITY, STRIKE COMMITTEES OVERCONFIDENT THEY CAN OPERATE PRODUCTION WITHOUT MANAGERS."

"... The [Donetsk] miners solved many urgent problems during the strike. This inspired them with confidence that they could also remove all other problems on their own, without the specialists' participation. Apparently that is the source of the rejection and nonrecognition of enterprise managers...."

to have none of these values, and on the contrary demand not only an immediate market system but also an increased income gap between themselves and the workers. Perhaps, then, one should gather that these attitudes are a class response to the conditions of workers' life, formulated with the aid of what made sense to the workers in the ideas they heard in the Communist rhetoric.

The socio-economic occupational groups that resulted from the Communist system of decisions on production correspond to the attitude division reported above. Not counting the Moslem and other economically marginal areas, the Soviet Union had a large class of low-paid workers who in certain respects were even more shut out of decision over their work than is the case in today's old capitalist lands: no strikes, no independent unions, tight control inside the plant by the party cell. There were relatively few unemployed, and little underclass; capitalism finds these useful for keeping labor under control, but Communist regimes had no need of such potentially disruptive elements. Furthermore, there was little of a middle class: much of the government bureaucracy and even the secret police and its many informers did not live as well as even the upper rungs of the lower middle class do in the major capitalist lands. The political leaders and major cultural figures lived in a manner comparable to the well-to-do in capitalism; but they were few. Moreover, the income gap between them and the bulk of the population was considerably less than that to be found in the West. Corruption, especially on the part of the bureaucracy, was rife but smaller in magnitude than in the West, if one counts the endless cheatings and political manipulations by business as comparable to bureaucratic corruption under Communism. Furthermore, under Communism the corruption was explicit, whereas such capitalist activities as cheating on prices or on claims about products are not recognized in the West as corruption.

For the common people under Communism life was drab, and people had little choice in goods and not much in occupation and in conditions of life. These conditions were notoriously worse than in the larger capitalist countries, but it should be noted that this applies more to the large middle class of capitalism. For the working class and even the lower rungs of the middle class in capitalism the substantive choice among product labels is largely vacuous or uninformed, the choice in occupation limited, and the drabness of life is only countered by the "idiot box" of television.

However, the evils of the Communist regimes are more visible to their populations than are the evils of capitalism to its population, partly because the monolithic power structure in Communism is more transparent and overt.

The major remaining characteristic of the Communist regimes is the dictatorial structure. One party, in most cases one man or one small self-perpetuating coterie, rules everything, by decree. This produces more or less of a police state (depending on the conditions in each country) with a political watch over the population, and a secret police with a widespread net of informers. All of this is not unknown in capitalism, though — outside the fascist regimes — to a lesser degree. The political structure produces a total silencing of dissidents, more than in ordinary capitalism, although this matter may not be of the greatest moment for the bulk of the population living its private life. It also gives a Byzantine character to the self-perpetuating ruling Communist party, in its internal machinations and in its decisions. This corresponds in capitalism to the Byzantine character of the also largely self-perpetuating corporate "executive suites," and somewhat differently to the "gentlemen's understandings" and conspiracies that control the politics and institutions of Western countries.

In respect to humaneness, the extremes of Communist dictatorship, from Stalin to Ceaucescu in Romania, to North Korea, to the Khmer Rouge in Cambodia and (among guerrilla movements) to the Shining Path in Peru, all fall (whatever their goals) into the same class as the fascist extremes in capitalism — Hitler, Franco, Pinochet, the Argentine colonels — and as imperialist actions in many of the colonies. One cannot really consider these, both in Communism and in capitalism, to be aberrations.

Dictatorship in Communism is the rule rather than the exception, and is permitted by the concept of Dictatorship of the Proletariat combined with the Party as vanguard of the Class. Furthermore, some of the most extreme dictators apparently saw themselves as true Marxists: the main work of Pol Pot, leader of the Khmer Rouge, is teaching Marxism in training cadres to do the work of the Revolution — in the way the Khmer Rouge did when it ruled Cambodia. Finally, the Chinese Communist government — the major remaining claimant to this kind of Marxism — finds excuses for the Burmese military dictatorship; and it supports the Khmer Rouge insistently, doing everything possible to return it to power, thus going even further than the businessmen and governments who helped Hitler's rise to power and supported him until he forced them into opposition.[14]

Nevertheless, there have been Communist regimes and guerrilla movements which while Leninist in their views had been primarily constructive and helpful to their population. Castro's Cuba, despite tolerating no dissidents, has operated in a way that apparently has retained the support of a large part of its population. The Sandinista government in Nicaragua, despite its economic failures[15] and its rejection of coalition, lost its majority probably because of the insurmountable economic and military circumstances imposed on it by the United States government. Where some middle-class "urban guerrillas" such as the Tupamaros in Uruguay or the Baader-Meinhoff in Germany carried out assassinations and kidnappings which could not be a contribution to social change, there have also been working class guerrilla movements such as in El Salvador (and in some respects the Philippines and Mao's insurgency in the Chinese west) that carried out constructive administration of rural regions that came under their control.

8.4 THE GLOBAL VIEW ON THE COMMUNIST REGIMES

Communism is usually discussed in terms of the specific histories of the Communist regimes, and the similarities among them. But the weakening and collapse of these regimes can be best understood in respect to the economic history of the whole modern world.[16] From this over-all perspective, many people, espe-

---

14. The vast literature on the Communist countries includes some responsible descriptions, such as N. Werth, *Histoire de l'Union Sovietique* (Paris: Presses Universitaires de France, 1990).

15. A. M. Cuenca, *Sandinista Economics in Practice* (Boston: South End Press, 1991). The author was an economic Minister in the Sandinista regime.

16. There have been other general views of Communism, which have had little explanatory value. A particularly irrelevant view is that Marxism or Leninism are simply religions (e.g., in J. M. Keynes, *A Short View of Russia* (London: Macmillan and Co.,1925). If nothing else, this position has been refuted by the very collapse of Communist regimes. For, religions and nationalisms do not fall by having been found wanting in some practical respect; they do not have to stand the test of anything and can therefore last for millennia. If they fall, it is because they have become irrelevant to the life conditions or hopes of the people. But the difficulties and fall of Communist regimes were clearly due to their failure to satisfy the promises of material goods and social liberation. Somewhat as a statement for which there are no conditions in which it is false is scientifically vacuous (tautological or metaphysical), an ideology or belief for which there are no material conditions in which it is rejected is irrelevant to human good. On this test, the collapse of Communist regimes showed that they were testable as a path to human good, and — in the form in which they were tested — failed.

cially in the non-Leninist left, have pointed out that historically the immediate task of the major Communist regimes was to construct an industrial infrastructure; without this there was no possibility of serious improvement in the consumption level of the population. To carry through such a program entailed that for many years a sizeable portion of people's labor would not yield them immediate consumer goods. Such a program, it was held, could be carried out only by a dictatorial government that could force people to work, and only by way of centralized economic planning and command.[17] Then, by the time the industrialization and modernization of each country had advanced sufficiently to make a rise in consumer goods possible, the political and economic bureaucracies of each country were so set in their ways as to thwart any reorganization toward consumers goods; and they were so entrenched as to preclude their replacement. The governments were thus unable to devise and operate a new socialist consumer-oriented economy. When the essential period of infrastructure development was coming to an end, and economic dissatisfaction was widespread, the Communist governments could only try to bring in capitalist economic methods while trying to retain their own political control — so Deng after Mao's death, and so Gorbachev.

There is little doubt that this scenario is descriptively correct as far as it goes. However, various questions remain. First, why was industrialization — with heavy military emphasis — and modernization addressed to the exclusion of all else? Lenin is often quoted as saying that the belly has to be filled first — the freedoms and things of the spirit can only be cared for later. But economic inequality and the poverty of the masses were not the only evils of the Czarist regimes — there was also the mistreatment and debasement of the population by all the authorities. One might think that even the much needed industrialization could be moderated and timed in a way so as to allow for a new respect toward the population and a new relation of the authorities toward it. Furthermore, even granted the industrializing dictatorial command economy, why could not the regime, including its

---

17. The social cost of industrialization was less dramatic in those countries such as Western European nations, Japan, and Korea, whose recovery or industrialization was eased by American support. Furthermore, in these countries the old ruling class, protected by the military occupation, shared in the new developments, so that the old social-cultural controls could hold sway less noticeably and with less overt violence than new controls required.

bureaucracy, modify its operation as the industrialization became less crucial, especially in the face of popular desires for more and better goods, for better organization of distribution, and for more freedom from direct surveillance and control? After all, capitalist governments were to some extent able to adjust to their populations. The usual explanation is that the monolithicity of the bureaucracy deprived it of flexibility; but the world of profit-making and later of corporate executives and junior executives is as complete a universe as is the world of the bureaucrats, and nevertheless these capitalist worlds were able to change when change became desirable. In the later years the Communist bureaucracies faced a clear and present threat to their continued existence, and it is hard to see why they failed even in these circumstances to recognize and correct such deficiencies as the falsity of plant managers' reports and the shoddiness of products and of distribution arrangements.

Some partial answer to these questions may lie in a modification of the industrialization scenario cited above. We may posit that capitalist success in production and more recently in achieving widespread improvement in standard of living creates a pressure upon the various populations of the world as they came in contact with the capitalist advance. "Contact" here refers not to the wars and conquests for markets and raw materials, as in colonialism or in the American opening of Japan in the 1850's, but rather the effect of non-capitalist populations' awareness of the material success of life in the modern capitalist countries. The responses to this posited pressure were of two kinds: to catch up with the capitalist modernity, or to shut it out. These responses depended on the kinds of ruling groups in each country, and on the historic circumstances; it will be suggested below that the Communist regimes constituted one set of responses.

Shutting modernity out was in general the response of the powerful religious establishments, as in the current Islamic fundamentalism, or in the combination of the Spanish Catholic hierarchy with military dictatorship under Franco. It was also the response of various local military dictatorships such as that in Burma (Myanmar). In addition to such responses from outside the modern capitalist area, there have also been attempts within that area to shut out the social modernity of capitalism while accepting its economic structure. Some of this may be seen in the most strongly Catholic countries (Ireland, Poland), and also in the

Protestant fundamentalism of the United States and the Jewish fundamentalism in Israel.

The other response was to catch up with modern capitalism. Here two assessments will be offered: first, that no country managed to catch up fully by its own efforts alone; and second, that the Communist way was objectively toward the same end as all the other catchings up — that is, directed only toward the point that capitalism had reached and no farther.

In some cases, the attempt was to catch up to the point of becoming an independent industrial and commercial power. Thus, after it was forced to accept capitalist infiltration, the well-organized Japanese government set out to do precisely that, with a program of conquest in Korea, China, and beyond. In other cases, the expectation was just to reach the point of being able to participate more modestly in the capitalist world, as was done in the Ataturk revolution in Turkey. The Sun Yat-Sen revolt of 1911 in China, the Russian uprising of 1905, and the Kerensky revolution of 1917 were of this character — in effect bourgeois revolutions against pre-capitalist authority.

In this catching up, there is one success story from which much can be learned. In the period immediately after World War II, America's program to confine the Soviet Union led it to strengthen the countries encircling the USSR — in Europe by Marshall Plan aid to capitalist recovery, and in the Far East by direct tutelage in establishing modern capitalisms, first in a failed attempt to organize Chiang Kai-Shek's China, then successfully in Japan, and to a much lesser extent in Korea. These attempts to build up independent capitalisms, even to the point of their becoming a threatening competitor, was an unusual operation; it succeeded because the United States government facilitated (and American industry submitted to) massive American purchasing of Japanese manufacture. It is relevant here to note that in the 75 years of Japan's industrialization and colonial conquests before World War II Japan did not approach competitiveness with the old capitalisms: its goods remained limited in scope and in many cases shoddy, and any future Japan might have expected could only have been as a regional capitalist center. Its ability to become one of the world's centers of capitalism came only with the exceptional help and accommodation of the United States. There is thus no case of any newcomer fully catching up with capitalism by its efforts alone.

The Soviet Union and most other Communist regimes also set out to industrialize and modernize, and succeeded in varying degrees. That they did not succeed better is not necessarily the fault of central economic planning, poor as it was, for the Soviet Union did well in infrastructure and military production. Post–World War II Germany and Japan had no military to create or maintain, and had American occupation forces to protect their governments and their economic steps. As noted above, Germany had Marshall Plan aid; Japan had from America both tutelage and a vast market. Both had a long industrial and commercial past, at different levels, before their economic "miracles." The Communist regimes had no such success, but neither did they have any of these advantages.

As to the other assessment above, that most Communist regimes were objectively geared only to catching up with capitalism: The general view is that this was the explicit purpose of Japan and the others, whereas Communism was directed at an anti-capitalist and post-capitalist "socialist" goal. However, one can argue that in reality the Communist regimes were not directed at any socialist goal. It is true that their statements, at least initially, were couched in Marxist terms. But this (and in China and Vietnam, also liberation from foreign occupation) was the basis for their arousing support in the population. This support is what enabled them to harness its energies for carrying out the industrialization. Talk aside, these regimes carried out only those activities relevant to economic modernization (and a large military economy) and to their own political impregnability (which they could argue was necessary to the economic program). In the way modernization was carried out there was no provision or preparation for any liberation of the population or for any development of the workers toward becoming a serious factor in decision-making, much less the controllers of their production (despite the limited Yugoslav workers' councils). And as basic industrialization was approached, there were no steps to modify the power and decision systems toward greater input from the producers as consumers, and no considerations of how Communist industrialization could lead to a liberated population.

As far as the structure and actions of the Communist regimes went, the only political courses available in the wake of their industrial infrastructure were either a continuation of the dictatorial regimes themselves or the introduction of that capitalism which reigned in the industrial countries. Indeed, the Communist leaders tried to do both, introducing capitalism within their political system.

In this general framework one can understand why Communist regimes arose in non-capitalist countries, why they were so centralized and dictatorial, why they ran into trouble when consumer issues became more prominent, and why they can offer no solution for these difficulties other than to introduce capitalist methods.

8.5 THE ROAD FROM COMMUNIST REGIMES

The "catching up" aspect of Communist difficulties involves not only consumption levels but also individual opportunities and freedoms (even if more in style than in substance), which in modern capitalism affect not only the business class to whom they originally applied, but also the "whole" population above the underclass. The absence of these freedoms in early industrializing Communism was "excusable"; for that matter, they had not existed in early capitalist industrialization, nor of course in the preindustrial societies. But later, the lack of both goods and freedoms weakened the hold of the Communist regimes, in different ways for the different parties involved. The governments felt primarily (e.g., during Perestroika) their inability to supply goods, but were aware of the way their failure to satisfy consumers related to modern freedoms (e.g., during Glasnost). The middle classes wanted great increases in both, since their counterparts in the West were the ones who most enjoyed the new developments in both areas. The workers apparently felt the lack of both goods and freedoms, but lacked the heady push of the middle-class elements who felt that they could rise to a higher position in society.

We therefore consider here four sociological participants in the (primarily European) Communist collapse: (1) the governments, (2) the middle-class elements, (3) the working class, (4) the "people" en masse.

(1) *The Governments.* In the monolithic and apparently unshakable Communist regimes, the first crack came from the failure of consumption arrangements especially as compared to the consumption levels of the main capitalisms. Newer leaders in the Soviet Union and China (and to a lesser extent elsewhere, as in Vietnam) came to recognize that the command system was not satisfying consumer wants in respect to quantity and quality and

distribution, and perhaps the system could not. The burden of military preparedness was a factor, at least in the Soviet Union; but clearly the system of arranging production was malfunctioning chronically. Khruschev's disavowal of Stalinism dealt with the political excesses, rather than with consumer economics. But after the ineffectual late years of Mao and after the Brezhnev stagnation, the new leaders no longer had the old "We will bury you" reliance on their economic system.

In this situation the new leaders tried to change the production system while retaining some planning and some non-market pricing (to assure people's basic needs), while maintaining political control. In China, Deng sought to increase production by agricultural privatization, as a precondition for a larger industrialization effort; this increase was needed to feed people who would be pushed into industry by the fact that they would receive no land in the privatization. The whole program was especially needed because of the population increase which resulted in part from the early improvements to Chinese life the Communists had brought. To this end, Deng divided much of the ill-used collectivized agricultural land among some of the peasants, but in a way that assigned the best land to a select group of people often with ties to the local Communist leadership and that therefore forced many others off the land.[18] In a short time some peasants became richer than others and locally powerful; they were enabled to employ farm labor privately, and to control existing local industries.

Meanwhile, selected capitalist enterprises were established by Chinese managers (often sons of the top leaders) jointly with foreign businessmen, resulting in quick wealth for the new Chinese entrepreneurs. Many of the enterprises did not do well, and advances in industrialization were fitful; but the new entrepreneurs became an important part of the economic landscape, being for example admitted into the special clubs reserved prior to this period for the top Communist personnel. Another device (or deception), used later also in Poland and the Soviet Union, was for the managers of a state enterprise to form a "cooperative" to which the management of their own enterprise was leased, whereupon the new management body fired workers and reduced wages and paid vast salaries to themselves. All these enterprises hired and fired workers on their own, while the rest of the workers con-

---

18. William Hinton, *The Great Reversal: The Privatization of China 1978-1989* (New York: Monthly Review Press 1990).

tinued to be assigned by the agencies of the command economy. In addition, small business activity was permitted, creating a class of well-to-do merchants.

In this situation, opposition to the government with its rampant corruption became pervasive among educated people and merchants, many of whom became completely pro-capitalist, and the opposition also reached urban workers. The opposition led to a confrontation in Beijing's Tiananmen Square in May-June 1989, culminating in a violent suppression (especially of the workers involved) by the government. The Communist leaders had to call in peasant army units controlled by leaders with peasant-area ties, after the Beijing worker-army units displayed an unwillingness to use their force. In post-Tiananmen China the main supporters of the hard-line leaders, most of whom still want to bring in capitalism while maintaining total political control, are the peasant areas — more precisely the wealthy farmers and local managers who are by now least involved in the command economy of the government.

In the Soviet Union, Gorbachev and his supporters in the Politburo first tried to reorganize production in accordance with the Perestroika proposal. When little happened (in the face of the plant managers' non-cooperation) they called for open criticism, Glasnost, largely as a popular pressure on the managers, somewhat as Mao's far more violent Cultural Revolution was a call for popular action against the bureaucracy. With this, the extreme control over the population was dropped, signalled for example by the release of the dissident physicist Sakharov from house arrest. This too did not lead to any massive push toward reorganizing production, and Gorbachev took a different step. Since World War III was too dangerous to be a possible move for either superpower, Gorbachev offered an end to the cold war, so as to reduce the economic burden of his military requirements and to gain technological and even economic help from the West (which he never received). This entailed ceding military control over the East European satellites.

All these actions had major political effects. The Glasnost call and the ensuing democratic elections opened up in the Soviet Union a Pandora's box of popular anger against the Communist economic and political structure. Gorbachev's statement in the summer of 1989, that the Soviet Union would not intervene to support the satellite Communist governments, led to immediate uprisings in those countries against the hated Soviet occupation

and the Communist system which it had enforced in the satellites. This led to their rapid independence from the Soviet Union
and to non-Communist governments almost throughout, even in
independent Yugoslavia and Albania.

Why did the top echelon's search for increased production and
consumer-oriented distribution fail? It is of course impossible as
yet to present an account of the forces and interests, and the
essential course of events. But some considerations seem clearly
relevant, especially from the point of view of what there is to
learn here in respect to the future of capitalism. It is clear that
while Communist regimes are not so monolithic as to preclude
mass uprisings, they are too monolithic to permit internal change
in the economic control system. For one thing, the managers
fought a rear-guard action against Gorbachev's Perestroika. More
basically there was no room for play between the political power
of the government and the productional power of the economic
bureaucracy (planners, managers). Their separation in capitalism
is a factor in its life-extending flexibility.

Second, there was no system of checks and balances neither in
the political nor the economic apparatus, such as might enable
different parts of the leadership or bureaucracy to respond differently to changing conditions. A democratic capitalist government
has checks and balances, in principle, though they are often circumvented, and business has something comparable in the lack of
hierarchic relations among enterprises.

Third, the top-down system had no bottom-up negative feedback, so that the low quantity and quality of goods and the dissatisfaction of the consumers could have no input into the further
decisions on production and distribution. Capitalism has a limited
range of such feedback mechanisms in the willingness or refusal
of market consumers to buy particular goods at particular prices.

Lastly, the supposedly reality-based decision system of the
command economy had no alternative system to fall back upon
when it was no longer able to make successful decisions. In contrast, the profit-based decision system of capitalism which calcu-
lates not the actual needs and resources of the population but only
the likelihood of making a profit can, when it has need, relinquish
some of its decision-making to government which can then act on
the basis of the people's needs and available resources.

The Gorbachev leadership was unable to overcome these difficulties: partly, because it was not prepared to go all the way to an

ordinary and inevitably West-controlled capitalism (in which it would lose its political status, and which might run it afoul of revolt from the people who would be yet further impoverished); and partly because it was an heir — though reform-minded — of the Communist system. It could therefore neither express (nor fully recognize) the anger of the people nor promote a radically different bottom-up decision system starting with workers controlling their workplace and federatively coordinating with other workers and with consumers.[19] This last move was unavailable to the government as a top-down decision-maker.

Whether such a wholesale revision of a Communist regime would ever be possible by reforms from the top is open to question. The 1968 "Prague Spring" group of Reform Communists under Dubcek — who temporarily became the leaders of Czechoslovakia at the time — might have been able to attempt it, and certainly the original Solidarity movement of the Polish workers — which became the spokesman of the Polish masses — proposed doing it; but both had been put down by force.

(2) *The Middle-Class Elements.* Although one may not think of an explicit middle class in Communist countries, there are various occupations in which work is not characteristically physical or massed, and whose consumption and social levels (or potential levels if they succeed) are in general higher than those of the working class: the administrative and political bureaucracy, the "intelligentsia," entertainers, farmers or petty businessmen who are able to sell within the small permitted market or on the black market. They correspond in various respects to the middle class of capitalism.

People in these economic positions were most prominent in the 1989-90 uprisings in the Soviet satellites and Baltic states, and we will survey their role there first. In countries with some socialist traditions, the initial public attacks on the Communist regime came from leftist intellectuals as in East Germany, or from workers as in the resurgence of Solidarity in Poland. But in countries with larger middle-class traditions, even the initial attacks came from apolitical or capitalist-minded writers and potential business elements, as in Czechoslovakia, Hungary, and the Yugoslav Slovenia, and with nationalist vehemence in Lithuania. Where the

---

19. The description of the Gorbachev government given here can be seen explicitly in its statements and actions at various stages from 1986 and on, e.g., in the *New York Times* of November 17, 1989. Cf. also Steven F. Cohen and K. Vanden Heuvel, *Voices of Glasnost* (New York: W. W. Norton, 1989).

Church was particularly strong — in Poland — it manipulated the uprising. In all of these countries, with large middle-class traditions, the right-wing middle class won governmental control immediately. The right-wing character is directly observable. In Poland, the new government's architects of the economic transition were American monetarists. In Russia, the economic advisers invited in by Yeltsin were not only the Hoover Institution but also such little known reactionary bodies as at the Pepperdine University.[20] In Czechoslovakia, the students who were very active in the uprising insisted that they would have none of Dubcek's human-faced Communism but demanded pure capitalism; the more moderate of them said with pride that they took the trouble to go to factories and urged the workers to join them. (In contrast, in the 1968 left-wing student uprising in France, many workers joined spontaneously.)[21] In Czechoslovakia, and to a lesser extent in Poland and Hungary, the new governments were explicitly committed to the extreme-right monetarist policies of Milton Friedman, and to strong anti-labor steps. The deputy prime minister in the new Czech government, attending the inauguration of the new Chilean president after the removal of the dictator Pinochet (whose regime had been infamous for tortures and killings), invited Pinochet to come to Czechoslovakia to advise the new government on peaceful transition to democracy; the invitation was rescinded after an uproar initiated by the Chilean writer Ariel Dorfman, who learned of this action.[22] As to the new Lithuanian government, almost its first act was to rehabilitate the

---

20. Cf. Jon Wiener, in *The Nation* (December 16, 1991).

21. The journal *Daedalus 121.2* (1992) p. 191 summarizes a 1991 Czech report as follows: "Among the least surmountable barriers to the creation of a civil society in most postcommunist countries are the inherited systems of values, which a group of Czech sociologists has succinctly described:

1. Society should not be overly differentiated; people's living standards ought to be as equal as possible.
2. Everyone must work, regardless of whether one's work is meaningful or productive.
3. State institutions know best how to satisfy people's needs; people need not care excessively for themselves.
4. The living standard need not be high, provided it is secure."

22. The Czech official was quoted in the Chilean press (*El Mercurio*) as saying "... sera muy interesante que grandes personalidades historicas, que trataron de resolver problemas, por vias quizas originales y especificas, relaten su experiencia" ("... it will be very interesting that great historical personages, who try to solve problems by ways perhaps original and specific, tell their experience.")

Lithuanian Nazi collaborators of World War II, no matter what mass crimes they had committed.

In contrast, the countries with smaller middle-class elements and traditions did not throw out all Communists from government: this holds for the Ukraine whose nationalism erupted in a big vote for independence but without excluding their own Communists. Communists also remained longer in the government in Romania (despite the mass uprising against Ceaucescu), Bulgaria, the independent Yugoslav Serbia, and Albania. One might argue that the more educated people could rise more quickly to the historical occasion. But it does not seem that the mass of East German voters who opted for immediate merging with West Germany and the Czech workers who were not motivated to be active in the students' uprising were acting differently because of differences in education.

Within the ethnic republics of the Soviet Union — in particular the Moslem ones, and Armenia and Georgia — the Stalin and Brezhnev governments had local Quisling leaderships under control. As the central government began to totter these local elements, comparable to the middle-class elements in the European Communist areas, pushed for national independence.[23] In all these cases nationalism may have been supported by most of the population but the middle-class elements actively used these issues, and became the rulers.

The special self-interest of the middle-class elements in Communist society is also evident in the Soviet center. The nature of this difference between middle-class and working-class responses can be seen more clearly within Russia proper, where the issues were economic and perhaps anti-dictatorial, without the nationalist motive. There, by all reports, the intelligentsia and the managers and the fledgling business people praise Reagan and Thatcher, favor immediate installation of a market system and privatization of the workplace, demand an increased gap between their incomes and those of the workers, and deride the welfare state or concerns for the unemployed as being economically wrong-headed; there is no mention of any shortcomings that capitalism might have.[24] These attitudes were explicit also in Deng's

23. Cf. Alexander Motyl, *Will the Non-Russians Rebel? State, Ethnicity and Stability in the USSR* (Ithaca: Cornell University Press, 1987).

24. Cf., for example, Boris Kagarlitsky, "Intellectuals against the Intelligentsia," in the New York journal *New Politics, vol.3 no. 1* (Summer 1990); Ivan Szeleny," The Intellectuals on the road to class power", *Politics and Society 15:2* (1986-87), 103-144.

China, which called for "a few people to get rich first," and where ideas about economic and social fairness are considered Maoist and obsolete. In almost all Communist countries, many managers and entrepreneurs have also taken control of enterprises by various devices, in effect to enter into the new capitalist class. As will be seen below, these attitudes and actions are very different from those favored by the Russian workers. In addition, these middle class occupational groups voice their opposition to Communism far more strongly than do the workers.

One may judge that the middle class is sharper in its opposition within Russia and more active in the uprisings and new governments in the satellites, because it is more focused in its anticommunism. And it is more focused because it has an alternative that exists and can be emulated, namely capitalism. Capitalism not only works better than the Communist system has worked but also promises the middle class in particular a higher economic position clearly above that of the workers.

(3) *The Working Class.* For their part, Russian workers are reported throughout to be strongly opposed to the price rises of a pure market system, to greatly increased unemployment and other steps in a "quick capitalism" program, to much of privatization and the fraudulent "cooperatives" formed by entrepreneurs and Communist managers, and to enrichment and private wealth in general, at the same time that they despise the Communist regime and also the great amount of corruption that developed within it.[25]

In some situations, indeed, e.g., in Romania, they acted unilaterally in workers' councils to determine the managing of their workplace. But the *New York Times* reported (10/7/90, p.14) that the Romanian government would "fire thousands of managers of Romania's huge failing state-owned industries...." The measures will include the dismissal of thousands of managers elected by workers' committees after the December revolution. The economic minutes asserted that most of the managers "act like union representatives. They do not understand that the government no longer sees itself as responsible for providing industry with raw materials and financing losses." It is of interest in this case that

---

25. The Western press sees these attitudes as due to brainwashing by Communist propaganda, and as constituting a childlike and unrealistic dependence upon government and search for cradle-to-grave security. But, as suggested in 8.3 above, these are reasonable attitudes for people in working class conditions.

there was no massive pressure by the workers against this action of the government. More generally, there has been no sustained attempt by workers to form workers' councils that would take over the managing of their workplace.

It was not that the workers were inert. They were active in early oppositions instituted from the left, as in the fall 1989 demonstrations in East Germany. And they were active in workplace opposition, as in the original Solidarity movement, or in the Czech metal workers' strike that helped topple the Communist government, or in the Siberian miners' strike.[26]

(4) *The "Masses."* It remains to note that aside from the distinct middle-class and working-class interests, the "people" as such were also an actor, in the street and in the voting booth.

In the satellites and other non-Russian lands, there were massive demonstrations that amounted to uprisings, after small-group initiatives, against the local Communist governments as soon as these lost their Russian umbrella. In the case of Romania, with its home-grown extreme Communist dictatorship, the uprising was more spontaneous against Ceaucescu's armed forces. In the Baltic states and the Ukraine the ethnic populations voted overwhelmingly for independence in support of local nationalist leaders. In Russia the political democratizations initiated by Gorbachev sufficed to let the anger of the bulk of the population dominate political developments. Even so, the "hard-line" Communist coup of August 1991 was stopped by a relatively small mass opposition, mostly in Moscow, rather than by a major uprising. In any case, while the independence seekers could replace the Communist regimes by nationalist ones, the Russian demonstrations could only reject the Communists without pushing for a particular replacement; in this they were more nearly like the peasant uprisings of the Middle Ages.

8.6 Assessments in Respect to Social Change

The thumbnail sketch above permits a few summaries or conclusions in respect to the possibilities of social and economic change.

---

26. When a Communist regime is fighting for its life, as in China but no longer in Russia, it understands that it can coopt the middle-class elements whereas the workers' opposition can be fatal (even though the Chinese regime rests primarily on the peasantry). At the end of the 1989 uprising in Beijing's Tiananmen Square, which was almost entirely a student activity with clear middle-class character, the suppression and executions were aimed particularly at the worker supporters more than at the students themselves.

(1) *On the Decision System of Communist Regimes:* Capitalism promotes competition, greed, and adversarial control over production, protected by governmental controls and often by political corruption. The single-party and governmental economy of Communism promotes a highly centralized, multi-layered bureaucracy and economic corruption under dictatorial controls. The overriding deficiencies in Communism were its inadequate production (in quantity and in quality) for consumer goods and services, and its police state.

More fundamentally, the system lacked incentives for individual initiative and independent innovations, such as could have made it flexible and able to change — for change was certainly needed in adjusting to a consumer economy. Such incentives and initiatives are not constrained to be the limited or unlimited monetary gain that capitalism offers; but to succeed in the long run a system has to offer the people — and preferably not just a small occupational range among them — real motivation in terms of their own needs. The system also lacked checks and balances such as are needed for stability. Negative feedback, not only for information but for input in determining the course of actions, is essential for a system's long-term effectiveness; quite the contrary, Communist regimes suppress all dissidents. Furthermore, its leader-centered monolithic structure precluded the kind of redundancy a system — somewhat like a living organism — must have if it is to be flexible and is to evolve. Otherwise it is harder for the system to react to changing conditions by revising some of its modes of operation or by alternating among them (as capitalism does by occasionally relinquishing authority to the government, Ch.3 above).

But there were also positive features which the West prefers to overlook. The Communist regimes kept at bay traditional national and religious oppressions, which rose to virulence as soon as Communism fell. The regimes decreased unemployment and did not create an underclass (at least not in their central areas). Large parts of the population, in particular the working class, developed a strong rejection of governmental and financial corruption, and an implicit valuing of economic equality and civic responsibility. American Sovietologists like to explain these attitudes as the result of Soviet propaganda. But, as noted in 8.3, the middle-class elements in the population did not share these attitudes, and were unaccountably impervious to the propaganda.

And the popular disgust at the Nomenklatura and at corruption were certainly no part of Soviet propaganda. Rather, we should judge that certain parts of the economic and social ideology of their Communism made sense to many in working-class conditions but not to those who had middle-class potentialities. Just as some of democratic capitalism's ideas of political equality arouse demands for this equality among its politically disadvantaged, so communism's ideas of economic equality and social responsibility arouse such expectations within its own population.

(2) *On the Failure of Communist Regimes:* The fact that a group (such as Lenin's in 1917) is instrumental in overthrowing a government does not give it the capability or effective status to reorganize the society or the economy successfully. Historically, it is only in rare circumstances and at great cost that the economic and social structures of countries have been wholly reorganized at a single juncture. Governments are unwise to make large-scale experiments, and to institute new economic policies and arrangements in one hasty action. A failure would be costly to the people involved and to their acceptance of the government's legitimacy. All Communist regimes have unavoidably made major economic miscalculations, only some of which were corrected. Central planning may have worked in rapid industrialization and in military production, but not for consumer goods. Prohibiting (or disregarding) oppositions may make life easier for the leaders, but prevents their understanding and estimating the needs of the people, and invites ultimate collapse or massive overthrow.[27] One may note in passing that the concentration of political and economic power in the hands of government allowed Communist regimes the ability to shift blame and decision-making between the economic system and the government. More generally, it is doubtful that detailed control of each individual's life, as Communism and Nazism attempted, can long survive in the modern world, Orwell's "1984" notwithstanding.

(3) *On the Collapse:* Failure in a system leaves open the possibility of corrections within the system. Collapse is terminal, even though some features of the system may be salvaged for use by its successor. Monolithic and superpower regimes can conceal a growing massive opposition that may cause any substantive weakness

---

27. Even in Nicaragua, where the regime was circumspect if for no other reason than the massive threat from the United States, the Sandinista failed to realize the people's attitudes, which brought them to electoral defeat.

to lead to an eventual collapse. "Mass" uprisings are still possible in modern society, though only in very special circumstances. Differences between middle class and working class may become relevant in the aftermath of a collapse or an overthrow. Just as fascism and socialism were two different reactions (largely in different classes) to pre–World War II capitalism, so the middle class and the working class have two different responses to the collapse of Communism. So also oligarchy and self-governed production are two different possible successors to tomorrow's capitalism.

Finally, it would appear that people who oppose a socio-economic system cannot effectively promote some other system unless that other system is available to them in their actual conditions — that is, exists in some measure within their knowledge and within conditions that are available to them. The middle-class elements of Communist countries can put all their efforts into attaining the capitalism that seems so promising to them in the neighboring countries.

Even the governments were not able to introduce successful new solutions. Lenin introduced a new system, but it only lasted some 70 years. Gorbachev was able to release the satellites (in his July 6, 1989, statement to the European Council that he would not intervene in their internal affairs); but he was not able to keep them from rushing back to their pre-communist state. He was able to release the Russian populace by Glasnost, but not to direct them to a "third way" between capitalism and communism — as he had clearly wished to do. In China, Deng was able to raise production, but only by opening the door to ordinary capitalism, rather than by any quasi-capitalist system that would fit into Communist governmental control such as he undoubtedly sought.

It would seem that in a large and complex society one cannot simply propose or institute a new broad arrangement from below. Governments may be able to do this from above, though with little long-term success. But when new economic arrangements arise from the participants themselves — from below — it may be that they can only grow piecemeal, with small-group activities becoming widespread and interconnected.

The reorganization of the main Communist centers may take long, and the attempt to transmute them into ordinary capitalist countries may fail in various respects. These countries may be left with various instances of worker control of their workplace, mixed with capitalist ownership and employment elsewhere in the economy. Plans for such arrangements of production have been put forward and local and piecemeal developments may in time produce results.

In spite of all the problems, it is not entirely clear that Communist regimes in Russia, China, and Vietnam will be permanently eliminated. Even if they are, they may be replaced by an economy and government that is truly mixed, containing economic areas of capitalism together with production and consumption areas of worker-control (possibly state-owned) enterprises. Russia and China are too big to be wholly bought even at bargain prices by their own Nomenklatura and entrepreneurs or by Western capitalism.[28] And the workers in many Communist countries are far from ready to accept capitalism in its entirety — not only all the economic misery that the transition to it entails, but also its economic inequalities and social injustices. An ex-Communist mixed economy may yet share the modern world with the three different capitalist centers of the United States, Western Europe, and Japan.

---

28. Even though home-grown capitalists can develop rather quickly in "moderate" Communism, as has happened in southern Vietnam.

CHAPTER 9

Intervening in the Historical Process

9.1 AWARENESS AND INTERVENTION

There is little evidence that people in the past were aware of the long-range course of history and social change, or that awareness was a factor in historical developments. If someone in 15th century Europe had devised a plan of development from commercial activities to a capitalist system, we might consider that to be a factor in the development which took place thereafter. Yet this whole directional course of development did take place, as though it was following a script, but without any such script having existed. Today it is possible to know in detail how social and economic conditions have developed, and to judge in part what are the possible courses of development from here on. Hence, to use our awareness in order to intervene in the course of history, in support of a desired direction, is something about which there is little experience. Societies, especially today, are too large to be determined permanently by any single group promoting a particular future course. Even those individuals or groups who have succeeded in playing a role in history did not succeed in imposing anything approaching their particular intended forms. This is seen not only in the collapse of the program introduced by the Bolshevik Revolution in Russia, but also in the long-range outcome of the French Revolution as compared to the intentions and programs of its leading groups.

In view of all this, it is necessary to consider carefully in each historical social situation to what extent intentional intervention in social-political change can have an effect on the historical outcome, and what sorts of intervention can have what kind and extent of effects. In any case, it is clear that to have any intended effect interventions cannot be arbitrary, but must fit into the existing social conditions and forms and into their possible directions of development — somewhat as an experiment in the physical sciences consists not in direct intervention into nature but in finding a way to observe the acting out of existing particular forces and conditions in nature. Intervening in social and political history thus requires a more detailed and more careful understanding both of history and of the current situation than is required for political propaganda or for general discussions.

Furthermore, while it is natural to suppose that historical and sociological understanding can affect our grasp of ongoing conditions, such grasp is also possible without that understanding. Sinclair Lewis, without having clear radical conceptions, was able to picture in his "Babbit" something comparable to what Arthur Miller, who did have such general conceptions, pictured in his "Death of a Salesman." At that, Lewis was more damning, while Miller was more pitying. In contrast, scientific knowledge and understanding are crucial for a grasp of events in the physical sciences: one might hesitate to go across a large bridge built without any engineering knowledge. The reason for the difference is that in history and sociology people's understandings are made out of the conditions and events in which they themselves are essential participants, so that a person can react (in his own interest) to a situation even without generalized understanding, though we may suppose that with broader and more careful understanding his reaction might be more effective.

9.2 AGAINST WHAT?

Since we live in capitalist society, the social ills that we see have a capitalist form. However, while many of these are indeed specific to capitalism, others exist in one form or another in all societies in which one group — governmental clique, economic class, caste, etc. — decides in its own interest the main socio-economic conditions of the rest of the population. One might claim that this distinction between social controls in general and the capitalist ones in particular is irrelevant, since in either case the conditions that we see are ones maintained by the capitalist relations and institutions; so that it is these relations and institutions that would have to change if those conditions are to be eliminated. But in opposing evils whose equivalent would be found in all "class" societies, it is important to oppose not only the capitalist form of them but their occurrence in any form — in particular in any possible post-capitalist society. One would have to guard against programs or changes that would remove the present form only to admit other forms. And in opposing evils that are uniquely capitalist, it is more responsible to oppose not capitalism as a whole but specifically the ills in question, for capitalism brought no little good to people in addition to all the harm. This is not merely an academic consideration for it affects the content and strategy of the opposition, as will be discussed below.

In any case, being "against capitalism" is not an adequate position. For one thing, as political radicals discovered when Hitler's "National Socialist" party claimed to be anti-capitalist, there is more than one direction in opposing capitalism. For another, capitalism like any societal order is a bundle of social arrangements, some of which we would not by any means wish to lose. We have to consider these ways and arrangements, and ask which we see as harmful and which as beneficial to people. We also have to ask which of these are interrelated, which ones are due particularly to capitalism, and how the loss of one property of capitalism might affect other properties of it.

Before considering the negative human properties of capitalism we have to recognize that this economic arrangement was the occasion of major advances in human life. Given what we can see so far, it is clear that historically man has moved, though with many setbacks, to better material conditions and higher cultural levels. What constitutes better material conditions is hard to formulate because some of them come with deterioration in the "quality of life." What constitutes higher cultural levels is also hard to formulate, because there are no clear or agreed scales of emotion and art, or thought and science, and there is no imaginable level which man is ultimately approaching, and no infinite future for man.

Nevertheless, both the material conditions of life and the richness of art and science and understanding are greater today than a few thousand years ago or a few hundred years ago. Some people today decry the notion of progress, partly because it is promoted as tantamount to the growth and product-proliferation of capitalism, and partly because they cannot accept anything which came under the banner of that same capitalism which has wrought so many wrongs. But whatever may be meant by "progress," there has been not only a slow progression but also some kind of qualitative progress in the long history of man, and for that matter in the evolution of life. And it is also undeniable that there has been particularly great progress in art and science and thought (including thought about a better society) during the last few centuries of European culture, and that the social conditions which grew with the ongoing development of capitalism were a causative factor in this.[1]

The two most prominent contributions are arguably individualism and technology.

The undoubted growth of individual independence during early capitalist development, which some have attributed to individuals being equal as customers in the market, may more reasonably be attributed to the opportunity for open entry into capitalist activity; that is, into the status of the burghers. Whereas in feudalism a person could own land only by birth or by royal grant or the like, any individual could enter capitalist profit-making if he could put together enough money to buy something, or to pay people to make something, which he could then sell at a profit. For some critics of society, individualism smacks of selfishness, aggressiveness, competitiveness, and disregard for others. This is certainly true of the economic individualism seen in the characteristic behavior of businessmen; it is fostered by the very condition of success in business. But culturally and politically, the individualist attitudes that spread with the growth of capitalist activity expressed a self-respect for one's own judgment as against authority and against the heavy hand of institutionally supported tradition. From the time when capitalism was just beginning to constitute a prominent part of the European economy, there were many oppositional or individualist innovations in many cultural areas: in religion with Huss, Luther, Calvin (for all the non-individualism of his own teachings), and the breaking of the Vatican's monopoly;[2] in art, in the Italian Renaissance; in music, Joaquin

1. Cf. Noam Chomsky, *Problems of Knowledge and Freedom* (New York: Random House, 1971), 57.
2. Cf. Max Weber, *The Protestant Ethic and the Spirit of Capitalism* (New York: Charles Scribner & Sons, 1978).

des Pres and Monteverdi, somewhat later, with Bach and the great composers during the 200 years after him; also the fast growing body of scientists from the 16th century and on; and the thinkers of capitalist economy and society from the 18th century.[3]

Some of the people involved exhibited their individual judgments in opposition to authority, or explicitly supported the new culture brought in by capitalism: Michelangelo's famous answer to the pope's decision that the Last Judgment's nudity was unsuitable ("Let him make the world a suitable place and painting would follow suit"),[4] Bach's strong Lutheranism, Mozart's attitude toward the Catholic hierarchy (not only in Salzburg), Beethoven's support for the French Revolution's ideals. Many bearers of the flowering in the arts and in the sciences had no personal opposition to the relatively frozen pre-capitalist society, but their independence and innovation in work would hardly have occurred without the social and cultural atmosphere that grew as capitalist activity became a larger factor in society.

As to the relation of capitalism to the development of technology, throughout human history there has been a slow and sporadic accretion of technology.[5] In the later periods of medieval Europe there was a recognizable growth of more massive and more complex technology, much of it for agriculture and rural manufacture unrelated to the early beginnings of capitalist activity in the towns. Some fostering of technology came from early commercial capitalism, as in the building of the large ships of that period. More came with businessmen's search for new sources of profit, in machinery that could be used in the contemporary agricultural environment (e.g., in the spinning wheel operated by farmers' wives in their cottages), and later in larger machinery that required new workplaces. The promotion of technology was not necessarily a specific fostering of new invention or application, let alone of new science; it came in part out of the utilization of existing knowledge and innovations. Later, capitalists and also the institutions of capitalist society explicitly encouraged technologi-

3. The argument here is not that the art of the western world is "greater" than the art of other societies, but that whereas in less individualistic societies art follows a preserved style within the limits of which the artist may develop his own expression; in the culture of modern Europe there was far more innovation and scope for individual variation, with results that have constituted a gain for human expression.

4. Cf. Giorgio Vasari's *The Lives of the Artists* (New York: Oxford University Press,1991).

5. Cf. Thomas P. Hughes, *The Development of Western Technology Since 1500* (New York: Macmillan, 1964).

cal innovation and scientific research, in their search for new products, cheaper processes, and ways of mass production. There was also some pressure, not only capitalist, for new technology in weapons. More recently the pressure was not only for weapons that could win wars, but also ones that could just make profits for the weapons industry.

The support for technology is not simple and direct in capitalism. No little of the technology that is developed in capitalism is more useful to profit-making than to the major human needs of the time. Much of it is in a wasteful and ecologically destructive form, for capitalism as a system is not interested in conserving for the future the goose that makes possible its golden eggs — it is only interested in the marketability and low manufacture cost of the product which the technology provides. Furthermore, much technology that could be of use for people's needs is not utilized because it would not increase profits, or would subvert existing profitable products, or because it can be saved for a later time when its profits would be needed more, or simply because the development that would bring it to the point of generating profits would take too long or be too costly. Despite these limitations, the development of technology and science and the increase in production during the last three capitalist centuries has been explosive.

The net effect of these social conditions has been vast. The individualism of capitalism plus the relative fluidity of social and cultural ways that came with the openness of entering into capitalist activity have supported a great flourishing and proliferation of the arts, science and political thought, with such broad ideals as are seen in Jean-Jacques Rousseau and in the Declaration of Independence. They have also created a system of democracy with the separation of powers in the United States Constitution. For all its limitations, flaws, manipulability, and capitalist bias this political system is valued by much of the population and any political advance should not seek to destroy but rather to extend and improve it (e.g., by making it federative, to express the interests of social subsets, as against being weighted toward majority rule determining limits on the behavior of all people). With democracy has come a degree of civil liberty, both in freedom of choice and in ability to dissent, far beyond what has been available in other societies even though it is far less than one might think is every human's due. Many of these liberties (and especially the extension of their domain beyond the original community of landowners and businessmen) came from the pressure of the "common people" — the customers and workers of capitalism — even though they are often honored only in the breach. Nevertheless, the initial intra-ruling class liberties and the very fact that they were amenable to extension under pressure (and under the needs of technology for a more orderly and competent working class) is characteristic of capitalism.

In addition, the incentive of potential wealth, the press of competition, the economic push to increase production and productivity, and not least the occasional accommodation toward the needs of the workers have all combined to make a great rise in production and a considerable rise in the standard of living of a large part of the population. That capitalism brought these contributions must be taken into account when considering its possible future changes and the desirability of such changes.

There is one further advantage to regarding capitalism as the latest period in the history of class societies, rather than as simply something to reject. For we can then see that capitalism, while a class-ruled system, has also created an example of a complex productionally interrelated society that operates with the principle of open initiative and without total centralization, in a quasi self-regulating manner. Though it is frequently destructive of human values, and latterly of the earth itself, one can ask whether these negative properties of the system can be changed while retaining and improving its non-centralized and self-regulating properties.

This question is important for two reasons:

First, no leader or movement is a demiurge, who can simply devise and create a wholly new system. The only option is to attempt to change some properties of the existing society while accepting the (possibly modified) continuation of the rest.

Second, a non-centralized structure is essential for any prospects of a more humane society. Modern production leaves little room for economic self-decisioning by individual units apart from others. Some kind of decision arrangement for interdependent production is unavoidable. The trend of capitalism itself and also of its relinquishings to government is toward centralization of ultimate decision-making. Any centralized system would have to be operated by participants in the very society which it is centralizing, and these participants could not avoid constituting within the society a special group with its own interests: there are no decision-makers who would not be interested parties in respect to the decisions made. Hence the only decision system that is a fair compromise among all group interests is one that is democratically controlled from below, by the welter of group interests that meet in society and must cooperate in order to produce and live together.

It is a corollary from the above that at no time can we lay down a social plan for all time. The system has to change through time. Hence, the only plan that avoids a class society throughout its history is not a particular design of society but rather a particular method of decision-making (for whatever society that may lead to at any given time): namely, that the decisions at any level be compounded by the groups affected, in some federative way from decisions or preferences which had been decided from "below."

In contrast to all the advances that have taken place with capitalism there is a host of injuries and sufferings created or maintained by it. Some have resulted from the unique way in which production is decided by businessmen. One is the separation of the decision criterion (i.e., profit-making) from the human considerations of production and consumption, which have led to shoddy goods, the proliferation of unproductive occupations that in some cases are not even needed for the rulers' social control, and false and misleading advertising. Another is the drive to expand, required for continued profit maximization, which constantly presses to increase wealth and decision power at the cost of the rest of the people and of colonial or quasi-colonial populations. This is the economic "individualism" of aggressive greed in "business as usual." Yet another is the cultural vacuity fostered by capitalism and its institutions, as well as the pervasive false fronts of virtually everything in business and government.

This obfuscation and falsification may be needed in capitalism more than in other class societies because the greater civil liberties in many capitalist countries limit the direct and selective control of dissidents and potential dissidents. Finally, there is the writing on the wall: the dangerous harm done to human ecology. As has been noted, the demands of profit maximization lead in various ways to pollution of the environment and depletion of the planet's resources, with effects that even the ruling groups will not be able to evade.

Most of the ills of capitalism, however, are common to all societies in which a ruling group wields power over the population.

First, in many of these societies, the means of production — land, water, rights to engage in particular productive activities —

are controlled by the wielders of power. In capitalism, property rights (always understood to include crucially private ownership of the means of production) are sacrosanct and taken for granted, as with land control in feudalism and hereditary status in royalty. This ownership, so often equated with a person's rights over his toothbrush, is perhaps particularly difficult to unmask as being none other than a power relation. Today, at least, people in republican countries no longer think that it makes sense for the son of a leader to become the next leader; but they take it for granted that the son of a factory's owner becomes its next owner.

Second, in all of these societies, the ruling group obtains some part ("surplus") of the product of other people's work, sufficient to enable them to live better than the ruled population. In obtaining this, the direct control over the activities of the producers ranges from tithes, taxes and profits (which leave the producers otherwise to their own devices), to slavery (as most recently in the wealthier Arab countries, and in effect in South Africa, but earlier in the southern United States, and in the Europeans' enslavement of the American Indians, and before that in the widespread slavery of the ancient world). In the case of capitalism, this surplus is obtained in the course of businessmen's dealings with their customers or with their workers — again, a method which is less transparent and more difficult to unmask as being a collecting of more than one's share. As has been noted, the victimization in respect to surplus is greatest when the customer has little or no alternative but to buy from the better organized businessmen. More important, the worker has little or no alternative but to accept employment from the relatively organized employers who have far more wealth and political clout and staying power than the job-seeking worker. But here again the objective of opposition would have to be not merely to the businessmen's selling or above all employing but also to any possible successor system in which the consumer has little say about prices and about the purveyors' misrepresentation of goods and in which the employee has little say in the wages and conditions of work.

A third property of ruling groups is the use of strong controls against dissidents, from exile to loss of livelihood to imprisonment and torture to execution. Capitalists, presumably, no more intend to allow dissidents to bring about their downfall than did any other ruling groups in the past or present. But, for all the intensity and virulence of their governmental actions, from the

American FBI and the English police's planted evidence (e.g., in planting bricks in the pockets of arrested peace demonstrators) to the police killing of blacks and the Sacco-Vanzetti and Rosenberg executions in America, the modern capitalisms have had their talons clipped by the civilization that capitalism introduced; mainstream capitalist governments are constrained to be less vicious in most of their policing than the fascist capitalisms (in a class by itself, the Nazi regime), the Third World quasi-capitalist dictatorships almost throughout (Chile, Argentine, Central America, the Philippines, Indonesia, many African countries), and the major Communist (Leninist) regimes, not to mention the medieval nobility and the old Asian regimes, and the Rome that crucified Spartacus' rebels after promising them safe conduct. Perhaps one hesitates to be thankful for small favors, but when one opposes the witch-hunts and thought-control of the modern capitalist governments, as one must if the world is to be Michelangelo's "suitable place," one should be contributing to the end of not merely the particular capitalist actions but the economic and social structure that enables any ruling group to function as it has.

To all these properties of ruling groups in their homeland, it is necessary to add the actions of many of them in countries which they come to control. Ancient and modern imperial rulers have usually been at their worst in this, whether as an imperial center exploiting the population and wasting the land beyond what they could do at home (e.g., the Dutch in Indonesia, the Belgians in the Congo, the English in India, the Israelis in the occupied territories) or by coming as colonizers and killing off or pushing out the population they found (the conquistadors in South America and the English in Tasmania and Australia, all of whom found it a sport to kill natives on sight; the Arab slave traders in Africa, the United States whites against the Indians, the Boers against the blacks). That after the withdrawal of the empires the new local rulers were as bad (as Jean Genet predicted in *The Blacks*) is a different matter.

In today's world, especially after the collapse of the Soviet empire, the United States remains the only large empire de facto. It maintains its power and the kind of local conditions it prefers by fostering whatever political elements are the most reactionary and repressive in the given country; compare the Chinese Communist insistent protection of the Pol Pot regime in Cambodia and their justification of the Burmese dictators. The control over empires has always been of import to the home country's rulers rather than to its people, and in many cases the import is primarily for their economic gain.

That the working class of the home country gained much from the colonies is doubtful, especially now. While there is great humanitarian reason to oppose empire, and while it is good material for exposing to the middle class of the home country the more naked character of their own government, it is not a major issue for the workers and will not in general develop their political understanding or arouse them to oppose their government. Nor is empire uniquely capitalist, though it was and is of major use for capitalist expansion.

Finally, the list of the major damages due to the power interests of ruling groups must include their stressing the loyalties of the ruled population, especially in religion and national identity and traditions. These last interests and attitudes — anthropological or "national" culture — do not have inherent validity or truth, and differ from the "high" culture in art and science and thought that expresses the emotional and intellectual condition of humanity with little or no regard to nation. The anthropological or national cultures express merely whatever has grown in earlier stages of development, whether from people's problems with the world or from inculcation by their rulers; it is generally backward-looking and unhelpful to most advances.

The traditional culture of one people means nothing to others, except as a curiosity; at its worst it can readily be manipulated by leaders to exaggerate loyalty to the home country (and its rulers) divisively against all outsiders and all different traditions. The high culture (despite its dubious name and its pre-emption by upper-class dowagers and investors) means much the same thing to persons of any nation, once they have some familiarity with its methods. European painters appreciated Chinese and African art, and Korean musicians can appreciate Beethoven; nor can this culture be used to set one people against another. This distinction is relevant to a discussion of class societies, because many progressives, seeking to free themselves from the conformity of their own national culture, have praised other national and tribal cultures or argued a cultural relativism in which all peoples' cultures were equally justified and respected. However, as suggested above, the political and sociological point is rather the converse: all tribal and national traditions, including our own, express the past of just one population, rather than general morality and the possibilities for human progress.

The extreme right demands that only western culture be taught to the exclusion of minority and foreign cultures, justifying itself by referring to the high culture of the West. But what they mean and promote is only the current "national" culture of capitalism, where individualism means "dog eat dog" and aggressiveness is (male) human nature and business profits are sacred. Rather than answering them by ascribing to other national cultures greater validity or interest than they have, one might first defend the human value of diversity in itself among cultures and among individuals, and then recognize the character of each culture, including the historic character of the big religions and the powerful states and economic systems. More than respecting the cultures, one can respect the rights of each social group to live by its lights (short of injury to its members), and the right of each individual to leave his group culture.

9.3 FOR WHAT?

The driving force in any major change of social power is a struggle against that which exists, as was surveyed above. But in many struggles for power, those in revolt have not only a definite view of what they are against but also some notion of what they are for. However, even the social innovations that rebellious populations have favored have been extensions and improvements on ongoing socio-economic arrangements rather than pure utopias unrelated to current reality.

Some may work to improve the socio-economic relations of the existing power system. Such struggles would presumably be carried out by middle-class elements, who would not be likely to take part in more fundamental social change but are willing to push their existing social environment in more humane directions or more in keeping with their nominal ideals. In the past, these impulses have included the principles formulated in the U.S. Declaration of Independence and later in the Bill of Rights, the abolitionist movement in America, electoral extensions such as the women's suffrage movement and proportional representation. In the present, the civil rights movement, the opposition to non-defensive wars (as in Algeria and in Vietnam) and to the U.S. system of client governments from South Korea and Taiwan to Pakistan and Israel to Central and South America. The main humanitarian issues of the present should also be included: homelessness (and the underclass in general), police brutality toward minorities, and the environmental dangers of today. A concentrated example of such issues of social justice and economic humaneness may be found in the "causes" (as he called them) espoused by Associate Justice Louis D. Brandeis of the U.S. Supreme Court.[6]

While it may be easy for middle-class people to hold liberal and humanitarian views, no effective action to change harmful features of the existing society is easy to achieve — even when not aimed against the power structure — because in most cases powerful groups have opposing interests. To take even a seemingly innocent example: entry into American colleges is based upon particular examinations (produced by particular organizations) which have been shown to be unfair and to an appreciable extent irrelevant. The organizations in question are able to disregard the public criticisms not because of some power of their own, but simply because the universities continue to require these particular examinations. But at this point the criticisms stop, because there are limits beyond which much liberal pressure will not go.

What we have here is a range of pressures within capitalism. The de facto idea of capitalism was control of production by others, by virtue of the entrepreneur's activity and of his owning "property" on which others had to work in order to produce. From the capitalists' point of view their activity required that they be free of feudal or royal restrictions, hence in general that they have freedom of action and that social constraints be decided by parliamentary law (in which they could have considerable input) and not by the specific interests of existing authority. These ideas were propagated by capitalism, and all of them (including the means of social production being accepted as private property) became embedded in the population's understanding of social life. Within this concept of society, individuals and sectors of the population not directly dependent upon making large profits out of others' work could afford to consider the human problems of the popula-

6. Brandeis identified himself with an array of public causes ranging from the "preferential union shop" in labor relations and savings bank life insurance, to maximum-hours law for industrial workers. The following give details on Brandeis and his remarkable career: *The Supreme Court vs. Civil Liberty: Dissenting Opinions of Justices Brandeis and Holmes in Cases Affecting Civil Liberty* (ACLU, 1927); Alpheus T. Mason, *Brandeis: A Free Man's Life* (New York: Viking Press) 514-518, 597-612; Phillipa Strum, *Louis D. Brandeis: Justice for the People* (Cambridge, Mass.: Harvard University Press, 1984); Lewis J. Paper, *Brandeis* (Englewood Cliffs, N.J.: Prentice-Hall, 1983); Elizabeth Brandeis, "Labour Legislation", in vol.3 of *History of Labour in the United States 1896-1932*, in John R. Commons, et al., eds. (New York: Macmillan, 1952-1955).

tion, and even the moral and environmental byproducts of their social system. In the spirit of the accepted social ideals, some people press for more humane conditions, more opportunity and freedom for the disadvantaged, but ordinarily do not consider whether these ideals conflict in practice with private control over others' production and with its central criterion of profit maximization.

This division in social-political attitudes within the existing system's world view (between progressives and conservatives) is hardly a new phenomenon in history and can be a factor in more far-reaching social change. People whose eyes are on ending the existing power relations may consider such "middle-class values" to be irrelevant. But, aside from their human value, the better living conditions, the greater amount of leisure, the stressing of egalitarian and humanistic principles, all make the disadvantaged people in society, and especially those who carry out the production, more ready and able to act effectively in their own interests. Nor is education irrelevant. Education cannot make more humane or egalitarian a person whose social interests are with the existing power wielders, but it can make a person whose own "objective" interests are for social change understand better both the problems and the possible solutions.

A quite different source of political struggle stems from new relations in the arrangements of production: interests of co-workers within capitalist manufacture. To this may be added in the foreseeable future a new arrangement, that of workers who control or own their production facilities. It was noted in 6.6 that the collaboration of workers in industry has created new arrangements of production which activated new economic and political interests for the more or less massed workers in their workplace.

These new attitudes and motives are not a matter of utopian goals thought out in principle, but an expression of new ongoing statuses and needs and perceptions on the part of a significant sector of the population. Although some thinkers, mostly in the 19th century, saw social and ethical issues stretching far into the future (as did, for their part, many of the thinkers of early capitalism), the interests and pressures of the growing industrial working class were the point of departure of these new ideas, and also the social basis of the political efforts in which many of the thinkers engaged. This applied both to the anarchists such as William Godwin, Pierre Joseph Proudhon, Mikhail Bakunin, Pyotr Kropotkin, and to the socialists such as Alexander Herzen, Ferdinand Lassalle, and Karl Marx and Friedrich Engels.[7]

The ideas of the social thinkers may have an effect on the points of view of the intellectuals and even of broad sectors in the population, but they can also be all but forgotten and can lose any role in the course of history: cultures can completely forget ideas that were once widely known. But the social conditions and new productional interests out of which those ideas came continue to press on the people who are affected. Shop-floor customs and practices, arrangements among co-workers, strikes and unions, and collective demands on the bosses cannot be eliminated, and with them there arise organizational methods, joint activities and interconnections ("networking") and ideas and attitudes. All of these may suffer reversals, partly due to manipulation and counterattack from the opposing economic and political powers. New anti-strike tactics are instituted when possible, unions become bureaucratic or corrupt, pension funds are mismanaged by union leaders or by company executives. But as long as there is the pressure of workers' interests in production arrangements there will be, from time to time, an overcoming of such reversals and a further development both of the activities engendered by the workers' interests and also of the more general ideas and attitudes that conform to these interests.

Further kinds of social actions and ideas may be expected from the further new relations of production whose coming was suggested in Chs. 6,7, namely control or ownership by workers of their own productional facilities. To the extent that such economic developments take place within the capitalist society, we may expect that the new productional interests of the participants will lead to new attitudes and readiness to act. The pressures, both from workers' interests within capitalist enterprises and from workers' control or ownership of whole enterprises, are likely to be felt only when they are ongoing conditions in the lives of part of the population. However, these social pressures can begin to appear at an early stage, as they did in the world view of the burghers (6.3, 6.4) and in the industrial workers' struggles from the early 19th century on. At such an early stage one cannot predict the course of development or the later specific interests and issues. Therefore, if we want to formulate at this stage a goal

---

7. Cf. Noam Chomsky, "Notes on Anarchism," in his *For Reasons of State* (New York: Vintage Books, 1973), 370-386.

toward which these new pressures are moving, we can only state it in terms of the infrastructure required for any satisfaction of these pressures. In effect, this infrastructure has to be some kind of system of control from below. For modern industrial production, this means something beyond the idea that each individual may decide his own work, and even more than each group of co-workers deciding their work with no other power-wielder inside or outside the group. The decisions of each producing group would have to come to terms with its suppliers, competitors, and consumers. The structure of such federative decision-making from below would leave no base for one group to develop institutionalized power over the production and consumption of the rest of the population, and is about as much of a goal as one can have so far in advance. To speculate on creating or devising social structures, and in particular decision structures, merely as an intellectual exercise is fruitless. One has to be as aware as possible of the dynamics, feedback properties, checks and balances, possible avenues for decay or corruption or for the growth of potentially dangerous leadership within the decision structure which can subvert it. One also has to be aware of how the new structure can grow, in terms of current interests and forces, out of the existing social structures and conditions. Provision is necessary at all times for constant and competent democratic oversight to guard the control-from-below character of any new structure.

Such a future goal can direct the choice of economic and political strategies even in the present, since it favors any action that increases control from below in the decisions on production, or that has serious promise of increasing it. These considerations apply not only to cooperatives and worker-owned enterprises but also to partial steps such as employee stock-ownership, employee participation in corporation decisions (e.g., the German Mitbestimmung), employee control over their immediate worksection (workplace democracy, and in part the English Shop Steward movement of the early 1900's) — provided these are not pro forma or trivial but have the structural promise of future extension. These considerations also apply to the general conditions of modern labor, indicating the importance — indeed the relevance to long-term goals — of effective democratic oversight by the rank and file over such entities as pension and health funds (whether union controlled or company controlled), and above all the importance of trade union democracy and of eliminating the possibilities of dictatorial leaders, corruption, and subversion of union leadership by the businessmen with whom they deal.

Above, we have sketched middle-class politically humane goals, and workers' goals both within capitalist production and on its fringes. Upon occasion, suggestions have been made of more abstract goals toward idealized or theoretical societies, embodied in concepts such as justice and equality. Here one must take into consideration the limitations on what social improvements are possible. Some goals that seem to be desirable may not be possible in any real world. Some ideals such as total justice, equality, truth may be definable logically but not in the universe of human lives. Others, such as complete fairness, or absence of interpersonal conflict, are precluded by the variety and complexity of the individual lives in a society — in any society. Such utopian ideas are made possible for us by the capacity to generalize and to reify abstractions available in our language and in our processes of thought. The existence of terms such as "equality" or "justice" may suggest an ideal in respect to which we judge a society or its change, but what the term indicates may not be a possible state of the world.[8]

One has to question the reality of such abstractions not because they are too idealistic, or too far from today's world, but because the very discussion of them as abstractions is not related to a current or future reality. In vague colloquial use such ideals can be valuable in "fixing the ideas" and in presenting a direction for desired improvement, but any attempts at global definitions of them and of a discussion purely in principle belong to intellectual and moral exercises rather than to social change and political action. These latter cannot wait for the intellectual discussion to clear the way.

9.4 STRATEGIES AND ISSUES

Any consideration today of how one can work for a better social future has to take into account the failure of the two major directions of political effort of the last hundred years or so. The

---

8. In the development of language, the underlying sentence structures indicated observable situations, normally by a verb (e.g., "equals," adjoined to one or two nouns stating that one weight equals another). But in becoming a more flexible and extendible means of communication, language developed the omittability of the nouns which the verb had adjoined (e.g., the omission of what it was that was equal), so that one could speak of equality in general as an abstraction even if such a relation can in fact exist only in certain situations (e.g., in the case of equality, as between quantities) but not in others (e.g., not, in the original sense, between people or between ideas).

socialist and communist parliamentary parties within capitalist countries succeeded in varying degrees in improving the life of the "common people." But they did not eliminate the general structure whereby workers and the bulk of the producing population were in many ways the victims of the capitalist controls which had called these parties into being in the first place. The Communist (Leninist, Bolshevik) revolutions and governments made certain important advances in favor of the working population, but settled down into dictatorships of individual or party that brought neither high consumption nor personal and political liberation to the great bulk of the population.

The more so because the poor record of the socialist parties and the collapsing Communist regimes have put socialist and Marxist political action into disrepute, it is important to recognize that promising long-term action of a different kind — economic and social and largely local rather than political — is available sporadically all over the capitalist world, and the methods for carrying it out are available for study even now.

The discussion in 9.2-3 was intended to sketch what directions of intervention in the possible course of the present capitalist society might lead to more humane and egalitarian social forms. Actions in this direction had been, since the beginning of the 19th century, the domain of what is now called the radical or leftist movement (mostly socialists and anarchists), whose main activities had been to discuss and analyze the capitalist economy and political structure, and when possible to promote oppositional action and organization by workers. It is of obvious value to maintain, advance, and bring up-to-date the rich culture of ideals and understandings that have been developed, especially within the Marxist analysis. However, in many periods and situations this activity can have little if any weight as an intervention in the course of history.

The Marxist tradition had an important offshoot in this direction, less publicly known than its political offshoot. Discussions of this direction are found in the writings of Anton Pannekoek, Karl Korsch, Paul Mattick, and such radical groups as the Council Communists and the French journal *Autogestion*.

The discussion above points to various possible interventions which seem to be available even when political activity may not be. The most important direction for any intentional intervention into the course of history appears to be economic — more precisely productional: specifically, to help workers develop ways to arrange and decide their own productional activity, in consonance with the other people involved in creating their product.

The first such intervention was the labor movement: the collective action of workers in an enterprise, industry, or region to take a hand in production arrangements. This includes the development among themselves of arrangements and allocations of work activity (including general principles to achieve this, such as solidarity and seniority), beyond what is decided by the boss, or in disregard of his decisions, or in opposition to his decisions. It includes workers' desires as to the wages, hours, and work-conditions they should have within the existing business situation, and their conflict with the boss or the government to get what they want instead of what is offered them. It includes creating institutions and organizations through which workers and other producers can act collectively — shop stewards, trade unions, labor education and research bodies, labor parties. Also, the current movements or struggles to increase workplace democracy (which in effect moves certain decision areas from the managers to the working groups), and to increase substantive input by workers into company decisions. For the future, it should mean a determined effort to put union and company pension and health funds under the effective democratic control of the workers involved.

Since all of these only limit but do not remove businessmen from profit-making and decision status, they are generally considered "reformist" rather than radical, and today are fostered within capitalist society by well-meaning liberals. However, they are all part of relevant social change, because they move some of the production decisions from businessmen to their workers, and increase the decision power of workers over their work, and above all create structures through which workers can act collectively in decisions over their work.

Indeed, though the labor movement operates within business or government ownership of the production facilities, it is nevertheless confrontational to each owner. More generally, it is confrontational in spirit to the business world because it advances the interests of the victims of that world; the profit maximization of businessmen gives them an adversarial interest in respect to their workers. Whereas the individualist profit-seeking of the capitalists had not been in direct zero-sum conflict with the feudal landlords, the attempts of workers to make decisions about their work (wages, conditions, etc.) come into direct conflict with the goal of profit maximization and with the decision domain of the bosses. It is for this reason that while the thinkers of early capitalism were not involved in struggles against the existing order, almost all the thinkers of the workers' movement after ca. 1800 associated themselves with practical efforts against the political or economic status quo.

A later and far more important movement for workers' deciding on their own production could open if opportunities for worker ownership and control were to expand appreciably. Even this would not be in immediate conflict with the capitalist system and its governments, since it does not try to dislodge the big capitalists from their strongholds, nor could it compete with the major and successful business concerns. Nevertheless, many businessmen would undoubtedly dislike such a development; and it is unlikely that middle-class liberals would find this a natural "cause," except for professionals for whom a declining capitalism would leave no jobs. However, if a political movement develops around workers' ownership it would have many functions to fill in helping the enterprises to organize and succeed and interrelate, and in maintaining their purely cooperative character. In addition, it would be important to build bridges between these enterprises and the trade unions, for example in union support for cooperative attempts when many of their members become permanently jobless, and in cooperatives' acceptance of trade-union principles and conditions for their own members.

Both types of workplace developments, cited above, create structures to enable people to have more say over their work — over whether they will have work at all, and in what conditions and with what income. They can thus be seen as different stages in the same direction.

Aside from the two workplace developments noted above, there are other types of movements which work toward a more humane and egalitarian society. Chief of these is the growth of "grass-roots" political activity, mostly in the U.S. where the freezing of politics into the permanent Republican and Democratic parties leaves no channel for issues and points of view that capitalism does not want to consider. The result has been the formation of many hundreds of organizations and efforts initiated by individuals who seek cooperation from like-minded individuals. These range from civil rights and minority and women's rights defense to environment protection and to criticism of government. Some of the organizations have become large and influential, such as the Nader groups, Amnesty International, Greenpeace, and the Human Rights Watch. But even the small groups are sufficiently numerous and durable so that the whole constitutes a pervasive component of the political scene. Aside from the attitudes that these groups promote and from the effects they may achieve, they are of great importance in that they bring into existence a new structure of political initiative and action from below, which does not have to wait for any institutional acceptance and wherein people do not need massive instruments that flourish by entering mainstream institutions and otherwise wither away. For this reason it would be counter-productive to try to merge the unwieldy mass of grass-roots initiatives into some hierarchical organization, despite the possible resulting efficiency, and because it would dampen some of the special groups' enthusiasms and above all the important character of initiative from below. Thus, a political structure rising from below is of a piece with the rise of workers activities from below in their workplaces.

9.5 Tactics and Tools

The question of tactics for intervening in social change is necessarily one to be decided separately in each situation. Nevertheless the discussion above suggests a few general considerations.

One is that the development into which one is intervening is sociological and economic (in production decision-making) more than political. This means that it is a matter of occupations, technology, and attitudes and understandings that have become common within relevant sectors of the population. It is more this than it is a matter of direct struggle for power. It also means that what is most important is to develop social structures — organizations or ways of interacting — enabling people to initiate and control activities relevant to their own life and work. Such structures would have to avoid leaving room for some individuals or groups to control the life and work of others, even via a back door.

The sociological view of social change makes it clear that the conflict between right and left is not a conflict of two propaganda lines or "value" systems. The motive forces behind it are two disparately situated class interests. One is that of the controlling group which wields power; the second is the interest of those over whom power is wielded. The power wielders can use propaganda because they alone can "make a word mean what they want." The U.S. administration can introduce into common parlance terms like the "war on drugs" at a time when it is increasing the drug trade as a step in displacing the Sandinistas in Nicaragua. It can introduce "political correctness" as a name for liberal attitudes on campus, to suggest without any serious evidence that the liberals have control, or even influence, on campus thought. The Reagan campaign introduced the term "L-word" to suggest that liberalism was so unspeakable as to be unnameable, with no more evidence than the term itself. False and indefensible as such namings may be, they become general coin because the media and publicly prominent people pick them up with relish. The opponents of the social order, and the voiceless sectors of the population, cannot do the like. They lack sufficient access to the media or to the attention of the population as a whole. Any term they wish to invent falls upon deaf ears, and any statement they make will be widely attacked even though true and all the more so if exaggerated or imprecise.

The lesser or deferred importance of the political aspect suggests that in the early stages the main activity of the left as an intervention in social change should be as little as possible confrontational or conspiratorial. Confrontation is of the essence in labor struggles against the bosses, though even here building the infrastructure of solidarity and democratic organization is the more crucial task. But confrontation in the political arena, though often unavoidable, is rarely an effective method for the left until its attitudes have become widespread and the political forces allied with it are massive. In any case, conspiratorial methods have little effectiveness. The structures of control from below will grow not because the power wielders are unaware of them, but because the power wielders cannot stop them — whether in producers' cooperatives where business is not sufficiently profitable, or in grass-roots initiatives across the country.

The ills of capitalism, and the exclusion of producers from decisions on their work, generally result from and are maintained by specific business, governmental, and institutional interests of control. The power wielders and those who act in their interests are always zealously on guard. It is they who are confrontational. The slowly developing movement for social change would do best to defer confrontation as long as possible and to put as much of its energy as possible into building the infrastructure of control from below, and into the ideas that accompany this infrastructure. The principle of control from below entails the recognition that this infrastructure cannot be imposed or created from above. Every cooperative attempt or method needs to be initiated by its participants, upon whom the risk of failure would fall.

Another general consideration, which fits in with the first, is that workplace change is the crucial change. It is not only that new self-interests of work groups, and new powers of decision on their own production, create the continuing attitudes and abilities for fighting against outside control. It is also that intervention is less difficult in the workplace than in the population as a whole. People act in their own interests and against outside control more intelligently and relevantly in the context of their workplace than in the context of street politics or the voting booth. Countering the propaganda of the power wielders is easier on workplace issues than on large public issues. And results of self-interest actions in the workplace do not have to depend on a change of the power distribution over the whole country or for winning over a majority of the population (or even of the "working class"). Given the sporadic structure of capitalism, results can be obtained piecemeal in workplaces and sometimes in localities, in a way that contributes to a later more general effect.

Stressing the importance of the workplace does not discount the possibility or value of other activities, such as the valuable grass-roots initiatives mentioned above, or the maintenance of radical thought. Such non-local and broad-spectrum activities as developing general opposition to the status quo ("class consciousness"), or unmasking its evils, are important but difficult. They may spread more easily, almost as a fad, in groups marginal to the social conflict — witness the explosion of student and youth radicalism in the late 1960's; but they can recede there as quickly, though many people who were affected by the 60's movement kept the faith. "Consciousness raising" may succeed more readily and have more permanent effect when it deals with narrower sets of problems, or when it does not conflict directly with the basis of status quo power, as was seen in the success of the feminist movement.

All of these discussions do not touch upon the harrowing problems of the Third World. In countries where a dictatorship closes all avenues to action, or where death squads silence any opposition, no local actions are possible except insofar as guerrilla warfare removes some areas from the reach of the existing government, as in the Philippines or in El Salvador. Even the worst dictatorships are not merely one-man or one coterie; there are always sectors of the population supporting the oppression — not only the (usually economically favored) army and the governmental bureaucracy (or in Islamic lands the clerics), but also merchants and other middle-class elements, as in the Philippines and South Korea, in many Latin American countries, or differently in the case of Hindu upper castes. When an imperial power can hand over local power to whom it chooses, even the vast majority of the population cannot unseat an oppressive local government, as when the Dutch government handed the Moluccas to the Indonesian government, or in the face of America's power over its client states (eliminating Arbenz in Guatemala and Allende in Chile, organizing the anti-Sandinista forces in Nicaragua, financing the ultra-right army in El Salvador, and so on indefinitely).

In Third World countries, even a guerrilla victory is unstable. The military or economic pressure of the larger powers, and the lack of infrastructure or sociological readiness for any socialist or cooperative society, make economic success doubtful. Even a guerrilla victory would be most effective in the long run if followed by a coalition government with opportunity for relatively peaceful economic and social development toward later political change. In the absence of such victory, the only serious choice for the left may be to try to unseat the dictatorship or army by a coalition with the middle class, for a period in which the existing governmental and military controls are replaced by the indirect controls of small-country capitalism, in which movements toward further liberation of the people become possible. Such coalitions are not excluded out of hand: In rural Philippines there are some merchant interests which favor the impoverished (Communist-led) peasants against the landowners because they can do better business if the landowners are removed.

In previous ages, and in some Third World areas today change has come slowly if ever, and then mostly from internal decline of the ruling groups. But in the modern world, change is certain, no matter how unshakable capitalist power may seem now, as did Communist power so recently. It is only after the collapse that one sees how fundamental were the fissures in the previously powerful social order. And for all their tenacity in any given period the understandings of society also change, especially with change in economic conditions: "Certainties come, certainties go." The promise for intervention toward people's decision power over their own production lies in a long-term consideration: Every advance in the power or decision status of the people is a local or partial victory, though some advances may be later nullified. Many defeats pave the way for later victories, because often they reinforce people's bitterness and desire for change, clarify their understanding of what has to be changed, and help them strengthen their opposition. Thus in either case the door for change is not closed. Only inaction — apathy, indecision, unreadiness to act — can keep the door shut.

accumulation of capital, 92
accumulations of urban wealth, 90
Ackerman, S.R., 61
agricultural privatization
    in China, 197
American Indians, 45
American Savings and Loan industry
    fiasco of, 147
Anarchist tradition, 108
anti-Bolshevik Marxists, 124
anti-slavery movement, 50
anti-trust laws, 38
anti-war movements, 50
Antweiler, O., 125
Applebaum, E., 137
assembly line, 142
Aston, T.H., 90
Avnat, A., 116
Avrich, P., 184

Bachtel, H.M., 130
Bacquet, B., 107
bailouts of failing businesses
    Chrysler automobile corporation, 39
Bakunin, M., 108
barter, 28, 158
    beneath the market, 27
Berkman, A., 108
Berle, A. A., 108
Berliner, J., 186
Beveridge Report, 73
Black nationalism, 149
Black self-help movement, 149
Blancherie, J., 107
Blasi, J., 131, 162, 171
Bloch, M., 87
Bodin, B., 107
Bolshevik Revolution
    collapse of the program introduced by,
        209
bottom line profit criterion, 40
Bottomore, T., 108
Bradley, K., 120, 133
Brandeis, L.D., 221
Braudel, F., 27, 77, 89, 96
Brecher, J., 149
Bresson, J.L., 107
Bricianer, S., 125

Briefs, G., 130
Briggs, A., 96
Brigl-Matthias, K., 125
Brinton, M., 125, 184
Broekmeyer, M.J., 130
Buckmiller, M., 125
Burawoy, M., 142
bureaucracy
    control from below as a preventative,
        170
    problem of, 170
business decision-making
    increased government involvement in,
        39
Buzgalin, A., 188

capitalism
    above the market, 27
    accumulation of capital from profit, 24
    advances in knowledge will decrease in
        late, 72
    adversarial position against customers,
        26
    adversarial position with respect to
        employees, 26
    basic legalism of, 100
    by the late 1700's, 96
    bypasses as temporary or permanent
        reductions, 79
    ceding decision-making to the govern-
        ment, 36-42
    cooperative successor to, 6
    cultural progress, 10
    culture disfavors in late intellectual
        inquiry, 72
    democratic successor to, 5
    destruction of the earth's resources and
        environment, 1
    difficult conditions for, 146
    dominant economy in England, 96
    early period, 36, 37
    effect of a stabilizing negative feed-
        back, 76
    evolution over centuries, 3
    expansion of, 3
    flexibilities of, 33
    foreseeable late, 152
    government decision on production as
        a bypass, 79

capitalism (cont.)
  governmental aids to, 75
  governmental bypass, 41
  governmental control of the economy, 5
  governmental intervention, 39
  growth of employee ownership, 5
  ills of, 10
  individualism, 10
  industrial capitalism, 10
  instabilities, 33-36
  Keynes's economic theories, 39
  lacks negative feedback to keep its sys-
    temic problems in check automati-
    cally, 78
  late period, 35, 88, 165
  latest period in the history of class
    societies, 215
  limits of the earth's available
    resources, 75
  limits of expansion, 75
  limits to, 74-76
  mixed economy, 5
  modern period, 37
  naked, 41
  network of middle-class occupations,
    32
  no intrinsic built-in stabilizing nega-
    tive feedback mechanism, 41
  non-capitalist production growing
    inside of, 4
  non-profit enterprises, 170
  oligarchic and dictatorial successor to, 5
  openness of, 25
  popular acceptance, 32
  principle of open entry to, 100
  principle of open initiation, 215
  problems of late, 3
  productional activism, 10
  profit-maximizing dynamics of, 99
  property rights are sacrosanct, 217
  prospect of capitalism replacing com-
    munism, 67
  quasi self-regulating manner, 215
  relinquishing behind, 146
  relinquishing decision-making on pro-
    duction, consumption, and socio-
    economic life, 41
  relinquishing of less profitable produc-
    tion domains, 100
  relinquishing to below, 146
  relinquishment to government, 3
  relinquishments of decision-making to
    the governments without a profit
    criterion, 81-82
  strengths and flexibilities, 32-33
  success of, 1
  systemic problems and limits of, 77
  trend toward centralization of decision-
    making, 215
  universalization, 63
  unorganized multiplicity of self-initiat-
    ing enterprises, 2
  use of its technology is damaging
    human ecology, 69
  wasteful technology of, 69
  wastefulness of capitalist technology, 6
capitalist accumulation, 157
capitalist control
  ownership remains the basic legalism
    of, 140
capitalist decision-making
  developments toward, 88-94
capitalist history
  capitalism leading to improvement in
    workers' consumption level, 31
  early period, 31
  late period, 31
  middle period, 31
capitalist ideology, 25
capitalist industrialization, 187
capitalist society
  ability of businessmen to decide pro-
    duction and consumption, 106
  alternative ways of deciding and
    arranging production, 99
  better material conditions, 9
  development of, 97-99
  higher cultural levels, 9
  values of individualism, property,
    profit, work ethic, 97
Captain Swing, 51, 126
Carby-Hall, J.R., 129
Carr, E.H., 184
cartels, 28
Case, J., 130
Catholicism, 45
caveat emptor, 26, 28, 35
Ch'en, C., 119
Chalmers, A.J., 25
Chartist movement, 105
chemical waste, 78
Childe, V.G., 110
Chomsky, N., 212, 223
Ciliga, A., 184
co-determination laws, 130
Coffee, J.C., 61
Cohen, L.B., 142
Cohen, R., 116

Cohen, S.F., 200
Cole, G.D.H., 107, 108, 128, 129
collectives, 114
collectivist commune, 118
colonialism
    of expanding 19th century capitalism,
        67
Comisso, E.T., 130
command system, 196
commerce
    growth of, 90
communism
    Bolshevik regime, 1
    failure of command economy, 40
    failures of, 1
    Leninist regime, 1
communist (Leninist, Bolshevik) revolu-
        tions and governments
    failure of, 225-226
communist China, 37
communist regimes
    command economy, 187
    corruption, especially of the part of the
        bureaucracy, 189
    dictatorial structure, 190
    global view on, 191-196
    immediate task to construct an indus-
        trial infrastructure, 192
    industrializing dictatorial command
        economy, 192
    monolithicity of the bureaucracy, 193
    no independent unions, 189
    no strikes, 189
    party as vanguard of the class, 190
    party dictatorship left no room for civil
        liberties, 187
    tight control inside the plant by the
        party cell, 189
    unexpected collapse of, 6
    workers radical ethic, 188
Communist Third International, 125
concentration of capital, 29, 31, 34, 93,
        155
conformity
    to the existing order, 45
Confucianism
    respect for authority, 45
conglomerates, 61
consciousness raising, 231
conspicuous consumption, 29
consumers' (supermarket) cooperative,
        120
contributions of capitalism to progress
    individualism and technology, 212

Cook, A.J., 107
cooperative decision-making
    possible first steps toward, 104-112
cooperative economy
    decision-model of a stable, 86
    democratic and reasonably humane
        system, 86
cooperative enterprises, 111, v
cooperative or communal (collective)
        enterprises, 103
cooperatives, 114, 224, 118-124
corporate management
    Byzantine structure, 60
    development of, 60
corporate raider(s), 60, 60, 61, 62, 73, 133,
        158, 160
corporation structure, 30
corruption, 34
Costello, T., 149
cottage handicrafts, 95
cottage industries, 100
credit-union-like cooperative bank, 120
Crouch, C., 129
Crystal, G., 159
Cuenca, A.M., 191
cultural relativism, 219
Cultural Revolution, 184

Dan, L., 116
Darin-Drabkin, H., 116
de Roover, R., 98
de Vries, J., 95
decision power
    general theory of, 18
decision system on production
    indirectness of profit, 59
decision-making on consumption, 16-17
decision-making on production, 16-17
decisions on production
    capitalist, 23-42
decline in productional knowledge
    in late capitalism, 70
Delage, P., 107
determinants of social changes
    sociological and productional develop-
        ments, 54
Deutscher, I., 184
dictatorship of the proletariat, 183, 190
dissidence
    prevention of, 15
divine right of kings, 18, 89
division of labor (occupations), 11
Dolgoff, S., 119
Duhring, E., 103

early capitalism
  thinkers of, 222
East European uprisings of 1989, 7
economic conversion
  legislation, 154, 156
economic decision-making, 12
economic democracy, 174
economic determinism, 98
economic political "system," 11
economic system
  development of business into, 94-97
economy
  as society, 19-20
  as system, 19-20
Edwards, E., 142
egalitarian democratic participation, 126
egalitarian society, 110
egalitarianism
  against human nature, 118
  ideology of, 120
elite-ruled societies
  attempt to lessen the inhumanity and
    dishonesty of, 180
Ellerman, D.P., 120
Elster, J., 105
employee buyouts, 140
employee loyalty, 131
employee ownership, 3, 162
  avenue to worker's control of produc-
    tion, 141
  broadens employee horizons to encom-
    pass explicitly the whole plant or
    company, 178
  business pressure for, 131
  clouds the difference between the
    owner and the worker, 173
  does not directly lead to self-govern-
    ment, 177
  employees' ownership of stock, 131
  form of privatization, 135
  in formerly communist countries in
    Europe, 135
  less profitable industries and compa-
    nies, 4
  necessary precursors for a humane suc-
    cessor to capitalism to come about, 86
employee participation in corporation
  decisions, 224
employee stock ownership, 224
employee-controlled enterprise
  freedom from profit maximization,
    157, 154
employee-owned companies, 102, 141

employee-owned enterprise(s),
  best promise may be in midsized pro-
    duction, 151
  climate for, 4
  danger of bureaucracy, 169
  decline in profitability and, 4
  hire business managers, 83
  history of such enterprises, 83
  learning how to oversee management, 4
  may prove viable even within capital-
    ism, 83-84
  organized in terms of control rather
    than ownership, 168
  preserving the participant character,
    165-171
  response to massive unprofitability and
    to decline of manufacturer in old
    capitalist countries, 84
  structural defenses against bureau-
    cracy, 169
employee-share ownership, 140
Engels, F., 103
English General Strike of 1926, 107
English Shop Steward movement, 128
environmental problems
  threats to capitalism, 69
equitable social order, 2
ESOPs (Employee Share Ownership
  Plans), 132
  advantages for the employer, 133
  capitalist values of ownership in con-
    trast to class-consciousness, 178
  employee buyouts, 134
  fend off hostile takeovers, 133
  no drive toward control, 177
  other reasons for establishing, 134
  passed by Congress on various occa-
    sions from 1974 and on, 131
  provide for worker participation in
    workplace decisions, 144
  proworker formulation, 134
  relation to unions, 136
  statement by an investment banker,
    171
  to protect employees, uncouple pen-
    sion and health funds from, 135
  use to advantage management and to
    disadvantage employees, 134
Estrin, S., 130
European Community, 64, 68, 76, 121
Evan, W.M., 130
extended families, 12

fascist regimes, 99
Febvre, L., 87
feminist movement(s), 50, 231
feudal economy, 90
feudal society, 92
feudal system, 94
feudalism, 19, 24, 44, 50, 101, 143, 212
  capitalism replaced by in stages, 99
  replaced by capitalism, not by peasant
    revolts, 111
finance capitalism, 61, 62, 145, 157, 187
Fordism, 142
Frankfurt School, 51
fraudulent "cooperatives"
  formed by entrepreneurs and communist
    managers in Russia after 1991, 203
free trade, 66
Freedom of Information Act in America,
  81
French Revolution, 209
Fyfe, H., 107

Garson, G.D., 130
GATT, 64
Gelb, A., 120, 133
Genet, J., 218
German Mitbestimmung, 224
Gimpel, J., 90
Glasnost, 196, 198, 207
global warming, 69
Goode, J., 137
Gough, J.W., 97
governmental decision-making, 42
Granrose, C.S., 137
Great Depression, 36, 38, 41, 42, 73
Greenberg, E.S., 129, 171
greenmail, 61, 63
Guild Socialism, 108
Guillebaud, C.W., 125
Gunn, C.C., 130
Gutkind, E.A., 90

Habakkuk, H.J., 89
Habermas, J., 171
Haimson, L.H., 184
Hardin, R., 171
Hare, A.E.C., 130
Herlihy, H., 90
Herzen, A., 108
high culture
  art and science and thought expresses
    the emotional and intellectual con-
    dition of humanity with little or no
    regard to nation, 219
Hill, C., 96

Hindess, B., 89
Hindu castes, 12, 45
Hinton, W., 197
Hirsch, P.M., 61
Hirst, P., 89
historical materialism, 87
historical process
  intervening in, 209-233
historiography, 87
history and social change
  awareness of the long-range course of,
    209
Hobsbawm, E., 89, 96, 127, 52
Hochner, A., 137
holding company, 62
Holton, R.J., 89
Horvat, B., 130, 173
hostile takeover attempts, 59
Hughes, T.P., 213
human ecology
  dangerous harm done, 216
human value of diversity, 220
humane and egalitarian society
  Amnesty International, 228-229
  grass-roots political activity, 228-229
  Greenpeace, 228-229
  Human Rights Watch, 228-229
  Nader groups, 228-229
humane and equitable society, 2
humane society
  possibilities of, v, 111
humanitarian issues of the present
  environmental dangers, 221
  homelessness, 220
  police brutality toward minorities, 220
Hunnius, G., 130
Hutterites, 114

Indian Untouchables
  higher castes' opposition to occupa-
    tional liberation of, 18
individuals and social change
  role as idea-makers, 48
industrial capitalism, 72, 127, 168
industrial cooperatives, 120
industrial democracy, 128
  federative decision-making from below,
    224
industrial policy, 38, 65
  modern Japan, 25
industrial production
  major new development within capital-
    ism, 95
industrial reconversion, 154

industrial revolution, 156
industrial waste
   disposal of, 80
industrialization
   social cost of, 192
information and communication systems, 70
informational technology, 66
infotainment, 72
innovation
   of technology, 156
insider trading, 38, 39, 62
intentional intervention in social-political change
   as little as possible confrontational or conspiratorial, 230
   building the infrastructure of control from below, 230
   most important direction appears to be economic — more precisely productional, 226-227
   oppose evils in capitalist society and any possible post-capitalist society, 211
   principle of control from below, 231
   what kind and extent of effects, 210
   what sorts of, 210
   workplace change is the crucial change, 231
inter-enterprise structures, 163
Islam, 45
Islamic fundamentalism, 193

Jewish fundamentalism in Israel, 194
Johnson, A.G., 120, 123
junk bonds, 60, 61, 62, 160

Kagarlitsky, B., 202
Kelso, L., 131
Keynes, J.M., 40, 191
Keynes's theory of capitalism, 42
Keynesianism, 80
Kibbutz industries, 115
Kibbutz movement, 114
Kibbutzim, 114, 115, 116
   egalitarian relations of production and consumption, 117
   principles preclude the employment of outside labor, 116
   social values, 117
   socialist belief, 117
Kirshner, J., 98
Klein, L.R., 40
Kolkhoz, 185
Korsch, K., 109, 125, 226
Kropotkin, P.A., 108

Kruse, D.L., 131, 162, 171
L-word, 230
labor movement, 107, 108, 126, 227
laissez-faire, 80
landed nobility, 95
Lasch, S., 108
latifundia, 43
Lefebvre, C., 107
Lefebvre, M., 107
Leninist vanguard communism
   ideologues of, 50
Leval, G., 119
leveraged buyout(s), 39, 62, 132
Levi, P., 184
Lindenfield, F., 129
Littler, C., 143
Logan, C., 120
Logue, J.B., 137
Lopez, R.S., 90, 94
Lowenstein, L., 61
Luddites, 51, 105, 126
Luxemburg, R., 184

Mafia, 33, 62
Magna Charta, 52
management buy-outs, 172
manorial lords, 89
Manske, F., 151
market
   as a system of exchange, 27
market mechanism, 4
market research, 58
market share, 29, 66
marketing cooperatives, 120
Martov, L., 184
Marx, K., 108
Marx's theory
   describes capitalism in terms of the social relations of production, 109
   sociologizing of economies, 109
   theory of the transition from capitalism, 108
Marxism, 174
Mason, A.T., 221
Mason, R.M., 129
Matouk, J., 172
Mattick, P., 109, 125, 184, 226
maximization of profit, 28
   decision-making criterion of capitalism, 2
Means, G., 108
medical research, 71

Medieval Europe
  new productional arrangements were developing before new social forms, 18
Mehring, F., 108
Melman, S., 38, 142
melting pot, 68
mercantile dynasties, 96
Michels, R., 170
microprocessors, 70
Mill, J.S., 107, 108
Miskimin, H.A., 90
Mitbestimmung, 130
mixed economy, 99
  capitalist, governmental, and self-governed all co-existing, 173, 152
  being forced to move toward decentralization and more room for worker participation in decisions, 143-144
modern corporations, 26
moieties, 12
Mollat, M., 89
Mondragon Cooperative Group, 119-124
Mondragon cooperatives
  consumers' cooperatives, 120
  cooperative bank, 120
  ideology of egalitarianism, 120
  industrial cooperatives, 120
  marketing cooperatives, 120
  producers' cooperatives, 120
  Ulgor plants, 122
monetarism, 80
monetary exchange, 92
money-based activities
  lending, buying and selling, 91
monopoly capitalism, 99
Mothe, D., 172
Motyl, A., 202
multinational corporations, 59, 76
  internationalisms of, 64
Mumford, L., 90

National Health Services in England, 73
nationalism, 67
nationalization
  see-saw fluctuations between privatization, 152
Nearing, S., 107
Needham, J., 88
negative feedback, 35, 41
  feedback mechanisms via market of, 199
  for a system's long term effectiveness, 205

lack of, 75
  to expansion and to misuse of the earth, 75
  top-down system in communist regimes had no bottom-up, 199
New Deal, 42, 73, 128
New Economic Policy, 184
Nomenklatura, 87, 206
non-centralized structure
  essential for any prospects of a more humane society, 215
non-profit production
  control-from-below character, 170
Nove, A., 173, 186
nuclear waste, 69, 78

occupational groups
  potential impact on economic system, 48
occupations
  advantages versus classes, 13
  decision-making on production, 16
  types and statuses of, 12
Olson, M., 171
Ombudsmen, 169
Orthodox Judaism, 45
Owenite colonies, 114
Owenite cooperatives, 119
ozone depletion, 69

Pannekoek, A., 125, 226
Paper, L.J., 221
paradigmatic criterion for monetary activity
  calculation of profitability, 93
participant-controlled enterprises, 163, 164, 175, 161
  retain their character and not slip into bureaucratic control, 162
Paton, R., 137
peasant revolts, 89
  of Medieval Europe, 51
Perestroika, 196, 198
Philipon, C.H.E., 90
Piore, N.J., 144
polarization of society
  large underclass, 75
  privileged power group, 75
political correctness, 230
positive feedback, 19, 28, 29, 91, 92, 94
post-capitalist developments
  potentially, 57-86
post-capitalist period, 88
Postan, M.M., 89
Postgate, R., 107

power
 wielders of social power, 22
power structure(s), 13
 changes in the character or strength of
  power, 14
 competing power bases, 14
 controllers of the economy, 15
 costs of power, 14
 grades of power, 14
 loci of, 14
 reigning culture of the society, 15
 social costs of power, 15
 sources of, 14
power wielders, 84, 142, 229, 230
Prague Spring group of Reform Communists, 200
prestige groups, 15
Preston, R., 143
Pribicevic, B., 128
producer-controlled cooperatives
 movement toward does not necessarily
  have to be confrontational, 161
producers' cooperatives, 119, 120, 137,
  230
producers' democracy, 166
productional decision-making
 importance of the form, 18
productional democracy, 164
productional self-government
 cooperate with labor union movement,
  165
profit criterion
 capitalist production, 24
 victims of, 35
profit-maximization, 4, 26
 dynamics of, 29
progress
 in art and science, 9
 in long history of man, 9
 notion of, 9
proletariat, 43
Protestant fundamentalism of the United
  States, 194
Protestantism, 18, 98
Proudhon, P.J., 108

Quilligan, J.B., 137

radical or leftist movement, 226
radicalism, 108
Reagan-Thatcher period, 33
Robber Barons, 62
robotics, 70
Rochdale cooperatives, 119
Ronan, C.A., 88

Rorig, F., 90
Rosen, C., 131, 134
Rosenberg, A., 109, 184
Rosner, M., 116
Rothschild-Whitt, J., 129
Rude, G., 51, 52, 97, 127
ruling entity
 business, 44
 landed aristocracy, 44
 military, 44
 priesthood, 44
ruling group(s)
 as exponents of national culture as traditions, 219
 as imperial rulers, 218
 obtains some part ("surplus") of the
  product of other people's work, 217
 prospects of, 216-220
 use of strong controls against dissidents, 217
Russell, B., 185
Russell, J.C., 90
Russian Menshevik Marxists, 184
Russian Revolution, 49

Sabel, C., 144
safety nets
 for workers, minorities, and the poor,
  73
Schumacher, E.F., 151
 a new decision system dependent on
  no ruling elite, 103
Scientific Socialism, 109
Scott, J.C., 89
self-governed enterprises, 173
 business opposition as threat to capitalism, 160
 competition (and to some extent complement) inside capitalism, 101
 midsize productional entities, 155
 natural technology for, 155
self-governed production, 160, 113-175
 based on cooperation rather than competition, 163
 could complement capitalism, 102
 democracy in production, 113
 help from social or political movement, 164
 invites inter-enterprise supports, 163
 next stage of labor movement, 106
 situations supporting, 148
 support within capitalism for starting,
  145-152
self-managed production, 146

Sen, A.K. and A., 12
serfdom, 94, 162
  dropouts from, 102
share system
  criterion of democratic decision-making from below, 169
  in employee-owned enterprises, 169
Shipway. M., 125
Simon, E., 137
Sirianni, C., 184
slavery, 217
  Caribbean Indians, 14
  southern United States, 14
Smart, A., 184
Smith, A., 96
  a particular design of society vs. a particular method of decision-making, 216
social change
  analysis of, 21
  collapse of communist regimes, 204-208
  communist regimes shift blame and decision-making between the economic system and the government, 206
  concentration of political and economic power in the hands of government, 206
  considerations in analyzing, 43-55
  continuity in forms of social life, 43
  decision-system of communist regimes, 205-206
  direction of, 53-54
  directions of change from capitalism, 183
  failure of communist regimes, 206
  internal change, 43-44
  more humane and equitable society, 172
  possible direction of, 11
  relevance of self-governed enterprises, 171
  social forces, 44-47
  to avoid a class society, 216
social forms
  economic effect on, 17-18
social relations
  economic political "system," 11
  occupations, 11
social relativism, 10
social status
  correlation between production of consumption, 12

socio-historical theorists, 44
soil and forest depletion, 69
Solidarity movement, 200
Sorel, G., 108
Sorge, A., 129
Soviet "insanity" convictions, 22
Soviet communism
  aftermath of, 183-208
Spanish Civil War, 108, 119
Stauber, L.G., 173
Stephen, F.H., 130
Stern, R.N., 129
stock market, 30
Strum, P., 221
Sturmthal, A., 130
subliminal advertisement, 58
successors to capitalism
  a fascist-style government directly controlling production and the lives and attitudes of the population, 112
  development of more egalitarian relations of production, 111
  Leninist communist regime, 111
successors to tomorrow's capitalism
  oligarchy and self-governed production, 207
suggestion box, 142
superstructure, 98
Syndicalism, 108, 124
systemic social forces
  stability and its changeability relation to, 44
Szeleny, I, 202

Tawney, R.H., 96
Taylorism, 142
teamwork science, 71
technology
  accretion of, 213
  development of, 213
  wasteful and ecologically destructive form, 214
Thimm, A.L., 130
Thomas, H., 120
Thompson, E.P., 107
Thompson, P., 143
Thorpe, W., 108
Tiananmen Square
  uprising, 204
tithes, 217
Toscano, B.J., 144
trade union democracy, 224

tribal or national culture
express the past of just one population, rather than general morality and the possibilities for human progress, 219
Udovich, A.L., 90
Ulgor plants, 122
underclass, 82
kept alive only by poverty-level welfare, 74
union and company pension and health funds
under democratic control of workers, 227
union democracy, 73
unions
decrease the militancy of, 73
universalization of capitalism, 67, 69
usury
biblical prohibition against, 90
utopia
impossibility of creating a permanent, 124

van Klavern, J., 96
Vanden Heuvel, K., 200
Vanek, J., 130
Vasari, G., 213
Veblen, T., 29
victimization of people
control from above by an "elite," 179
Viola, L., 185
von Oertzen, P., 125

Wagner Act, 81
watch-dog committees, 169
Webb, S. and B., 107, 128
Weber, M., 170, 212
Weissman, B.S., 137
welfare state(s), 35, 39, 41, 85
of Sweden ("capitalism with a human face"), 73
Werth, N., 191
whistleblowers, 169
White, L.J., 62
White, R.J., 96
Whyte, K.K., 120
Whyte, W.F., 120, 123
Wiener, J., 201
Wilpert, B., 129
Wolf, H., 151
Wolff, P., 89, 90
worker buy-outs, 172
worker decision-making
business moves toward accepting, 141-145

worker empowerment
due to their own struggle, 143
needs of modern technology, 143
worker ownership and control, 228
worker participation
pressure for, 129
worker-controlled enterprises, 2
worker-controlled production, 2
worker-owned enterprises, 224
workers' control of their workplace, 114
workers' councils, 130, 124-126
workers' decision power and ownership
accretive development, 172
working class
depoliticization and weakening of, 73
workplace democracy, 224
pressures for, 128
workplace self-government, 128-129
works councils, 130
World Bank, 39

Young, K.M., 131, 134
Yugoslav workers' councils, 195

zero-sum situation
making of profit, 26
Zimbalist, A., 143
Zwerdling, D., 129

ABOUT THE AUTHOR

Zellig S. Harris was born in Balta, Russia on October 23, 1909. Shortly thereafter his family emigrated to the United States. He received his B.A., M.A., and Ph.D. at the University of Pennsylvania. Starting his illustrious linguistics career in the field of Semitics, he wrote *A Grammar of Phoenician Language* in 1936 and *Development of the Canaanite Dialects* in 1939. As of 1940, Harris shifted his scholarly focus to the field of general linguistics, to which he made numerous path-breaking contributions.

Among the many books Harris published are *Structural Linguistics* (1951), *String Analysis of Sentence Structure* (1962), *Mathematical Structure of Language* (1968), *Papers in Structural and Transformational Linguistics* (1970), *Notes du cours de syntaxe* (1978), *Language and Information* (1988), and *A Theory of Language and Information: A Mathematical Approach* (1991).

After World War II, Harris founded the Department of Linguistic Analysis at the University of Pennsylvania. This was reputedly the first department of linguistics in the United States.

Harris was the recipient of many honors. He was elected member of the American Philosophical Society, The National Academy of Sciences, and the American Academy of Arts and Sciences. He was also a Corresponding Fellow of the British Academy and President of the Linguistics Society of America. In 1986 he delivered the Bampton Lectures at Columbia University. Between 1967 and 1980 Harris was the Benjamin Franklin Professor of Linguistics at the University of Pennsylvania. He died on May 22, 1992.